Mobile Europe

Mobile Europe

The Theory and Practice of Free Movement in the EU

Ettore Recchi
Sciences Po, Paris

© Ettore Recchi 2015

Softcover reprint of the hardcover 1st edition 2015 978-0-230-27447-1

All rights reserved. No reproduction, copy or transmission of this publication may be made without written permission.

No portion of this publication may be reproduced, copied or transmitted save with written permission or in accordance with the provisions of the Copyright, Designs and Patents Act 1988, or under the terms of any licence permitting limited copying issued by the Copyright Licensing Agency, Saffron House, 6-10 Kirby Street, London EC1N 8TS.

Any person who does any unauthorized act in relation to this publication may be liable to criminal prosecution and civil claims for damages.

The author has asserted his right to be identified as the author of this work in accordance with the Copyright, Designs and Patents Act 1988.

First published 2015 by
PALGRAVE MACMILLAN

Palgrave Macmillan in the UK is an imprint of Macmillan Publishers Limited, registered in England, company number 785998, of Houndmills, Basingstoke, Hampshire RG21 6XS.

Palgrave Macmillan in the US is a division of St Martin's Press LLC, 175 Fifth Avenue, New York, NY 10010.

Palgrave is the global academic imprint of the above companies and has companies and representatives throughout the world.

Palgrave® and Macmillan® are registered trademarks in the United States, the United Kingdom, Europe and other countries.

ISBN 978-1-349-59147-3   ISBN 978-1-137-31602-8 (eBook)
DOI 10.1057/9781137316028

This book is printed on paper suitable for recycling and made from fully managed and sustained forest sources. Logging, pulping and manufacturing processes are expected to conform to the environmental regulations of the country of origin.

A catalogue record for this book is available from the British Library.

A catalog record for this book is available from the Library of Congress.

Contents

List of Figures vi

List of Tables viii

Preface and Acknowledgements x

Introduction – Between Individualization and Globalization: The Long-Term Premises to Free Movement 1

Part I Theorizing Free Movement: History, Policies, Demographics 15

1 A Frontierless Continent: History of an Idea and Its Realization 17

2 Why Free Movement? Assessing Policies and Rationales 35

3 EU Movers: How Many Are There, Where Are They, What Do They Do? 49

Part II Practising Free Movement: Sociological Perspectives 79

4 'Old' and 'New' EU Movers: Integration Pathways Compared 81

5 A Sterile Citizenship? Intra-European Mobility and Political Participation 105

6 Intra-EU Mobility and European Identity: Towards a Sense of Shared Belonging 123

Conclusion – Free Movement in Europe: Epitomizing the Age of Mobility? 145

Methodological Appendix 155

Notes 159

References 175

Index 201

List of Figures

0.1 Economic globalization: international trade flows in 50 countries (1980 and 2009) — 9

0.2 Social globalization: transnational personal contacts in 50 countries (1980 and 2009) — 10

3.1 European citizens residing in a member state different from their own, 1990–2012 (in thousands) — 53

3.2 EU movers and third-country citizens residing in the EU, 1990–2012 (in thousands) — 54

4.1 Structural characteristics of Western EU movers in France, Germany, Great Britain, Italy and Spain (2004): multiple correspondence analysis — 88

4.2 Sociocultural characteristics of Western EU movers in France, Germany, Great Britain, Italy and Spain (2004): multiple correspondence analysis — 90

4.3 Structural, sociocultural and identitarian characteristics of Western EU movers in France, Germany, Great Britain, Italy and Spain (2004): multiple correspondence analysis — 92

4.4 Structural, sociocultural and identitarian characteristics of EU movers in France, Italy, Spain and Greece (2012): multiple correspondence analysis — 100

5.1 EU movers at the polls for national general elections: turnout rates (%) — 116

5.2 EU movers at the polls for the European Parliament: turnout rates (%) — 117

6.1 Feeling European: EU movers and stayers who declare themselves to be 'very attached' to Europe (2004 and 2010–2011) (%) — 130

6.2 Identity spread: difference between level of attachment to Europe and average level of attachment to nation/region/city (or town or village) among EU movers and stayers (2004 and 2010–2011)   133

6.3 Distribution of the index of individual transnationalism (in %)   139

7.1 Income inequality between countries and intra-EU movers' stocks in EU15 (1986–2010)   147

7.2 Mobility more than migration: Growth of world population, migrant stocks and international arrivals, 1960–2011 (1960 = 100)   149

List of Tables

1.1	Milestones of the EU free movement regime	18
2.1	Main European policies favouring intra-EU mobility	36
3.1	The rise of Central-Eastern Europeans residing in other EU member states, 2000–2011 (2000 = 100)	57
3.2	EU movers in 2001: % of each nationality by country of residence	60
3.3	EU movers in 2012: % of each nationality by country of residence	62
3.4	EU movers in 2001: % of countries of residence by nationality	64
3.5	EU movers in 2012: % of countries of residence by nationality	66
3.6	Dispersion of intra-EU mobility by nationality in 2001 and 2012 (Lieberson index)	69
3.7	National patterns of geographical mobility in the EU between 2001 and 2012	70
3.8	Mobility and work during the crisis: occupational positions of 'stayers' and 'movers' from the EU15 and from new member states (NMS) of the first and second enlargements, 2007 and 2010 (as % of workers per occupational category)	71
3.9	Stocks of EU movers in selected EU countries: growth rate (2006 = 100)	76
5.1	The political participation of EU movers and stayers: components of the politicization index (%)	110
5.2	Determinants of political involvement of EU movers in 2004 (EIMSS) and 2011 (Moveact): OLS regressions of the politicization index	113

5.3	Determinants of voting for the European Parliament among EU movers in 2004 and 2011: logit regressions	119
6.1	Determinants of attachment to Europe in 2004 and 2010–2011: logit regressions ('very attached' vs 'fairly, not very or not at all attached')	134
6.2	Determinants of identity spread in 2004 and 2010–2011: OLS regressions of the difference between attachment to Europe and attachments to nation/region/city (or town or village)	136
6.3	Determinants of attachment to Europe among EU movers in 2004 and 2010–2011: logit regressions ('very attached' vs 'fairly, not very or not at all attached')	137
6.4	Mobility experiences, individual transnationalism and attachment to the EU in the EU population: multi-level logit regressions ('very attached' vs 'fairly, not very or not at all attached')	140

Preface and Acknowledgements

> *Notre nature est dans le mouvement.*
> (Blaise Pascal, *Œuvres*, Vol. XIII, Paris, 1928)

While writing this book, three memories periodically resurfaced in my mind. The first was the recollection of when I watched television for the first time. It must have been a summer evening towards the end of the 1960s. On air was a programme which fascinated my grandfather, who was sitting beside me. The main characters were high-spirited young people, representing modest (and for me largely unknown) provincial towns from various countries as they competed in a series of zany games. Two impeccable judges announced the scores in several languages with a sort of Olympian aplomb. The scoreboard – I seem to remember – gave precedence to the names of the towns over their respective countries. *It's a Knockout!* was the title of this weekly programme. For my grandfather and me it soon became unmissable.

The second memory has a definite date: 1 May 2004. On that day the right of free movement was extended to the citizens of the ten new member states of the European Union. At a motorway service station on the *Autostrada del Sole* in Italy, I parked next to a car bearing a Polish number plate. I made a rapid calculation: it was morning, so they must have set off shortly after midnight to have already reached Tuscany. I ventured 'Welcome' in English, and the driver – aged about 50 and who must have spent most of his life behind the Iron Curtain – smiled at me with complicit pleasure. He told me, more by gesture than with his broken English, that he had crossed the once impassable Polish frontier holding his breath, without stopping or being stopped.

The final memory goes back to the summer of 2007. Romania and Bulgaria had just joined the EU. After a spate of petty crimes, a television crew had entered a Roma encampment on the outskirts of Rome and found itself surrounded by a swarm of children, who with a mixture of cheek and defiance chanted to the television camera: 'We are Europeans, we are Europeans.'

Yes, like 500 million other people, those Roma children were 'Europeans' – and today this adjective no longer denotes a mere geographical location. Since 1993, after the Maastricht Treaty, the citizens of the EU member states have been *also* European citizens. Being

European has assumed a political meaning. And in the absence of a fully accomplished Europe-wide democratic game, it has consisted principally in a right: the entitlement to move and settle at will across the entire EU with the same rights enjoyed by the national citizens of the receiving country. In this book I shall first reconstruct the social and political conditions in which this right has been affirmed. I shall then illustrate the experiences of those who exercise it in a systematic manner – that is, the approximately three per cent of Europeans who live in a EU member state different from that of their origin[1] – and whom, for the sake of brevity, I shall henceforth call 'mobile Europeans' or 'EU movers'.[2]

Their history closely follows the developments of European integration in recent decades. Since the 1990s, with the progressive and substantial removal of the EU's internal borders following the Schengen Agreement and with transformation of free movement rights as a part and parcel of European citizenship, migrating in Europe has become an easier choice than it used to be in the years of post-Second World War mass migrations. Besides free movement policies, this change has been favoured by technical progress, which has considerably reduced the costs of mobility: high-speed trains, low-cost flights and infrastructural networks have greatly facilitated movements across the continent. In keeping with the transformations typical of late modernity, which have compressed distances and times, an increasing number of Europeans have started to imagine a flexible kind of international mobility which serves a variety of purposes. Moreover, the improved quality of life and welfare in Mediterranean Europe has reduced the incentives for migration along the South to North axis typical of mobility in the post-war period, and it has increased the incentives to move in the opposite direction – from North to South. After the enlargements of the 2000s, earnings differentials have spurred conspicuous flows from East to West and South. Labour migration, which has assumed various forms in the old continent's history since the beginning of the modern age (Bade 2003; Livi Bacci 2012), has been revived by these latter movements, but also flanked by less-structured patterns of mobility that can be only partially interpreted using the categories of traditional studies on migration.

Mobile European citizens constitute a 'strategic minority' that warrants attention from different perspectives: as migrants *sui generis*, as social agents epitomizing a fluid society and as beneficiaries of that atypical form of citizenship which is European citizenship. Each of these categories raises questions that this book seeks to answer.

From the first perspective, *as migrants*, EU movers seem to be the protagonists of innovative migratory projects because of the wide array of factors which motivate them, and because of the political framework in which they organize their lives. In a certain sense, they are 'post-migrants'. By moving across an international space without borders, they enjoy a position of privilege in the global population of migrants – usually subject to disadvantages and discrimination – and they embody the utopian dream of the cosmopolitan citizen free from the constraints imposed by state sovereignties (Pécoud and De Guchteneire 2007a). To be clarified, though, is the extent to which EU movers evade the dynamics typical of the migrant experience: for instance, social segregation and downward social mobility.

From the second perspective, *as agents*, by their sole act of moving, mobile Europeans actively contribute to redefining the political spatiality that characterizes the contemporary age, pioneering a 'borderless world' (Ohmae 1990; Beck 1997; Sassen 2006). Assumed as the distinctive feature of our time (Urry 2000, 2007), mobility – of goods, information but also people – makes the political, economic and cultural boundaries of nation states porous, generating a process of deterritorialization and the development of a 'network state' whose most advanced breeding ground is the EU (Castells 2000; Beck and Grande 2004). Other authors suggest that transnationalization recasts the social and political coordinates of society through constant 'de-bordering' and 're-bordering' (Rumford 2006). On a constructivist view, the geographical, political and cultural dimensions of boundaries – which traditionally overlapped – are disarticulating and recomposing themselves (Delanty and Rumford 2005; Delanty 2006; Eder 2006; for a post-Marxist reading see Balibar 2004). However, these suggestive – and sometimes highly imaginative – interpretations of social change lack empirical bases. How many truly transnational individuals are there? Where do they go? What do they do?

From the third point of view, *as citizens*, EU movers are the champions of European citizenship insofar as this concept acquires full meaning through the exercise of the right to free movement. As Joppke points out (2010a, 28 ff.), citizenship has three facets which reveal themselves in migrants' experience. Firstly, it is a package of rights; secondly, it is a status that solicits participation in collective decisions; thirdly, it is a shared identity. This is also the case of European citizenship. Hence, mobile Europeans highlight the importance of these rights, the political import of EU citizenship and its impact on European identity. European movers lend themselves to a reasoning *a fortiori*: if European integration is not important for them, for who else could it be so? Answering this question may perhaps bring us closer to understanding whether European citizenship is destined to serve as a model for a post-national world, or whether it will amount to nothing more than an experiment leading to a side road of history.

***

This book draws on a far-reaching research programme which began in the early 2000s and has combined my interests in the themes of migration, European integration and elites (understood as 'strategic minorities' in the reproduction and change of social structures). More specifically, I have had opportunities to conduct empirical analysis of mobility in Europe as the coordinator of three international research projects, generously funded by the European Commission, whose findings are constantly cited in this book: the Pioneur Project (2002–2006), the Moveact Project (2011–2013), and the Eucross Project (2012–2014).[3] The contents of this book have also benefitted from related funding from the University of Chieti-Pescara (2010–2013) and from the *direction scientifique* of Sciences Po for the Space-Set project (2014–2016) which develops a more general approach to individual spatial mobility.

I wish to thank all the people who, in different ways, have helped me advance this research agenda. As I conceive it, social research moves back and forth between teamwork and individual speculation. On the team side, I have always been very fortunate. My gratitude goes, in no particular order, to Antonio Alaminos (and family), Oscar Santacreu, Mari-Carmen Albert, Michael Braun, Nina Rother, Anne Muxel, Damian Tambini, Camelia Arsene, Tina Nebe and Emiliana Baldoni, who embarked with me on the Pioneur project. I have had the privilege of working on the Moveact project again with Antonio and Oscar, but also with Anna Triandafyllidou, Sylvie Strudel, Michaela Maroufof, Karolina Koc Michalska and Luca Raffini. Finally, once again with Michael Braun, to whom I am greatly indebted, and with Adrian Favell, Juan Díez Medrano, Mike Savage, Dumitru Sandu, David Reimer, Ann Zimmermann, Steffen Pötzschke, Laurie Hanquinet, Irina Ciornei, Fulya Apaydin, Janne Jensen, Monica Serban, Alin Croitoru, Deniz Duru, Nazli Sila Cesur, Valerie Steeb, Theresa Kuhn, Lorenzo Grifone Baglioni, Thea Rossi and Justyna Salamońska I have undertaken the Eucross project. They have been much more than colleagues. Matteo Abbate and Valentina Bettin have bolstered me with their emotional intelligence during the most difficult phases of the teamwork.

Throughout this time, Adrian Favell has shared with me his unique ideas, perspicuous visions and inspired disenchantment. I enjoyed Juan Díez Medrano's insightful comments, especially during my stay at Universidad Carlos III in Madrid in 2012–2013. Gianfranco Bettin

Lattes has relentlessly encouraged me at every turning point. Finally, I am intellectually thankful, on many grounds, to Massimo Livi Bacci, Yossi Shavit, Rainer Bauböck, Virginie Guiraudon, Niilo Kauppi, Miguel Maduro, Russell King, Martin Kohli, Saara Kokkalainen, Patrick Le Galès, Marco Oberti, Alain Chenu, Tommaso Vitale, Mirna Safi, Louis-André Vallet, Yannick Savina, Bernard Corminboeuf, Aurore Flipo, Mathieu Ichou, Margot Delon, Anne van der Graaf, Milan Bouchet-Valat, Willem Maas, Philippe van Parijs, Ferruccio Pastore, Valeria Bello, Gloria Pirzio, Vincenzo Cesareo, Michel Poulain, Antoine-Emmanuel de la Sayette, Patrick O'Mahony, Cosimo and Giovanni Recchi. I am also grateful to all my colleagues and staff of the Observatoire Sociologique du Changement at Sciences Po, and particularly to Marie Ferrazzini and Sylvie Lesur. Adrian Belton translated the first half Italian-half English version of the manuscript with patience. Lauren Pugh added her sagacious reading to the second version. At Palgrave Macmillan, I welcomed Philippa Grand's wise support and understanding as well as Dharmendra Sundardevadoss and his SPi Global team's most careful editing.

This book is dedicated to my grandparents Luigi and Clara, who long ago crossed the Appennines *controcorrente*.

Introduction
Between Individualization and Globalization: The Long-Term Premises to Free Movement

1. **Framing free movement: the concept and the context**

When Paul, Pablo and Paolo think about a united Europe, what do they see? According to the Eurobarometer, which has repeatedly put this question to a sample of citizens from all the countries of the European Union, there are no doubts on the matter. 'Freedom to travel, study and work anywhere in the EU': this is the answer given, year after year, by the majority of the interviewees. It is not the euro, nor democracy, nor peace among nations, but rather free movement which epitomizes the EU in the minds of Europeans.[1]

Indeed, what portion of the globe can boast a space with no frontiers among 28 sovereign states? Such an achievement is all the more striking in a continent which was the cradle of the nation state, and in which for centuries, war after war was fought to defend or change its borders. European citizenship – whose cornerstone is free movement – allows Europeans to move to, and reside in, whatever country of the EU they wish, and to receive the same treatment afforded to the national citizens of that country. This is a regime *sui generis* which still technically takes the form of international migration, but it does so on the conditions typical of internal migration. In order to mark this change semantically, EU documents increasingly refer to intra-EU movements as 'mobility', rather than as 'migration', restricting the latter term to the movements of people from third countries. In everyday terms, 'mobility' means migration 'in first class', without the nuisance of documents nor the risks that characterize the journey and settlement of traditional migrants.

In the general sense, 'individuals enjoy freedom of movement [. . .] when there are no laws or administrative controls that prevent them from leaving a current place of residence and from taking up residence elsewhere' (Bauböck 2011, 350). Bauböck also specifies that freedom of movement consists of three separate rights: exit, entry and settlement at the destination. In this book, however, I shall concentrate on free movement within the EU, considering these three rights as a single package, with the addition of the right to non-discrimination with respect to the national citizens of the state of residence.

As Michael Walzer (1990, 11–12) points out, freedom of geographical mobility sits at the top of the 'four mobilities' that substantiate liberalism (the others being 'social', 'marital' and 'political' mobility). Thus, granting freedom of movement to regular residents within *national* boundaries is quintessential to a liberal polity. But in the case of the EU – and herein lies its exceptionality – the right to free movement has an *international* scope. This freedom belongs within a broader framework whose rationale is the 'freedom of movement of goods, capital, services and *people*' to which the EU Treaty (in its various versions) makes constant reference as the 'engine' for the construction of a united Europe – or, in the lexicon of European studies, the principle that has made it possible to 'deepen' integration. In EU law, reference is made to the 'four freedoms' of the EU (see, for example, Barnard 2007), an expression which echoes – notwithstanding substantial differences of content – the four freedoms which Franklin D. Roosevelt, in his famous State of the Union address of 1941, set as the fundamental goals of American society (freedom of speech and worship; freedom from want and fear). Roosevelt's proclamation represents a manifesto for modern citizenship; indeed, it was subsequently reprised almost word for word in the preamble to the Universal Declaration of Human Rights of the United Nations. More modestly speaking, the four freedoms of EU law aim to build a supranational market – or, in other words, a 'single market' without customs or tariffs on imports (freedom of movement of goods), without currency controls or constraints on foreign investments (freedom of movement of capital), without national barriers to professional and business activities (freedom of movement of services) and without limitations on the movements of individuals from one state to another nor discrimination with respect to the citizens of those states (freedom of movement of people).

Making it a component of the single market, however, does not do justice to the legal and practical implications of the EU free movement regime. Its significance is decidedly broader, for people are not merely producers and consumers. Freedom of movement in the EU alters the traditional notion of national citizenship, which is intrinsically both a privilege and a spatial constraint (Berezin 2003). Maurizio Ferrera has grasped the revolutionary nature of this change by noting that national citizenship was historically conceived as an 'instrument of closure' (2005, 206). As has been noted, 'the first step to the state system we know today was the monopolization of the legitimate means of movement' (Mau et al. 2012, 23; see also Brubaker 1992, 31; Torpey 2000, 4 ff.). Especially with the advent of welfare in the twentieth century, the solidarity ('risk-sharing') implicit in common citizenship led to an emphasis on the spatial dimension of belonging to a state – that is, the physical boundaries which separated those who were citizens from those who were not. Exiting those boundaries meant losing nearly all the rights and duties of solidarity; entering did not afford access to them. Still today, if European citizens do not exploit their freedom to cross the borders of the member states, their citizenship rights and guarantees continue to derive from national laws. Technically speaking, 'without the movement of EU citizens, there is nothing actually to trigger EU law rights and the situation is thus described as wholly internal' (Foster 2011, 350). When European citizens move, however, the traditional tie between rights and territory is severed, so that 'for most civic and social rights, the filtering role of nationality has been neutralized' (Ferrera 2005, 207).

Free interstate movement is thus a fundamental ingredient – if not indeed the lever – for dismantling the nation state and constructing a post-national political order. But what is the origin of this principle, and what are the historical processes that have led to its success in contemporary Europe? I shall reconstruct its historical genesis in Chapter 1, describing – in broad outline – the main stages of its intellectual diffusion and its gradual incorporation into European law. As a preliminary step, in this introduction I wish to consider the principle in light of macro-changes that have had an impact on the basic values and social relations of the societies in which the principle of free cross-state movement is manifest. I maintain, in fact, that from a strictly sociological point of view, the right to spatial mobility and settlement beyond the confines of the nation state is the point of intersection between two great tendencies which traverse advanced human societies. The first tendency is cultural. It consists of the growth of subjectivity and the parallel granting of an increasingly broad array of individual rights to make choices and take action: in a word, *individualization*, in the sense that I shall shortly clarify. The second tendency is structural. This concerns the expansion of economic and social interactions among actors based in different national societies: in a word, *globalization*. Prior to late twentieth-century Europe, nowhere and in no historical era had such tendencies overlapped to produce a legally protected situation in which people could organize their lives on an international scale – that is, across the borders of states – without particular controls and restrictions by those states. This phenomenon is unprecedented and it has revolutionary potential. For analytical clarity, before proceeding I shall conduct a separate examination of each of the two tendencies – individualization and globalization – that constitute the cultural and structural matrixes of the frontierless Europe described in the rest of this book.

2. Europe as the outpost of individualization

Research and theory on citizenship rights stand at the crossroads of history, political theory, philosophy of law and political sociology. In the vast literature on the topic, there is a connecting theme on which I shall concentrate here because it concerns an extremely long-period trend: the progressive expansion in time and space of the rights of individuals *qua* individuals, and not as members of groups and communities. For the sake of brevity, this can be termed *individualization*. The process is all but recent. Its centuries-old genesis and development arose from a

> radical reversal of perspective [. . .] in the representation of the political relationship, that is, in the state–citizens or sovereign–subjects relationship: a relationship increasingly considered from the point of view of the rights of citizens no longer subjects, rather than from the point of view of the powers of the sovereign, in line with the individualistic vision of society, according to which to understand society one must start from below, that is, from the individuals of which it is composed, in opposition to the traditional organic conception, according to which society is a whole which comes before individuals. (Bobbio 1990, xi–xii)

For Bobbio, this process gave rise to the wars of religion which, at the beginning of the modern age, affirmed the right of 'man as such' to profess his faith without the sovereign's approval. It unfolded, with interruptions and resumptions, along a still continuing path 'from recognition of the rights of the citizen of a particular state to recognition of the rights of the citizen of the world, as first proclaimed by the Universal Declaration of Human Rights' (ibid.).[2]

Bobbio's view is explicitly grounded in a Kantian-inspired philosophy of history (ibid., 48 ff.) and resonates with Marshall's (1963) well-known theory of citizenship, in particular with its division into stages of the expansion of individual protections in the Western world (and especially in Europe). The first generation of civil and political rights was followed by a second generation of social rights and then by a third generation of further rights, such as 'the right to live in an unpolluted environment' (ibid., xv), and among which rights such as the recognition of cultural differences (for example, use of one's native language) and differences in sexual orientation (for example, the formation of homosexual families) can certainly be included as well. Eventually Bobbio envisages a fourth generation of rights connected with the manipulation of genetic heritage, in accordance with a pattern of progressive 'specification' of rights-holders (ibid., 62 and 69 ff.).[3]

The perspective that characterizes 'the age of rights' entails that 'the state is made for the individual, not the individual for the state' (ibid., 59). A fundamental corollary to this is the reversal of the relationship between rights and duties: 'in regard to individuals, henceforth rights come first and then duties; in regard to the state, first come duties and then rights' (ibid., 59–60). The person has primacy, not the sovereign. But, as Bobbio warns in another essay, a 'potential right' is one thing, while an 'actual right' is quite another (ibid., 86). Are human rights truly taking on the role of a compass for European law or are they still subordinate to *Staatsangehörigkeit*?

The classic model of national citizenship foresees a rigid territorial containment of individual rights (Bendix 1977). If, therefore, the tendency towards the individualization of rights is indeed growing, we can expect it to generate 'de-territorialized' or 'frontierless' rights.[4] Consequently, the status of mobile individuals – migrants – is the litmus test by which to determine whether rights are granted to an individual as a person or as a member of a national community.

This line of inquiry has also been pursued in an important – but also controversial – study by Soysal (1994) on the advent of a post-national citizenship in Europe (and elsewhere). Soysal's comparative analysis reaches two conclusions. The first is that there is an ongoing standardization of the rights of non-citizens in Central and Northern Europe's states, with a progressive conferral of entitlements on migrants which partially alters the Marshallian sequence of citizenship – first come civil rights, then social rights and finally, but more cautiously, political rights (Soysal 1994, 120 ff.). Her second and more audacious conclusion is that when the demarcation line between citizens and non-citizens becomes blurred, 'the individual supplants the national citizen' (ibid., 164). Soysal therefore sees the emergence of a new model of post-national citizenship in which the rights and duties of individuals are defined on the basis of a 'higher order' with respect to nationality. The proliferation of international conventions – promoted by the United Nations (UN), the Council of Europe, the United Nations Educational, Scientific and Cultural Organization (UNESCO), the International Labour Organization (ILO) *and the EU* – stands in the background to this process. But, overall, '"European citizenship" clearly embodies postnational membership in its most elaborate legal form' (ibid., 148). As Soysal has subsequently glossed, the advent of European citizenship echoes an 'expansive institutionalization of human rights' in the post-Second World War period by which 'dispensation of rights is not simply a matter of *national* citizenship' (Soysal 2012, 16; see also Meyer 2010). The European project is an incarnation of a broader cultural trend of individualization.

The next step in this reasoning – which, however, Soysal does not take – is that the right to mobility precedes the other rights and duties of the post-national citizen, insofar as the free choice of residence determines the state and substate legal order of reference, especially in a system of multi-level governance in which the implementation of policies – and therefore the protection of rights in the first instance – is also always attributed to the nation states and their local governments.

A number of criticisms have been brought against Soysal's arguments. Firstly, they have disputed the alleged standardization of the rights of non-citizens, citing substantial differences among national policies for the integration of immigrants (see, for example, Joppke 1999).[5] Secondly, they have stressed the continuing capacity of contemporary states to curb migration and to raise new barriers between national and third-country citizens, thereby asserting their sovereignty (Guiraudon and Joppke 2001; Geddes 2003; Hansen 2009). Thirdly, they have underlined that migrants themselves, in many contexts, are averse to post-national protection and prefer to acquire national citizenship through naturalization – that is, they trust more in the recognition and protection granted by states than those by international bodies (Joppke 1999, 262–3).[6]

Must we therefore conclude that the model of post-national citizenship is merely a hypothetical construct and that the state – via national citizenship – is still the main source of protection for individual rights? To complete the picture, account must be taken of two further, relatively recent, developments. The first is the exponential growth of 'multiple citizenship' since the 1990s. Until not long ago, 'dual citizenship used to be regarded as an evil of the same kind as statelessness' (Bauböck 2011, 347), because it could engender conflicts among states and contradictions or accumulations of duties (consider conscription, for example). Today, however, prohibition of dual citizenship is more the exception that the rule around the world (Blatter et al. 2009). The phenomenon can be seen as a sort of equilibrium point between the aspiration of migrants to naturalization and the individualization of rights in post-national terms. Multiple citizenship gives mobile people a 'made-to-measure' dual presence, normally in the country of origin and in that of destination. It thus fuels the transnational, rather than post-national, character of citizenship (Fox 2005). This factor, as Bauböck (2010), for example, maintains, may have the virtue of keeping citizenship's affective and participatory component alive, while preventing the prevalence of a purely instrumental conception of it – which, according to some, is the principal flaw of European citizenship (Weiler 1996). On the other hand, the phenomenon concerns Europeans only on paper, because European citizenship is conceptually *supra*national rather than *trans*national, so that possession of dual citizenship within the EU is pointless (Bauböck 2003; Faist 2007). Not by chance, the naturalization rates of mobile European citizens in EU member states are close to zero (Bauböck et al. 2006; see also Reichel 2011).

The second development has been described by Joppke (2010b), who at first was openly critical of Soysal, but a decade later acknowledged that European citizenship has borne out the post-national model. European citizenship, in other words, was not post-national at the time when Soysal was writing, but it has become such with the extensive interpretation that the European Court of Justice (ECJ) has given to it, decision after decision, uncoupling it from national citizenship as an autonomous source of individual rights (see also Chapter 1). As the notion is now defined, European citizenship almost ideally distinguishes between citizenship and nationality, thereby exhibiting a tendency that affects citizenship in all liberal democracies: its 'lightening'. 'The future of citizenship is bound to be light, and lighter still with the help of "Europe"' (Joppke 2010b, 29). This lightness derives from the removal of the duties component traditionally associated with citizenship (the military service, which is no longer compulsory in almost all democracies; taxation, which depends on residence rather than citizenship) and, in parallel, from the scant identity salience of citizenship – as demonstrated in Europe by the minuscule proportion of EU citizens who call themselves 'European'. But is this really the case? However suggestive his view may be, Joppke reaches hasty conclusions. Indeed, he even forgets what he himself has pointed out, namely, that mobility is the 'trigger' of European citizenship. As we shall see in Chapter 6, mobility is associated empirically not only with full enjoyment of European citizenship in legal terms, but also with its greater appreciation in identitarian ones. The individualization of rights – which in Europe finds important expression in the free movement of persons and in the recognition of their equality regardless of state borders – is a major step towards recasting citizenship in post-national form. But in doing so, it does not necessarily strip citizenship of its symbolic charge.

3. Europe as the outpost of globalization

Towards the end of the twentieth century, 'globalization' came into general use as the term encapsulating the distinctive features of the contemporary age. The success of the concept was rather sudden, yet it was not brief. In 1980 there were no more than four published articles and academic books with 'globalization' in their titles; in 1990, there were already 165; ten years later, fully 3,230; and in 2010, yet again 3,210.[7] Just as publications on globalization proliferated, so did the definitions of the concept. Albeit with different nuances,[8] the lowest common denominator which social scientists largely agree on is the spread of network-like relations conducted at a distance and disembedded from national societies. There is a similar consensus in the literature on the multi-dimensional nature of globalization: it is a process consisting of economic, social and political dynamics (and also, according to some authors, technological and ecological ones). On these grounds, numerous attempts have been made to construct empirical indices by which to compare levels of globalization in different periods and geographical areas. The index most frequently used, and which is perhaps also the most complete – both for historical coverage (from 1970 onwards) and for the range of countries analysed (208) – has been developed by a group of researchers at the Zurich Polytechnic: the KOF Index of Globalization (Dreher et al. 2008). The KOF Index consists of three subindices which measure the 'economic', 'social' and 'political' dimensions of globalization. The third subindex seems comparatively less convincing, since it draws on indicators measuring a country's capacity for international representation (in terms of embassies, treaties signed, participation in UN peacekeeping operations and membership of international organizations), but does not record the penetration of supranational governance into national societies – which is perhaps the most distinctive feature of political globalization. I will therefore restrict my treatment here to a rapid survey of changes in the levels of economic and social globalization across one generation, that is, from 1980, in the wake of what is commonly considered the acceleration phase of contemporary globalization (Chase-Dunn et al. 2000), to 2009. The data refer to 50 countries, these being the 27 member states of the EU at the time and 23 others of significant size and historical–political influence distributed across the remaining four continents.[9]

With very few exceptions, the economic and social globalization of the countries examined stood at higher levels in 2009 than in 1980 (Figures 0.1 and 0.2). In point of fact, the growth rate of economic globalization was greater; on calculating an average per country (that is, without weighting for the different country size), the most recent figure is 25 per cent higher than it was three decades earlier. Instead, the social globalization index is 'only' seven per cent higher. Moreover, the correlation between the same country's levels of globalization at the two historical moments considered is decidedly smaller on the economic dimension ($r = 0.63$) than the social one ($r = 0.97$). Some countries (Russia and China, but also Spain, Sweden and the former communist countries in Europe) have moved up in the economic globalization ranking. The growth path of social globalization is more modest and smooth. The difference may be due to the role of policies, which can intervene to attract foreign capital or favour international trade more directly than

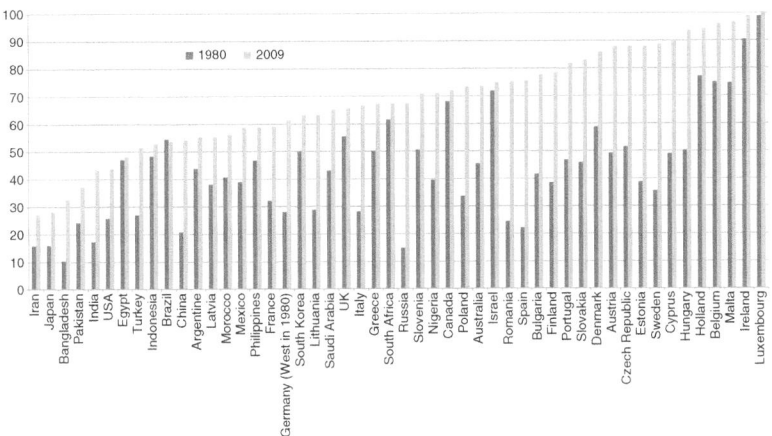

Figure 0.1 Economic globalization: international trade flows in 50 countries (1980 and 2009)

Source: KOF Index (international trade indicators only). For a detailed description, see http://globalization.kof.ethz.ch/static/pdf/variables_2012.pdf (consulted 16 July 2012). When the 1980 figure was not available, the closest possible year was used.

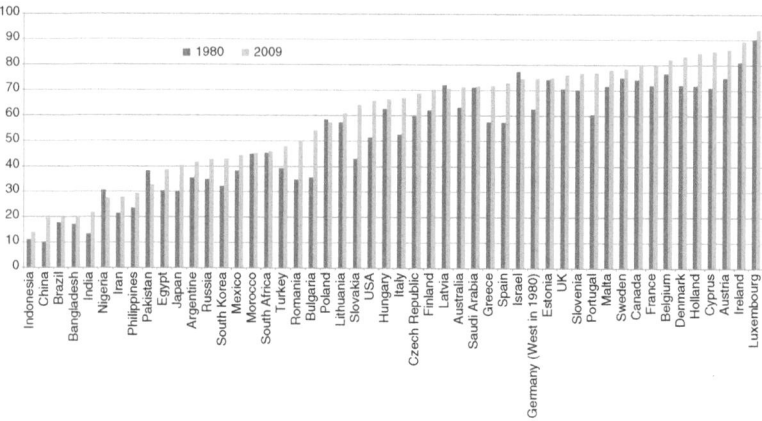

Figure 0.2 Social globalization: transnational personal contacts in 50 countries (1980 and 2009)
Source: KOF Index (international interactions only). For a detailed description, see http://globalization.kof.ethz.ch/static/pdf/variables_2012.pdf (consulted 16 July 2012).

they can influence population movements or personal transnational practices. For this reason as well, it is not always true that countries with a larger share of international trade are also more globalized socially (for instance, Hungary); nevertheless, the correlation between the two dimensions of globalization has clearly increased (from $r = 0.68$ in 1980 to $r = 0.96$ in 2009).

Perhaps the most striking – though not generally known – result of these elementary analyses is its geographic feature. In both figures 0.1 and 0.2, where countries are arranged on an increasing scale of globalization, EU member states appear on the right-hand side – that is, among the most globalized. On the economic dimension, the highest-ranking non-European countries occupy only nineteenth and twentieth places (Israel and Australia); and on the social dimension, the ninth (Canada) and the seventeenth (Israel). No EU member state is less economically globalized than the USA; socially, only five are. Although the mass media celebrates high-growth economies as the champions of globalization (first Asian Tigers, then BRICS), when globalization is measured in a rigorous way, its epicentre is evidently Europe. This depends to a large extent on the process of European integration, which exemplifies an institutionally regulated and sustained form of internationalization absent in other regions of the world.[10] The creation of a common market and a harmonized legal system has greatly facilitated economic and social exchanges among the countries of the EU. At the economic level, the key evidence is that, for all member states, more than half of their foreign trade takes place with the rest of the EU. Moreover, the main trading partner of all EU member states is another member state. Overall, the EU market absorbs goods of a value two-thirds higher than the level recorded for exports from the EU-28 to non-member countries (Eurostat 2014). In regard to social globalization, one likewise finds that 87 per cent of the tourists who visit a country of the EU originate from another member state (European Travel Commission 2012). After the enlargements of 2004 and 2007, as Chapter 4 will show, intra-EU migration flows have also outstripped those originating from third countries. Within its borders, the EU is the most denationalized and interdependent world region.

4. Free movement in Europe: policies and actors

If at the beginning of the Cold War, had someone told an Italian, a Pole, a Romanian or a Finn that one day they would be able to put away their passports and move to the other end of the continent with their families, without asking anyone's permission while maintaining all their rights, the prospect would have seemed as fanciful as the conquest of Mars or an air-propelled car. There is little doubt that 'the European experience is the most comprehensive attempt to establish free movement in a large supranational space' (Pécoud and De Guchteneire 2007b, 24) – a utopia becoming a reality. A similar regime of open borders is only to be found in much smaller portions of the globe: the Trans-Tasman Travel Arrangement between Australia and New Zealand, the Caribbean Community (although with greater restrictions) and the Nordic Council (which by now is largely included within the EU) (Casey 2009). While international cooperation agreements have been established in almost all continents, from the North American Free Trade Agreement (NAFTA) in North America to Mercosur in South America, the Economic Community of West Africa (CEAO), the Arab Maghreb Union (AMU) and the Association of South-East Asian Nations (ASEAN), only a few of them contemplate free movement for labour purposes, and none grant political rights to movers (Meyers 2002; Mau et al. 2012, 128 ff.). Indeed, the EU case looks even more extraordinary when considering that state permission to change one's place of residence is still formally needed *within* some countries – most noticeably China, where the *hukou* system has been de facto relaxed but not abolished and limits the rights and life chances of a sizeable part of its approximately 200 million internal migrants (Chan 2008).

Europe presents itself to the world – and above all, to its citizens – as a bastion of individual freedom, part of which is its spatial variant (namely freedom of movement). With the progressive extension of free movement (see Chapter 1), Europeans have seen their individual rights increase, and so too their experiences of the 'Other'. Yet there is no lack of criticism of this transformation, in particular, by the Marxist scholars who argue that all efforts to create a 'Europe of flows' (Hajer 2000) are in fact functional to the expansion of capitalism – and, therefore, to the exploitation and the destruction of community social relations, with the correlated psychological and social damage diagnosed by authors such as Deleuze and Guattari (1980), Harvey (1982) and Sennett (1998). In parallel, Foucauldian critics of European integration also highlight the centrality of 'spatial governance *within a frame of seamless mobility*' in the EU integration project, conceiving of it as a form of governmentality geared to moulding citizens' conduct and ultimately homologating their subjectivities (Jensen and Richardson 2004, 3; emphasis added). Europeanization is 'European space-making' which entails 'imagined mobilities' staged by 'transnational social actors' (Jensen and Richardson 2007). Ultimately, as 'Europe's new political constituency is fundamentally grounded on the privileges of the mobile investor, service provider and worker', the EU's power is predicated on the free movement regime (Vigneswaran 2013, 108; for a comprehensive view of Foucault-inspired approaches to the EU, see Zimmermann and Favell 2011).

In a less intellectually sophisticated fashion, it cannot be denied that a frontierless Europe is an outcome which Europeans themselves are not particularly content with, at a time when the contradictions of monetary union occupy centre stage. Never before has European integration been viewed with such suspicion and scepticism as in the first half of the 2010s. As Hooghe and Marks (2009) point out in a much-cited article, public opinion struggles to perceive its benefits and expresses a 'constraining dissensus' in regard to any further steps forward. In the discourse of Eurosceptic movements and political parties, free movement is demonized as being potentially subversive of idealized self-sufficient societies – a 'two birds with a stone' kind of target that compounds anti-immigration and anti-EU sentiments.

***

The chapters that follow seek to illuminate the history, characteristics and social impact of the EU free movement regime. More specifically,

Chapter 1 examines the visions and first proposals – somewhat utopian – of a Europe without frontiers, and then reconstructs the successive stages of the introduction, application and extension of the right to free movement from the European Coal and Steel Community Treaty to the transitional measures for free movement by the citizens of the countries which joined the EU in 2007. Chapter 2 unpacks the array of EU policies which facilitate free movement, focusing on the Schengen system, the Erasmus Programme and the European Job Mobility Portal (EURES) as exemplary actions. In the following chapters, the attention shifts to the individuals who systematically exercise the right to free movement, that is, the European citizens who move their residences to a different member state. Currently, Eurostat data record about 13 million mobile Europeans or, otherwise put, around one European citizen in 40 – an underestimated figure which does not include commuters or people who move for brief periods (for example, Erasmus students). But who are the mobile Europeans? What do they do? When did they migrate and why? Chapter 3 tries to answer these questions on the basis of aggregate demographics on EU movers. Moving on to sociologically more informed analyses, two broad international surveys that were coordinated as part of research funded by the European Commission are drawn on: the Pioneer Project and the Moveact Project (see Methodological Appendix). Chapter 4 highlights the profound difference between the social integration of 'old' and 'new' EU mobile citizens in the receiving societies. Chapter 5 explores the consequences of mobility on the actual exercise of political citizenship rights. Finally, Chapter 6 specifies the empirical association between the experience of mobility and European identification. The chapter resumes the initial theme of free movement as the driver of social and cultural change, considering it within a theoretical framework which links 'practices' and 'values' via *habitus*, and comparing it critically with the dynamics of socialization outlined by classical political sociology. The Conclusion frames the book's results in a wider perspective. In the context of a historical trend towards greater international movements (of which migration is only one component), the EU emerges as a regional and paradigmatic human mobility system that – sustained by the economic and cultural forces described in this Introduction – approximates a possible model for a denationalized and open world predicated on the primacy of the person over territorially defined polities.

Part I
Theorizing Free Movement: History, Policies, Demographics

1
A Frontierless Continent: History of an Idea and Its Realization

1. European integration and the right to free movement: an inextricable tie

Although it has never aroused the collective fervour typical of great changes, European integration is the most revolutionary political transformation that has occurred in the West since the Second World War. The exceptional nature of this process is also evident if one adopts a longer diachronic perspective. Rarely – perhaps never – in history has sovereignty been *peacefully* transferred from polities as strong as the modern European nation states to other and broader organizations.[1] Should the world one day achieve a post-national order, it is very likely that Europe will have marked out the path.

The uniqueness of the process of European integration is even more evident if one assumes the standpoint of migration scholars. European Union citizens have opportunities unequalled in comparison with those of migrants in other parts of the world: they can travel, live, study, work and retire in whatever member state of the EU they choose, and once they have settled in that state, they are entitled to the same rights as its citizens – with the only significant exception of the right to vote in national parliamentary elections.[2] In cases of possible discrimination (in the workplace, in the property market, in access to health care and so on), they may appeal to the European Court of Justice (ECJ), which acts to ensure that citizens of the Union residing in another member state receive equal treatment.[3]

This does not mean that all EU citizens have the same rights wherever they decide to live, since each member state has its own set of civil, political and social rights (Hix and Høyland 2011, 280–1). Moreover, in practice EU movers' rights are implemented and 'contextualized' through differing national policies (Carmel 2013). In technical terms,

Table 1.1 Milestones of the EU free movement regime

Year	Event	Description
1951	European Coal and Steel Community Treaty	Free movement across member states granted to miners and steelworkers with recognized qualifications
1957	European Economic Community Treaty	Free movement across member states granted to workers in all occupational sectors
1968	Council Regulation 1612/68 and Council Directive 68/360	Abolition of all restrictions on the movement and residence of member state workers and their families and prohibition of any discrimination based on nationality
1973	Accession of UK, Ireland and Denmark	British, Irish and Danish citizens entitled to free movement rights immediately
1981	Accession of Greece	Greek citizens subject to seven year transitional measures for full free movement rights
1986	Accession of Spain and Portugal	Spanish and Portuguese citizens subject to seven year transitional measures for full free movement rights (then reduced to six)
1990	Directives 90/364, 90/365, 90/366	Free movement is extended to non-workers (retirees, students, others)
1992	Maastricht Treaty	Free movement defined as part of European citizenship
1995	Accession of Austria, Finland and Sweden	Austrian, Finnish and Swedish citizens entitled to free movement rights immediately
1990s (various dates)	Schengen Treaty	Abolition of border controls between member states
2004	Accession of Poland, Hungary, Czech Republic, Slovakia, Slovenia, Estonia, Latvia, Lithuania, Malta and Cyprus	New member state citizens entitled to full free movement rights immediately in UK, Ireland and Sweden, in 2006 in most EU15
2004	Directive 2004/38	Permanent residence rights for long-term EU movers
2007	Accession of Romania and Bulgaria	Romanian and Bulgarian citizens entitled to full free movement rights immediately in ten member states, simplified procedures elsewhere
2011	End of transitional measures (2004 enlargement)	Citizens of 2004 accession member states entitled to full free movement rights all over the EU
2014	End of transitional measures (2007 enlargement)	Citizens of 2007 accession member states entitled to full free movement rights all over the EU

both legal and statistical, the citizen of one EU member state who settles in another is still a foreigner. His or her position matches the standard definition of 'migrant' as proposed by the United Nations: 'a person who moves to a country other than that of his or her usual residence for a period of at least a year' (Alfieri and Havinga 2005, 2). Compared with all other international migrants, however, EU movers' status does not automatically entail having fewer rights than nationals.[4] To a large extent, mobile European citizens are international migrants with the same rights as internal migrants.

Migrating in the free movement regime means migrating 'in first class'. But it has not always been thus. Until a few decades ago, even after the introduction of the free movement regime, the Southern Europeans who worked in Central-Northern Europe were still *Gastarbeiter* in the eyes of the natives. Their legal emancipation has been coupled with a terminological shift. Noticeably, since the 1970s and 1980s, in the documents of the European Community and subsequently of the EU, 'migration', once used to refer to the movement of citizens of one member state to reside in another European country, has been replaced by 'mobility' – a more neutral term. In parallel, both the content of free movement rights and the categories of people entitled to them have expanded (Table 1.1). The successive stages of this change are reconstructed in the rest of this chapter.

2. A brief history of the right to free movement in Europe: the first steps

Differences in historical experience notwithstanding, the abolition of mobility constraints within national borders has been an essential part of the 'invention' of modern citizenship (Brubaker 1992; Torpey 2000). From the French Revolution onwards, the right to territorial mobility has been enshrined in the bulk of democratic constitutions. Correspondingly, since Kant's *Perpetual Peace* project, free movement across national boundaries was seen as the keystone of a future cosmopolitan order – though with some ambiguity concerning its implementation and limitations (see Archibugi 1995; Habermas 1997; Kleingeld 1998). Federalist thought, and especially the ideas of the British federalists of the early twentieth century, further elaborated this view to make it politically feasible in the European case (Pinder 1996). A direct heir to this cultural tradition and promoter of some of the most influential integrationist initiatives of the immediate post-war period was Winston Churchill. In the autumn of 1942, on the eve of the decisive battle of El Alamein, the then British prime minister wrote thus to Anthony Eden: 'My thoughts rest primarily in Europe [. . .]. I look forward to a United States of Europe in which the barriers between the nations will be greatly minimized and *unrestricted travel will be possible*' (Critchley 1996, 85; emphasis added). A few months later, in 1943, in an entirely independent manner and following the lead of socialist Europeanism (Landuyt 2004, 16 ff.), in *Gli Stati Uniti d'Europa e le Varie Tendenze Politiche* (which followed the more celebrated *Manifesto di Ventotene*), Altiero Spinelli gave to a future unitary European state, of which he outlined the features, the principal task of 'ensuring full freedom of movement for all citizens within the federation'.[5]

As we shall see, the history of European integration is inextricably tied to the history of realization of this vision of a continent without frontiers. To be noted in this regard is that the founding fathers of a united Europe shared the characteristic of being 'frontier men' by birth, as has often been pointed out: Schuman, a native of small Luxembourg poised between German and French influence; De Gasperi, from the Italian Trentino occupied by the Austro-Hungarian Empire; and Spaak, from a family of mixed Flemish and Walloon origins (Mayne 1996). All these men, and even more so Monnet, were also 'mobile Europeans' in every respect. Schuman studied in France and in Germany (whence he was conscripted into the French civil service during the First World War); the young De Gasperi sat in the Habsburg Parliament in Vienna, to be then elected to Rome, where he lived in the Vatican under fascism; Spaak was exiled to France, Spain, Portugal and Great Britain during the Nazi occupation. Finally, the biography of Monnet perfectly matches the portrait of a transnational European. Born into a bourgeois family in a small French town, as a young man he moved to London to learn English, and then travelled widely on business in Sweden, Russia, Egypt, Canada and the United States, where he lived for many years with his Italian wife (Duchêne 1996).

It was these men who launched the process of European integration. After some false starts (in particular, the aborted European Defence Community), the first successful initiative was the creation of the European Coal and Steel Community (ECSC), one of whose priorities was establishing the right to cross borders.[6] In the treaty instituting the ECSC – signed in Paris in April 1951 by representatives of the six states (Germany, France, Italy, Belgium, the Netherlands and Luxembourg) which would subsequently form the European Economic Community – Article 69 assured removal of 'any restriction based on nationality upon the employment in the coal and steel industries of workers who are nationals of Member States and have recognised qualifications in a coalmining or steel-making occupation'. Section 4 stipulated that member states 'shall prohibit any discrimination in remuneration and working conditions between nationals and migrant workers, without prejudice to special measures concerning frontier workers; in particular, they shall endeavour to settle among themselves any matters remaining to be dealt with in order to ensure that social security arrangements do not inhibit labour mobility'.

Historical reconstructions of the negotiations which for almost an entire year preceded the signing of the treaty, inducing Great Britain to withdraw, show that the Italian delegation, headed by Paolo Emilio Taviani, pushed strongly for Article 69 because of unemployment in Italy and the will to improve the living conditions of Italian migrants abroad.[7] In response to the reluctance of some delegations to include the article, Taviani raised the spectre of an international authority which would regulate the wages of miners and workers in heavy industry – an institution which would have been especially unwelcome to the Netherlands and Germany, where industrial relations in the mining and steelworking sectors were particularly difficult (Maas 2007, 13–14). In the definitive version of the article allowing nationals of the six countries to work abroad in the sectors specified by the treaty, and therefore indirectly guaranteeing their right to free entry on the national territory of the firms hiring them, the Italian delegation had to recognize a clause safeguarding state authority which was eventually borrowed by the Treaty of Rome, the Schengen Treaty and Directive 2004/38 on the right of free movement and establishment: the removal of restrictions became 'subject to the limitations imposed by the basic requirements of health and public policy'. Left ambiguous was the notion of 'recognized qualifications' in coalmining or steel-making – so that governments had another device with which to exclude unwelcome foreign workers. Finally, the free movement of miners and steelworkers was also subject to stipulation of a framework agreement on the right to free movement.

The ECSC Council only approved this last agreement in December 1954. As Maas notes, the drafting of the document required 'more than the time it had taken to negotiate the Treaty itself' (ibid., 16). As ratification by the last member state – Luxembourg – came in June 1957, the mobility of workers only became possible from September of that year. In the meantime, Italian migration to the other signatory countries continued to be regulated by the already existing bilateral agreements. Still in force in the mining sector was the Italo-Belgian agreement of 1946, on the basis of which the Belgian mining companies recruited two thousand Italian workers a week, receiving coal supplies at advantageous prices in exchange (Morelli 2004). The delayed implementation of Article 69 was irksome to the Italian representatives in the ECSC and also, apparently, to Jean Monnet himself, who as president of the ECSC High Authority declared: 'It is essential to tear down borders between European nations [. . .] we unite Europeans and we do not keep them separated. *We are not joining states, we are unifying men*' (Monnet 1955, 130–1 and 132). But such a lofty aspiration was certainly not a priority on the agendas of the governments of member states, who were fearful of the social, even more than the economic, consequences of this first step towards integration.

The tug-of-war between the young Community institutions, generally open to an extensive and rapid implementation of free movement rights, and the national governments, which were much more cautious, continued in the following decades. It centered in particular on the social security of migrant workers, which challenged the 'exclusiveness' of national citizenship as the source of welfare rights. The *modus vivendi* solution was inspired by the idea that the Community institutions would concern themselves with the 'coordination' of the national social security systems, rather than with their standardization. The Community regulations of those years, which only later decisions by the Court of Justice would modify, established four key principles: (a) non-discrimination and equality of treatment; (b) recognition of all insurance periods independently of the country of employment; (c) exportability of acquired rights; and (d) application of the law of the country of employment (*lex loci laboris*) (Ferrera 2005, 100–4). The primacy of national law was thus – at least apparently – preserved.

The positive experience of the ECSC opened the way for the subsequent European Economic Community Treaty (signed in Rome in March 1957) and, in parallel, for the re-proposal of the principle of mobility of workers in all occupational sectors. Article 48 of the Treaty of Rome affirmed the right to accept offers of employment from another member state; to move freely within the territory of the Community for that purpose and to reside in another member state once employment had been obtained. Article 48 also stipulated 'the abolition of any discrimination based on nationality between workers of the Member States as regards employment, remuneration and other conditions of work and employment' (section 2). The only limitations on this right concerned employment in public administrations and possible restrictions 'justified on grounds of public policy, public security or public health' (section 3). As a corollary to these provisions, Article 52 introduced the right of residence in the member states for self-employed workers, and Article 59 the possibility to furnish cross-border services.

Application of this package of principles came about slowly and gradually in the following decade, beginning only in 1961, when a first procedure was established for the acceptance of job offers by citizens of other member states: such offers had to be made public for three weeks to give priority to potential national candidates, after which the government authorities issued the work permit. Simultaneously, however, entry and exit visas were abolished for travel within the Community. In 1964, further Community legislation eliminated the three weeks' clause; and it extended the free movement right to the family members of workers moving abroad. It also established the important principle that member states could deny the crossing of their borders to individuals whose behaviour threatened public security or public health.

The definitive implementation of the free movement principle came in 1968, when Regulation 1612/68 and Directive 68/360 abolished all restrictions on the movement and residence of Community workers and their families. Regulation 1612/68 prohibited any discrimination based on nationality for migrants from other member states as regards remuneration, conditions of employment and unemployment benefit. It also established the right of Community workers to equal treatment by guaranteeing to their families the right to reside with them and take up any type of employment in the host country. Directive 68/360 considerably reduced the bureaucratic formalities necessary to cross intra-Community borders by granting workers and their families the right to enter a member state simply by producing a valid identity card or passport. Community migrants were also granted residence permits (of five-year duration and automatically renewable) on producing a certification of employment, and entitlement to remain in the host country if involuntarily unemployed. Free movement throughout the Community thus became a fundamental right for the *workers* of the member states. This leap of quality was greatly favoured by the economic conditions of the time: since economic growth had abated migratory pressure from Italy to the other member states, 'the mobility of the European workers was no longer socially and politically dangerous' (van der Mei 2003, 26).

The measures introduced in 1968 concluded the transitional regime envisaged by Article 49 of the Treaty of Rome (earlier than the anticipated term of 1970), and created the conditions for full exercise of the right to free movement within the European Community. They therefore represented an indisputable turning point. It is true that they tied the right of movement to work contracts, expressly relating it to 'workers' rather than 'citizenship', which was entirely in keeping with the economic focus of the process of European integration in its early years. But it is also true that in a period when migratory movements in Europe were subject to bilateral agreements centred on 'guest-work',[8] the Treaty of Rome inaugurated a legal regime of equality between migrants and national citizens which the vice-president of the European Commission during the early 1960s, the Italian socialist Lionello Levi Sandri, far-sightedly described as 'an incipient form – still embryonic and imperfect – of European citizenship' (cit. in Maas 2007, 21): an implicit citizenship, therefore, which derived from the labour market, and not from the recognition of individual rights.

3. Towards European citizenship

Since the 1970s until today, EC laws and decisions by the Court of Justice of the European Communities (subsequently Court of Justice of the EU) have decidedly widened the content and extent of the right to free movement as originally set forth in the Treaty of Rome. In particular, the ECJ has performed a key role in extending the scope of the general principle by shifting entitlement to the free movement right from *workers* to *persons*. On the basis of appeals lodged over time by individual citizens, the Court has been able to furnish a broader interpretation of Article 38 (ex 48) of the Treaty of Rome and Regulation 1612/68, which emphasizes the material dimension of citizenship included in the concept of free movement.[9] The ECJ has constantly interpreted the right of free movement as the right to 'all-around' equal treatment – not just in the labour market, but in society as a whole, and therefore in regard to the social, cultural and educational aspects of the lives of workers and their families in the host country (O'Keeffe 1998, 20–5). Its jurisprudence was decisive in extending the principle to encompass, in the 1970s, all self-employed workers, and then in the 1980s, seasonal workers, paid apprentices and university students who had entered employment in the host country – as also provided for by subsequent Community directives (Baldoni 2003, 8–9).[10]

During the 1970s and 1980s, European institutions put forward several proposals for the free movement regime to be linked with some form of supranational citizenship. The first proposal was mooted by the Italian government, with the support of the Belgian government, during the Paris European Summit of 1972. Such citizenship would have been additional to national citizenship and, after a certain period of residence in one of the member states, it would have allowed citizens of the Community to exercise political rights such as the right to vote in municipal elections. The question was taken up again and developed at the Copenhagen Summit of 1973, at which the foreign ministers of the member states issued a final declaration on European identity. Discussion of the proposal was postponed to the 1974 summit, again held in Paris, during which establishment of a 'passport union' was envisaged, as well as the possibility of granting citizens of member states special rights as members of the Community (Olsen 2012, 36). The only outcome, in fact, was the proposal of a common passport. Nevertheless, the debate had been opened, and the dogma of the exclusiveness of national citizenship – defended with particular vigour by Raymond Aron (1974) – had been explicitly breached. As Olsen observes (2012, 37), this novelty entailed that 'all European citizens were construed as *equals*, not only in terms of the specific rights bestowed on them from the Community, but also through belonging to the Community as such', thus configuring an 'external' dimension of common identity.

European citizenship was again mentioned by the 1975 Tindemans Report and, in the same year, by a Commission document bearing the eloquent title *Towards European Citizenship*. In 1977, a European Parliament resolution likewise expressed favour for the introduction of Community citizenship, thus opening the way for the 1984 *Draft Treaty Establishing the European Union*, with which the same Parliament (this time, however, democratically elected), and largely through the efforts of Altiero Spinelli, proposed that 'citizens of the Member States shall *ipso facto* be citizens of the Union' (see Olsen 2012, 50 ff.).

The appointment of Jacques Delors as president of the Commission gave new impetus to the process. It was associated with the neoliberal idea of giving great openness to the Community market in the 1986 *White Paper on Completing the Internal Market*, which formed the basis of the subsequent Treaty of Maastricht. In the meantime, the Commission headed by Delors promoted further initiatives to support mobility, such as the Erasmus Programme (see Chapter 2), while the Economic and Social Committee drew up the *Community Charter of the Fundamental Social Rights of Workers* (also known as the 'Social Charter'), adopted in 1989 by eleven of the twelve member states (Great Britain only adopted it in 1997 under the first Blair government). Although not directly operational in regard to free movement, the Charter harmonized the protection of Community workers against any potential attempt to discriminate against member state citizens on grounds of nationality.

As a logical consequence of the 1986 Single European Act – intended to create 'an area without frontiers in which free movement of goods, people, services and capital is ensured' – a significant step forward came in 1990, when Directives 90/364, 90/365, 90/366, and subsequently 93/96, explicitly extended freedom of movement to economically inactive persons: students, pensioners and the unemployed.[11] Unlike workers, however, individuals in these three new categories were required to fulfil two conditions to enjoy the right: they had to have health insurance and they had to possess sufficient resources so as not to impose additional costs on the host country's welfare system.

The idea of European citizenship assumed greater vigour and a more political dimension with the fall of the Berlin Wall. In 1990 and 1991, the debate intensified, involving all the Community and national institutions. In July 1990, the European Parliament approved a resolution on the matter which required the inclusion of provisions intended to develop 'real European citizenship' in treaties. In October of the same year, the Commission resumed its proposal of European citizenship, justifying it as a means to strengthen the Community's democratic legitimacy. Shortly thereafter, in November, the European Parliament approved a series of proposals for modification of the Treaty of Rome and foresaw inclusion of an article which defined anyone possessing citizenship of one of the member states as a European citizen. The institution of European citizenship now became an explicit goal, formulated and voted in immediately by the Conference of the Parliaments of the European Community. In December, a European Parliament resolution on the constitutional bases of the EU defined its contents. In the European Council meeting held in Rome during the same month, member states unanimously concurred that the issue of a European citizenship should be examined by the Intergovernmental Conference on Political Union convened for February 1991. As a result of that Conference, in June 1991, the proposal prepared by the Luxembourg government became definitive. In February 1992, finally, the heads of state and government of the member states signed the Treaty on the European Union in Maastricht.

The Maastricht Treaty entered into force in November 1993. It represented the culmination of a long process towards the full accomplishment of free cross-border mobility by officially introducing the status of European citizen. In concrete terms, European citizenship consists of a set of rights to which the citizens of every EU member state are automatically entitled: (a) the right to vote and stand as candidates in elections to the European Parliament and in local elections in the member state wherein they reside, regardless of their nationality; (b) the right to petition the European Parliament and appeal to the EU Ombudsman; (c) the right to diplomatic protection by any other member state of the

EU in third countries where their own country does not have diplomatic representation; and (d) the right to free movement and residence throughout the territory of the EU.

It is evident that a person can exercise the first three rights to only a modest extent compared with the last one. Although formally significant, the possibility to vote and stand for election to the European Parliament or to local governments only becomes of interest once a person has enjoyed the right to cross-state mobility. Whilst it is true that the right to vote is the most classic and evident discriminant between the status of citizen and foreigner, in this context it is a second-order right conditional upon residence. Petitions to the European Parliament, appeals to the Ombudsman and recourse to diplomatic protection are decidedly remote options for ordinary people. Freedom of movement and freedom of residence, by contrast, are immediately accessible rights which influence people's life opportunities. The free movement regime, in short, is the true keystone of the edifice of European citizenship.

4. **After Maastricht: citizenship, social rights and enlargement of the Union**

Spurred by the Maastricht Treaty, which seemed to steer the integration process in a bolder political direction, several member states drew up proposals to extend the range of rights associated with citizenship and to transfer traditionally national powers – in particular, those regarding social rights and naturalization procedures – to the EU. Portugal drafted a *European Citizens Charter* which enumerated the rights of citizens, its purpose being 'to provide citizens a clear picture of the advantages and added value of European citizenship' (Maas 2007, 69). This and other initiatives, however, were thwarted when unanimous consensus was not reached on a further treaty, mainly due to the intransigent opposition of the Danish and British governments. Hence, contrary to the expectations of many observers, the Amsterdam Treaty of June 1997 added little to nothing to the array of already existing citizenship rights – to be specific, only the right of European citizens to communicate with EU institutions in any of the EU's official languages. By contrast, the treaty introduced a clause designed to reassure Eurosceptics and nationalists: 'Citizenship of the Union shall be additional to and not replace national citizenship.' For their part, the Europhiles obtained incorporation of the Schengen Treaty which eliminated internal border controls into the new EU Treaty.

However, the Cologne European Council of June 1999 and the Tampere meeting held in October of the same year saw the strong return of integrationist forces, with a Constitution for Europe being set as the new objective. The task of drafting this document was given to the European Convention, a constituent assembly consisting of representatives of heads of state and government, the national parliaments, the European Parliament and the Commission. This was installed in December 1999. The draft Constitution of October 2000 included the Charter of Fundamental Rights of the EU, which specified in great detail the meaning and the effects of European citizenship in the social and economic spheres. The European Constitution was signed in Rome in October 2004, but its ratification was beset by extraordinary difficulties which eventually led to its suspension. The referenda held in France and in the Netherlands in May 2005 rejected it, and the open opposition mounted by some of the new member states subsequently prompted the drafting of a less ambitious treaty to reform European institutions.[12]

In the meantime, debate continued on how to adapt European institutions to the EU's imminent eastward and southward enlargements. Primarily devoted to this purpose was the Treaty of Nice signed in February 2001 and ratified two years later. This treaty contained an important innovation, as it established that decisions by the Council on free movement could be made with the qualified majority mechanism rather than by unanimity. This change made it easier for the European Commission to prepare a directive consolidating legislation on free movement without the risk of veto by hostile member states.

Directive 2004/38 established the general conditions for European citizens to exercise their right to move and reside on EU territory, not only by unifying the previous legislation scattered among two Regulations and nine different Directives, but also by adopting conclusions from ECJ jurisprudence. It thus gave full effect to European citizenship as conceived in abstract by the Maastricht Treaty: 'Although continuing to differentiate quite sharply between economically active and inactive citizens, the Directive made the right to free movement in the Union a fundamental and personal right, potentially unconstrained by strict dependence on a market logic' (Giubboni and Orlandini 2007, 7).

In detail, Directive 2004/38 established the right of European citizens to reside permanently outside their own countries and the responsibilities of the host country in regard to their social security, exempting them from additional formalities, such as, for example, a residence card. For the first time, three distinct categories of mobile Europeans and their family members were legally defined: short-term (up to three months), long-term (from three months to five years) and permanent (more than five years of continuous residence), in regard to which diversified benefits were to be disbursed by the welfare system of the host state (De Bruycker 2006).[13] For the first category, no formalities or restrictions were imposed on mobility (unless on exceptional grounds of public safety or public health). For the second category, the right to settle was made conditional on employment, enrolment in education or otherwise the possession of sufficient economic resources and health insurance so as not to become a burden on the welfare system of the host member state. After five years of continuous residence, mobile Europeans entered into the third category: that of citizens with the right to permanent residence. This right was no longer subject to conditions and therefore entailed the direct responsibility of the member state of residence to furnish the mobile citizen with social assistance.[14] As Ferrera notes (2005, 138), 'The implementation of this directive is bound to circumscribe severely not only the legal autonomy of member states in delimiting the sphere of social assistance, but also the actual exercise of this autonomy, through the "proportionality" qualifications for expulsion measures justified in financial terms.'

Compared with national citizens, mobile European who permanently reside in another member state do not have the right to vote in national elections, are excluded from employment in certain public administrations that require the exercise of state authority (see Barnard 2007, 481 ff.), and have decidedly more complicated access to certain benefits furnished by national welfare systems (especially social security: see Giubboni 2010).[15] If on the one hand the limitation of political rights is the unequivocal legacy of a citizenship which first came into being and developed as an expressly national institution, on the other hand there seems to emerge a 'derivative' system of supranational solidarity, not without controversies or conflicts, which tends to erode the exclusive sovereignty of individual member states (Giubboni 2007).

As has been shown, ever since its first formulation – at the outset of the process of European integration with the creation of the ECSC in 1951 – the right of Europeans to cross the boundaries of nation states has been flanked with further rights which extend the scope of those entitled to them: from only miners and steelworkers at the beginning of the 1950s to all workers at the end of the 1960s, and finally, to all economically self-sufficient persons in the 1990s. In the jargon of European studies, in short, the right to mobility has progressively 'deepened'. But the European integration process has developed in the sense not only of a deepening of contents but also of geographical enlargement. This was most markedly and significantly apparent in 2004 and 2007 with the accession of twelve new member states to the EU, ten of them located in Central-Eastern Europe and for around forty years separated by hostile and militarily garrisoned frontiers – mainly to prevent the inhabitants of those countries from moving *en masse* to the West.[16] In the space of fifteen years, there occurred an upheaval hardly imaginable during the Cold War: the Iron Curtain disappeared and free movement began over an area extending from the Atlantic to the Carpathians. What had been a forbidden dream for the citizens of the communist regimes became a subjective right exercisable simply by buying a railway ticket at any station from Transylvania to Silesia.

In point of fact, the free movement of the citizens of Central-Eastern Europe's new member states has been subject to a transitional regime of constraints and restrictions which has allowed each state to limit access by new EU citizens to its labour market as employees for a maximum of seven years (with a commitment to evaluating whether or not to renew the transitional regime, first after two years and then after five years). The measure, already applied on the occasion of the previous enlargements to Greece (1981), Spain (1986) and Portugal (1986), has officially served the purpose of abating possible 'migratory shocks'. Once again, this testifies to the unwillingness of nation states to delegate immigration policies, even partially, to supranational authorities. In 2004, moreover, the reluctance of the governments of the 'old' Europe found support in the bogeyman of the 'Polish plumber' evoked by some politicians and sections of the press (particularly in France), so that, on the occasion of the first Eastern enlargement, only Great Britain, Ireland and Sweden decided not to apply the transitional regime, thus becoming – as we shall see in Chapter 4 – the main destination countries of the intra-EU migration flows which ensued. Nevertheless, the British, Irish and Swedish example was imitated by the majority of the other member states in 2006 under pressure by the European Commission as it celebrated the European Year of Workers' Mobility. Even Austria, Germany, Belgium and Denmark, which decided to maintain the transitional regime, gradually admitted a series of exceptions to the rules applied to the recruitment of new EU citizen-workers in sectors with labour shortages (for instance, engineering in Germany). For citizens of the 2004 enlargement countries, the transitional regime expired in May 2011.

The situation proved even more complex when the transitional measures were applied to the intra-EU mobility of Bulgarian and Romanian citizens. Ten countries (among which, however, only Finland and Sweden were from the former EU15) offered Bulgarians and Romanians unrestricted access to their labour markets after the enlargement of 2007. The majority of the other member states introduced facilitations, simplifications or derogations in order to grant work permits in employment sectors with high demand for foreign workers. Likewise for this second enlargement, however, the transitional measures followed the '2 + 3 + 2' formula: they were subject to a first re-examination after two years; to a second one after a further three years; and, if not before, had to be removed after a total of seven years. The deadline for the elimination of every constraint on the free movement of Romanian and Bulgarian citizens in any other EU member state was thus set for 1 January 2014. By that date at the latest, every distinction on a national basis in the mobility rights of European citizens within the whole EU was definitively removed.

5. Conclusion: from utopia to routine to controversy

Free movement across national borders in Europe was envisaged as a utopia in the first half of the twentieth century; then it emerged as a long-term objective in the post-war years of the European integration process, finally becoming a tangible reality by the turn of the millennium. During this multi-decade process, the most significant events have indubitably been the abolition of restrictions on movement for workers and their families in 1968 and the introduction of European citizenship in 1992. Similarly fundamental has been the adoption of the Schengen system, which progressively came into effect during the 1990s, eliminating EU's internal borders (presented in more detail in Chapter 2). No less important, though less visible, has been the action of the ECJ, which has extended and reinforced the rights of mobile workers in the member states and has tenaciously combated – ruling after ruling – every discrimination based on nationality (Poiares Maduro 2002). Especially when European legislation on the matter has seemed indecisive, the Court has been inflexible in its removal of existing (or re-emerging) nationality-based privileges. It is the ECJ which has affirmed that free movement rights *already* entail the transnational solidarity that national governments have been unable to translate into political practice. There is little doubt that 'the activism by the European Court of Justice has transformed EU citizenship from a derivative status to a free-standing source of rights' (Joppke 2010b, 22).

As Foster writes (2011, 373): 'It is clear that the legal regime regulating the free movement of persons has come a long way from the near-empty and little-used original Treaty provision for it. It is ironic, then, at the present stage of the evolution of free movement rights, that the concern is whether those rights have now actually gone too far and encroached too much on areas of the member states' own national laws more than is universally acceptable.' This sort of preoccupation resonated particularly in connection with the euro crisis of the late 2000s–early 2010s and the increasing success of neo-nationalist parties. On several occasions and in different countries, plans were made for a restrictive revision of the Schengen rules. A scale-back of free movement rights was threatened by several political leaders, either to win Eurosceptics' votes as Nicholas Sarkozy did during his presidential campaign of 2012 or to protest against other member states' migration policies as France did when Italy granted six-month residence permits to illegal migrants from Northern Africa in the spring of 2011, allowing them to travel freely in the Schengen area, and as several member states proposed to do in March 2012 in reaction to Greece's supposed incapacity to stem illegal immigration from Turkey. Even more serious (because it was less clearly founded on critical events) was the April 2013 joint letter to the European Commission written by the governments of Austria, Germany, the Netherlands and the United Kingdom asking for restrictions on the free movement regime due to 'cheats' and 'abuses' in access to host countries' welfare systems. Marking a semantic shift, the letter referred to 'immigrants from other member states' rather than to 'movers' (Pascouau 2013). Opposition to free movement also creeps in through the national interpretations of the EU regulatory framework (Carmel and Paul 2013). Indeed, it is reported that in Belgium – although still quite exceptional and limited in absolute terms – the number of EU movers notified of expulsion as 'unreasonable burdens' to national social assistance 'more than tripled in three years', culminating in 2,712 such letters in January 2014 (Euronews 2014). Romanians and Bulgarians were the two largest nationalities affected. Meanwhile, in France, following a controversial dismantling of Roma camps in the summer of 2010, 'evictions and expulsions [of EU Roma citizens] have not only continued since the end of 2010, but they have gradually increased throughout 2011, 2012 and the first half of 2013' (Carrera 2013, 1). In May 2013, a popular referendum induced the Swiss government to introduce immigration quotas on long-term residence permits for EU citizens, invoking a 'safeguard clause' mentioned in the 1999 free movement agreement with the EU.[17] Restrictions or the total abolition of the EU free movement regime also figured in the platforms of rampant nationalist parties (such as UK Independence Party, Front National in France, Partij voor de Vrijheid in the Netherlands) at the European Parliament election of 2014. Although predominantly launched for electoral purposes, these proposals signal that the EU free movement regime is not irreversible should a contrary political will emerge. But, given the centrality of free movement illustrated in this chapter, such a scenario would strike a fatal blow to European integration altogether. Europe can hardly be one if Europeans cannot move and mingle across national borders.

2
Why Free Movement? Assessing Policies and Rationales

1. Pro-mobility policies in the EU: a classification

Since their early days in the 1950s, European institutions have devised a wide range of policies designed to encourage the free movement of citizens. These can be arranged within Lowi's (1972) well-known classification of public policies as 'constituent', 'regulatory' or 'distributive'. By contrast, there are no policies which encourage mobility that are of an openly 'redistributive' kind – that is, intended to shift resources from some social categories to others (Table 2.1).

The most important *constituent* public policy affecting transnational geographical mobility within the EU is indubitably European citizenship. Introduced – as already illustrated in Chapter 1 – in 1993 when the Maastricht Treaty entered into effect, European citizenship qualifies freedom of movement as an individual and universal right. An analogous symbolic and substantial value is associated with the Schengen system. Progressively implemented from the mid-1990s onwards, this system facilitates individual mobility between member states by eliminating border controls within the EU – with some exceptions. Likewise, the creation of a single currency can be considered a constituent policy which enhances free movement. The euro reduces transaction costs to the advantage of a population that appears increasingly interested in cross-border activities, and it helps workers and consumers compare wages and prices among countries – from the online purchase of cheap goods to job vacancies. European institutions themselves bring about cross-state mobility by attracting personnel from member states. Moreover, specific agencies and tools have been devised to support employment and health insurance coverage across Europe, such as the EU job-search website (EURES: European Employment Services) and the European health insurance card,

Table 2.1 Main European policies favouring intra-EU mobility

Constituent policies	Regulative policies	Distributive policies
• Community institutions (ECSC, EEC, Euratom, EU: since 1951) • European citizenship (since 1993) • EURES (since 1993) • Schengen Information System (since 1995) • Euro (since 2001) • EHIC (since 2006)	• Free movement, settlement and non-discrimination rights (since 1968) • Recognition of educational and professional qualifications (since 1990) • Harmonization of higher education (Bologna Process, ECTS: since 1990)* • Abolition of internal border controls (Schengen agreement: since 1995)**	• Student, teacher and researcher mobility grants (Erasmus, Marie Curie: since 1987) • Regional programmes of transborder cooperation (Interreg, European Territorial Cooperation: since 1990)

Notes: * The Bologna Process stems from non-binding state agreements without the direct involvement of EU institutions. Whilst these agreements are in line with the principle of harmonization of national systems, legally the Bologna Process is not an EU policy. ** In the first stage, Schengen agreements were signed independently from European law. Since the Amsterdam Treaty of 1997, they have become part of the *acquis communautaire*.

which guarantees emergency health care throughout the Union (EHIC: European Health Insurance Card). Both of these measures – in different yet complementary domains – are significant cases of constituent policies designed to facilitate intra-European mobility.

Other initiatives, such as the historic Directive 68/360 and Regulation 1612/68 on freedom of movement and the equal rights of migrants from member states, are examples of *regulatory* policies. Likewise belonging in this category are measures relative to the recognition of EU-wide equivalence of educational and professional qualifications. Equally significant are the ECJ's persistent interventions to defend such equivalence. In some cases, decisions by the Court have given broader interpretation to existing rules and thus further expanded the range of application of the right to free movement (Guild 2004; Carlier and Guild 2006). Indirectly, the harmonization of education systems – part of the so-called 'Bologna Process' – can also be considered a regulatory policy facilitating the mobility of EU citizens, insofar as it is aimed at the Europeanization of educational qualifications so that they are valid beyond national borders (see the note to Table 2.1).

The *distributive* policies with effects on the geographical mobility of EU citizens are instead more circumscribed, in that they consist largely in the awarding of study and research grants. Some of them, although they do not promote mobility in the first instance, encourage it through the enhancement of cross-country curricula and the international expansion of the labour-market prospects of their holders. Others instead avowedly pursue mobility as their main objective – as in the case of the Erasmus Programme, which, indeed, even extends beyond the boundaries of the EU (including Norway, Iceland, Liechtenstein and Turkey). Although the Erasmus Programme is endowed with relatively limited financial resources, it moves some 250,000 undergraduate and post-graduate students a year for periods varying between 3 and 12 months.[1] In addition, while addressed to a category of movers with more advanced qualifications, the Marie Curie Programme involves around 3,000 researchers a year. Finally, in a more indirect way, mobility is also encouraged by the policies of the European Regional Development Fund (ERDF), particularly when they aim to strengthen cross-border cooperation through the creation of new transport links, information and communication networks, and companies with multinational capital in border zones (from 1990 to 2006 termed Interreg programmes and thereafter European Territorial Cooperation). In the words of Johannes Hahn, European Commissioner for Regional Policy, 'European Territorial Cooperation is central to the construction of a common European space, and a cornerstone of European integration. It has clear European added value: helping to ensure that borders are not barriers and bringing Europeans closer together' (European Commission 2011b, 4).

For each category of policies, one specific measure among those mentioned will now be examined: EURES, the abolition of internal border controls (the Schengen system) and the Erasmus Programme, respectively. They are illustrative of how free movement issues span across different policy areas, such as labour markets (EURES), border control and police (Schengen), and education and youth (Erasmus).

2. A constituent policy: EURES, the European job mobility portal

EURES was launched in 1993 with the purpose of creating a Europe-wide organizational and Internet-based network to support European citizens who intend to move to work in another EU member state (as well as Iceland, Liechtenstein, Norway and Switzerland).[2] Belonging to the network (coordinated by the European Commission) are national public employment services (PES), trade unions and employers' organizations in the countries concerned. EURES has more than 850 advisers available to users throughout Europe. The advisers – tellingly termed 'Euro-counsellors' – are experts on legal, administrative and logistical questions having to do with intra-European mobility and who work in PES or for other partner organizations.

The dynamic heart of EURES, however, beats on the Web, where those seeking jobs abroad or those offering them to immigrant labour (but from within the EU) can showcase themselves.[3] The services of the EURES web portal – free of charge and updated in real time – can be personalized through *My EURES* individual accounts by those seeking or offering jobs.[4] Candidates can post their CVs online just as is done on job-search websites managed by private companies. Employers can browse the profiles of candidates and make job offers. Jobseekers can receive email alerts on job vacancies which match their profiles, subscribe to thematic newsletters and contact the EURES advisers.

The typical users of the portal are students who are looking for information about the labour markets of other European countries, recent graduates looking for work experience placements and internships, workers prepared to move abroad for a medium-long period time with a good knowledge of one or more languages besides that of the country of origin and companies unable to find what they need on the local labour market. The majority of vacancies are available in Germany, the UK and France, and job offers are concentrated in information technology (systems engineers and programmers), catering (cooks, kitchen helpers, bartenders, waiters), marketing (sales and marketing managers) and mechanical engineering (engineers, technicians and welders).

The services furnished by the EURES network – both traditionally through the advisers and in the more up-to-date form of online contact – are intended to match labour supply and demand in a manner that is not only efficient but also fair and respectful of the rights of the parties. Through EURES, the European Commission endeavours to promote a 'fair mobility' based on the struggle against migrant worker exploitation and the black economy, to ensure protection and safety at work, as well as respect for the legal rights of workers and employers. EURES also organizes informational meetings on labour-market trends and specific occupational profiles – basically, job events with an EU-wide connotation (also online: www.europeanjobdays.eu).

In 2003, in recognition of the effectiveness of the EURES network, the European Commission decided to reform its legal bases so that EURES would become the European body which links together national PES and assumes responsibility for yearly European job fairs. Job vacancies on display on the web portal hover around 1.5 million, individual CVs around one million and companies offering jobs around 30,000.[5] The portal receives some 3.6 million visits per month and delivers approximately 150,000 job placements abroad per year – two-thirds of which are without face-to-face mediation (Ackers 2012). EURES performs a particularly important role in cross-border regions by responding to requests for information and proposing *ad hoc* solutions to problems arising from this specific and complex type of intra-European commuting. As stated by the EURES website, it is estimated that more than 600,000 Europeans live in one country and work in another, and they constantly encounter legal, administrative and fiscal obstacles. Thanks to the EURES network, today more than 20 cross-frontier partnerships[6] respond to the information and coordination needs of mobile labour in border regions. They constitute the linkages between local authorities, national administrations, employment centres and the social partners (that is, in the EU's jargon, employers' organizations and trade unions) on the two sides of the border. Thus created, EURES is 'an undisputable example of "stratarchic" interaction directly linking supranational rulers pursuing deliberate and distinctive spatial objectives, and subnational developmental coalitions interested in responding to new local needs and at the same time seeking resources for strengthening the institutional foundations of their communities' (Ferrera 2005, 188).

3. A regulative policy: Schengen, the abolition of border controls

The Schengen agreement, which was incorporated into the EU Treaty in 1999, is a fundamental complement to the right of free movement. From the agreement stem the abolition of internal borders among signatory states and the creation of a single external frontier, the unification of entry conditions and the issue of visas, the sharing of rules on the right to asylum (in application of the Dublin Convention), the coordination of external frontier surveillance to combat illegal immigration, the duty to communicate third-country citizens' movements from one state to another (recorded through the Schengen Information System),[7] the strengthening of judicial collaboration and the right to tail and pursue criminals from one state to another. As of today, the dispositions of the Schengen *acquis* are fully applied by almost all EU and EFTA member states: Austria, Belgium, Cyprus, Denmark, Estonia, Finland, France (and through it the Principality of Monaco), Germany, Greece, Iceland, Italy (and through it San Marino and the Vatican), Latvia, Liechtenstein, Lithuania, Luxembourg, Malta, Monaco, Norway, the Netherlands, Poland, Portugal, the Czech Republic, Slovakia, Slovenia, Spain, Sweden, Switzerland and Hungary.[8] Thus a map is drawn of a Europe without borders which extends from the North Pole to the Mediterranean.

The most visible effects of Schengen are the end of the obligation to show a passport when crossing borders among member states, and the separation at ports and airports between persons travelling within the Schengen area and those arriving from outside, the purpose being to concentrate police controls on the latter. Citizens of the Schengen area countries therefore have the right to enter all other member states without particular formalities: possession of a valid identity document is sufficient. The right to travel in the Schengen area can be restricted only for reasons of safety, health and public order upon express decision by the national authorities according to the so-called 'safeguard clause'.[9] A third-country citizen can enter and travel in the Schengen area for a maximum period of three months provided that s/he possesses a valid travel document and a transit or short-stay visa (the 'uniform Schengen visa'),[10] can justify the purpose of his/her journey, has sufficient means of subsistence for the duration of the stay and for the return journey, is not signalled in the Schengen Information System and is not considered a threat to the public order or national security of one of the member states.[11] Those wishing to stay for more than three months must have a long-term stay permit (the 'national visa'), which each state can grant in conformity with national law.

Historically, this regime has come about little by little; and it initially did so separately from the *acquis communautaire*. Schengen was created in 1985 as a cooperation agreement among Belgium, France, Germany, Luxembourg and the Netherlands. Its convention of implementation was signed in 1990, and it entered into effect in 1995. It should therefore be stressed that the objective of a Europe without border controls was initially defined and pursued within the framework of an intergovernmental covenant which, over time, has come to involve a total of 30 countries. Schengen was then incorporated into the EU legal system after the 1997 Treaty of Amsterdam.

The formation of the Schengen area is an example of the incrementalism through which European integration typically advances. The discussion on the need to extend free movement to include persons (and therefore not just goods, services and capital) dates back to the early days of the Community, but it was only in the 1980s that the debate began to consider eliminating surveillance on movements among the member states (see Chapter 1). The outcome was the creation of a restricted area consisting of the first Schengen signatory countries, in which controls on internal borders were abolished, as well as the requirement to possess a passport for expatriation. The original intention was that these measures should concern only citizens of the contracting countries. But control procedures were not significantly accelerated, because it was still necessary to verify the nationality of persons arriving at border crossings. It was to remedy this situation that controls at internal borders were eventually eliminated for all passengers while those at external borders were strengthened in parallel.

As Guiraudon (2003) puts it, Schengen balanced free movement with the securitization of external borders by implementing a common policy on immigration and asylum and a more efficient coordination of national security agencies. The Schengen system thus reproduces the classic model of national citizenship in which borders perform the role of physically distinguishing between insiders and outsiders (Olsen 2012, 77). Yet the system's logic also confronts European governments with a constant challenge: that of forcing member states to trust each other, in order both to share the benefits of free movement and to prevent its undesired effects.

4. A distributive policy: Erasmus, mobility in higher education

The purpose of the Erasmus Programme (where 'Erasmus' is not only a reference to the sixteenth-century Dutch humanist Desiderius Erasmus Roterodamus but also an acronym for *EuRopean Action Scheme for Mobility of University Students*) is to promote student exchanges among European universities through the awarding of grants and the recognition of examinations taken abroad. In concrete terms, the programme allows all students of the EU member states (but also Iceland, Liechtenstein, Norway, Switzerland and Turkey) to study at a foreign university, and/or undertake an internship at a foreign firm, for a period varying from 3 to 12 months. More than the grant – which is decidedly modest (approximately 250 euros a month) – Erasmus entitles participants to attend courses and sit examinations, take a language course and use sports facilities at the host institution. The budget for the years 2007–2013 amounted to some three billion euros.[12]

The Erasmus Programme was launched in 1987 with the adoption of a Community action programme for student mobility. It came at the end of a long period of gestation which began in the mid-1970s, and it was inaugurated by the *Joint Study Programmes Scheme*, a pioneering short-range initiative (it involved around 600 students between 1976 and 1986) intended to support joint study programmes adopted by universities in different countries. In the first year (1987–1988), 3,244 students from 11 countries participated. In 1995, Erasmus was incorporated into the Socrates community action programme as a specific chapter devoted to higher education.[13] In 2002–2003, the year when the threshold of one million participants was surpassed, there were 123,957 Erasmus student grant-holders from 30 different countries. In 2007, coinciding with the twentieth anniversary of Erasmus, the programme entered a new phase when it was incorporated into the *Lifelong Learning Programme*.[14] Eighty per cent of the budget for the sector was allocated to Erasmus, thus emphasizing the prime function of mobility in the growth of the EU, and superimposing – in public opinion, but also in EU budgets – Erasmus and the EU's interest for mobility in Europe. In 2010–2011, 231,408 students participated in the programme, and 33 different countries were involved. The total number of Erasmus students then reached 2,300,243, with an almost constant annual increase in participants.

Since the first Community student mobility programme of 1987, Erasmus has undergone profound quantitative and qualitative changes. The programme's initial purpose was to train a European elite consisting of young people able to operate beyond their national and cultural borders. In a field like education, in which the European Commission does not have specific competences – and with a strategic objective as particularly difficult to pursue as the Europe-wide harmonization of higher education – student mobility is regarded as a powerful device with which to foster the emergence of a labour market extending across the continent and open to highly qualified professionals and workers.

With its incorporation into the Socrates framework, the range of goals pursued by the Erasmus Programme has been extended to encompass the Europeanization of a broader array of training systems and individuals. Student mobility is seen as a factor which also, directly and indirectly, brings people not involved in mobility schemes (other students, teachers, family members) closer to Europe. The Erasmus Programme thus stands at the crossroads between formal and informal learning: besides institutional education, it offers opportunities for more general personal enrichment. The inclusion of Erasmus in the *Lifelong Learning Programme* further emphasizes this crucial aspect by offering opportunities alongside formal education – or as an alternative to it – to develop experience at firms, training centres, research institutes, organizations and institutions. Living, studying and working in another

European country are presented as occasions not only for movers to put their skills to the test, but also to participate in cross-cultural activities which stimulate a shared sense of belonging. On observing the development of Erasmus in the two decades of its history, one discerns a gradual shift of emphasis from the professional dimension to the cultural one. A typical case of spillover from a tool for the enhancement of human capital, Erasmus has progressively turned into a policy with an explicitly broader non-economic purpose.

5. Conclusion: mobility for what?

Free movement has been relentlessly encouraged by European institutions through a variety of policies. As examples of differing types and realms of EU pro-mobility policies, this chapter has illustrated the cases of EURES, Schengen and Erasmus. What can explain this wide-ranging and persistent policy efforts by the EU to spur its citizens to move? What does the EU expect out of enhanced cross-state mobility of people? The prevailing answer is this: a more integrated and efficient economy. The mainstream view among economists is that intra-European mobility is the necessary labour-market complement to monetary union. Within a vast area that uses the same currency, the mobility of workers is functional to the absorption of imbalances due to the possible decline of some national production systems (in economic jargon, 'asymmetric shocks'). This appears especially important because, since the monetary union, it has no longer been possible to counteract these shocks through state intervention – by devaluing the national currency or providing state aid to industries in difficulty. In short, the facility of moving labour from one country to another is regarded as a sort of *employment insurance* against the labour-market imbalances that may occur in a supranational economic system. This argument was first put forward by Robert Mundell (1961), the Nobel Prize winner for economics in 1999, and it provides the most solid macroeconomic basis for free movement in the EU (see Braunerhjelm et al. 2000; Sapir et al. 2004). In times of crisis, it has been revived in Brussels to justify the EC continuing commitment to foment free movement (Reding et al. 2013).

A complementary argument, which is also particularly dear to the European Commission (2007a, 2007b), emphasizes the importance of workers' geographical mobility for a more efficient allocation of human capital on a Europe-wide scale. Job opportunities across borders not only mitigate the risks of localized unemployment and underemployment, but also allow more fruitful use to be made of professional skills, thus acting as a *productivity enhancer* by improving the match between labour supply and demand.

A variation on the theme concerns the stimulus for innovation imparted by the mobility of knowledge workers. The argument is inspired by the Lisbon Strategy of 2000. In this case, reference is made not so much to the mobility of average workers in general as to R&D specialists. If talented people can move freely, they can contribute better to R&D in the firms and institutions best able to make their abilities bear fruit. Intra-European mobility thus acts as a sort of *innovation trigger*, boosting the technological progress on which solid and enduring economic development notoriously depends.

Finally, from a political point of view, freedom of movement is regarded as a powerful driver of European integration 'from below', capable of taming nationalism and amplifying a supranational collective identity. In substance, mobility is considered a *legitimacy tool* of the EU. This idea appears in embryonic form in the classics of federalist thought (see Chapter 1). In the social science literature, it has been defended in Ernest Gellner's *Nations and Nationalism*:

> If this freedom of international movement became general, nationalism would cease to be a problem; or at any rate, communication gaps engendered by cultural differences would cease to be significant and would no longer produce nationalist tensions. Nationalism as a permanent problem, as a Damocles' sword hanging over any polity which dares to defy the nationalist imperative of the congruence of political and cultural boundaries, would be removed. (Gellner 1983, 118)

From a policy-oriented perspective, in the history of European integration such a tenet has perhaps been made explicit for the first time in the two so-called Adonnino reports on *A People's Europe*, produced by an *ad hoc* committee of the European Parliament upon request of the European Council in 1985. These reports coupled the encouragement of free movement with other more mundane proposals – such as a euro-lottery – to strengthen Europeans' collective identification (Shore 2000, 46–7; Theiler 2005, 60–2). The approach has recurred in numerous documents of European institutions since then. For example, in the *Action Plan for Mobility*, the European Commission (2002) expressly stated that individuals who use their rights to free movement are expected to appreciate European citizenship and support European integration with more enthusiasm than non-mobile Europeans. This is explicitly reiterated in the most recent legislation. The preamble to the Directive 2004/38, which consolidates and extends the rights to free movement, states as follows: 'Enjoyment of permanent residence by Union citizens who have chosen to settle long term in the host Member State would strengthen the feeling of Union citizenship and is a key element in promoting social cohesion, which is one of the fundamental objectives of the Union.' Implicit in this statement is the claim that mobile Europeans are a population crucial for tempering nationalisms and embodying the vision of a united Europe as the forerunner of a cosmopolitan society.[15] In short, European movers are seen as the champions of an 'ever closer Union'. Potentially, free movement across the borders of the EU member states, associated as it is with the status of European citizen, gives individuals great awareness of the role of the European institutions and of the potentially ampler life chances created by EU policies, thus strengthening the sense of belonging to Europe.

Although all the arguments outlined above seem correct in principle, are they indeed well-founded, and therefore such as to justify the public policies and investments devoted to the mobility of European citizens? Let us review them again in the light of empirical analyses. As we shall see, studies able to give precise answers are fewer than might be expected, and their findings are anything but unanimous.

As regards free movement as *employment insurance*, migration among European countries has been a traditional response to unemployment – just consider the flows from the South to the North of the continent in the post-war period (see, for example, Bade 2003, 204 ff.; Recchi 2006). Nevertheless, this has been less true in recent decades than it was during *les trente glorieuses*. Puhani (1999) has estimated that in the 1980s and 1990s, the extent of unemployment offset by European migration was only 8 per cent in France and 4 per cent in Italy, with a maximum of 30 per cent in the German labour market.[16] On the basis of similar data, Mouhoud and Oudinet (2004) maintain that the migratory response to unemployment differentials is so weak that it would take decades to rebalance them through intra-European mobility. Even in the aftermath of the euro crisis that started in 2009, it was found that Southern Europeans, and particularly Italians and the Portuguese (the two largest communities of intra-European migrants only a couple of decades ago), resisted the allure of intra-EU migration (Recchi and Salamońska 2015). Overall, EU cross-state mobility figures have increased quite modestly in the 2009–2013 period. In the national economy that has suffered the most and made the most dramatic cuts to social welfare schemes – Greece – the proportion of citizens who left hovered around 5 per 1,000 in 2010–2011 – that is, proportionally as many as Poles, who were in fact experiencing uncommonly solid economic growth.[17] Hence, at least so far, intra-European labour mobility has been an economic adjustment mechanism of little significance in regard to growth disequilibria, despite the presence of sizeable wage and employability differentials among countries and sectors.

In regard to free movement as a *productivity enhancer*, it is to be noted that the poorer macroeconomic performances of some countries is also blamed on a systemic mismatch between individual abilities and the national division of labour. According to this diagnosis, the European economies would improve if only they allocated human capital more efficiently through a greater labour mobility among firms and therefore often among geographical areas (Padoa Schioppa 1991; Kostoris Padoa Schioppa 1999). More mobility would mean less unemployment, but above all less underemployment (like that of young graduates working in call centres or fast food outlets), which also entails productivity losses. Yet the proposition that workers' geographical mobility generates higher productivity is still entirely to be proved – for example, by comparing the wages (assumed as a proxy for productivity) of mobile and non-mobile workers. Unfortunately, it is difficult to obtain systematic empirical data enabling such comparison. Interesting, though indirect, results are reported by studies on the relationship between occupational mobility and productivity inasmuch as changing jobs entails a change of residence. Numerous econometric analyses show that productivity suffers in the case of frequent job changes (Auer et al. 2004), while it increases with tenure, albeit at a declining rate. The reason for this is that productivity derives from two distinct forms of human capital: 'general', which stems from school education, and 'specific', which relates to experience accumulated in a particular workplace. The former type of capital is fixed, while the latter tends to grow with the continuity of employment. The more productivity depends on specific human capital, the greater the benefit of job stability – and therefore also of spatial immobility. In short, whilst unrestrained geographical mobility seems able to ensure that the right person has the right job, it is equally true that many occupations need a stable workforce to guarantee maximum productivity.

At first sight, the argument that free movement acts as an *innovation trigger* can be tested by considering the relationship in a given interval of time between the inflow of workers into a geographical area (on whatever scale: national, regional or local) and the number of patents issued in that area. In the USA, Richard Florida did not find a significant statistical association between the total flow of immigrants and innovation in metropolitan areas (Florida 2002, 254–5). However, this simple measure may be misleading because patents depend on the activity of an extremely small and select group of workers – namely, researchers and inventors. Even if the areas of high immigration and strong innovation happened to coincide, this would not necessarily be convincing proof of a causal relationship between the two phenomena. What instead fuels technological progress is the 'density of human capital',[18] which, according to Florida (2002), can be achieved through the mobility of high-skilled workers. Thus, the ideal test of the mobility–innovation causal link would require measurement of innovation (for example, the number and utility of patents) by scientists and researchers *after* their employment in geographical areas different from those in which they worked previously. A test of this kind has apparently never been conducted in Europe. At any rate, the measures for researchers' mobility – such as the already mentioned Marie Curie Programme – launched by the EU are at least justified on another ground: Even when R&D people's mobility is not a direct cause of innovation, it facilitates the construction of social networks and epistemic communities which constitute added value for research in the long run.

Finally, the argument that free movement is a powerful *legitimacy tool* has been put to test in a research project conducted between 2004 and 2006 in the five main EU15 countries – the Pioneur Project (whose data will be analysed in more detail in Chapters 4, 5 and 6). The project found that intra-EU mobility goes together with stronger legitimation of the integration process – at least among Western European citizens (Rother and Nebe 2009). In other words, EU movers show stronger attachment to the EU, have a decidedly more positive image of it and perceive themselves as better informed about European policies and institutions than people who continue to live in their home country. Although a self-selection problem in the data, whereby anti-EU individuals either do not move or do not remain in the countries to which they have moved, cannot be ruled out, evidence is that favourable attitudes to the EU are stronger the longer people have lived in another European country. Repeated experiences of easy border crossing and the enjoyment of denationalized rights as EU citizens, even when occasionally problematic, are likely behind a greater appreciation of the benefits of the European integration process altogether. The argument shall be taken up in greater detail in Chapter 6. On balance, considering the available evidence, the economic returns of intra-EU mobility are more controversial than its legitimacy dividends.

3
EU Movers: How Many Are There, Where Are They, What Do They Do?

1. The precursors: intra-European mobility before citizenship

When the train left Milan station one morning in September 1957, its passengers thought about their mothers, their wives, their children and their mountains disappearing over the horizon behind them. They certainly did not know that one day they would be remembered as the first Europeans who could exercise their right to free movement – albeit in the limited forms envisaged by the ECSC Treaty. In the testimonies collected over time by historians, most of them admitted that they had no idea of where their destination, Belgium, was situated; even less were they aware of the incipient process of European integration. As touchingly recounted by a second-generation Italo-Belgian: 'The journey was for them but a minor logistical episode, embedded somewhere among poverty, hunger, war, and silicosis. Never in their talk did they claim to be heroic; never did they describe the journey as difficult and decisive' (Canovi 2011, 10). The night before their departure, they had been examined by a Belgian doctor and, on being deemed fit, had signed a work contract which stipulated their pay and lodging. Like so many before and after them, they travelled without stopovers to Brussels, where they alighted on the platforms allocated to goods trains so that they would not mix with other travellers. From Brussels, they were taken by lorry to the mines where the jobs that they had so long sought awaited them – and for too many of them, also a tragic death in the accidents and disasters that, counting the casualties in the fire at the Marcinelle colliery in 1956, claimed 868 victims between 1946 and 1963 (Rossini 2006).

Even in this dramatic context, the Italian workers who settled in Europe during the 1950s and 1960s were the precursors of the mobile Europeans of today. Thanks to two belatedly implemented clauses in the constitutive treaties of the ECSC and the European Economic Community (EEC) which were strongly promoted by the governments in Rome (see Chapter 1), the journeys of these Italian workers came about under the aegis of free movement. And even though free movement rights did not receive complete legal recognition until 1968, their migratory project exhibited a pattern which already prefigured the intracontinental mobility of the following decades: relatively short-range, circular or for commuting purposes. It was thus quite different from the transatlantic migrations which hitherto had preceded definitive settlement. In the 1950s, Italian emigrants still divided equally between those who crossed the Atlantic and those who crossed the Alps. In the 1960s, however, the intercontinental journeys became rarer: over 80 per cent had a European country as their destination (Livi Bacci 1972, 114). In the meantime, another phenomenon emerged: strong expatriation flows were matched by equally large movements back to Italy. In the 1946–1951 period, less than half of all Italian emigrants returned to the homeland; however, almost 60 per cent did so in 1952–1957; 63–65 per cent in 1958–1963 and 88 per cent in 1964–1969 (Romero 2001, 412).

In those decades, Italians were the first and the most numerous of intra-European migrants. Between 1946 and 1970, over one and a half million Italians settled in another country of the continent (Pugliese 2002, 21–2).[1] But they were soon followed by the Spanish, the Portuguese and the Greeks, along the same South–North route, and in response to the same socioeconomic conditions, as well as to a similar demand for blue-collar labour in Europe's industrial heartland. Spanish emigration took off in 1960, as a result of the agreement signed by Franco with the German government to deal with the shock to the Spanish economy caused by the 1959 Liberalization Plan (Ródenas Calatayud 1994, 63 ff.). During the 1960s, emigration from Portugal also grew apace, especially to France, which hosted more than 800,000 Portuguese citizens at the end of the decade (Moch 1992, 185), and from Greece, with Germany as its main destination. However, being a citizen of a member state of the EEC gave greater freedom of movement to Italians – as testified by the fact that in Germany, in 1966, 69 per cent of Greeks and Spaniards and 80 per cent of Portuguese had immigrated on the basis of official recruitment programmes compliant with intergovernmental accords, while only 8 per cent of the Italians had done so (Romero 2001, 413).

At the beginning of the 1970s, immigrants in the industrialized societies of Central and Northern Europe accounted for between 5 and 10 per cent of the resident population, with peaks of 15 per cent in Switzerland and 25 per cent in Luxembourg (Recchi et al. 2003, 6). It is not easy to estimate the number of Europeans among them, but it must have been greater if – as in the cases of Germany, Luxembourg, Sweden and Switzerland – the receiving country did not have a reservoir of labour in its former colonies.[2] At the beginning of the decade around one and a half million Italian, Spanish, Portuguese and Greek citizens were resident in Western Germany (Rogers 1985, 5–9). The statistics on workers alone record 1,800,000 member state citizens employed in another of the nine EEC member states in 1973 (Molle and Van Mourik 1988, 326).

As is well known, the 1973–1974 oil crisis marked a watershed in the history of continental migrations. With the crisis, the demand for foreign workers collapsed, and immigration policies were made more restrictive. Paradoxically, despite the numerous repatriation programmes introduced in France, Germany and the Netherlands, the outflows were less than expected, owing to the immigrants' fear that they would be unable to re-enter the country in the future. In this regard, migrants from EEC member states – in that period, the Italians – were at an advantage, because the free movement regime gave them a chance to go back and forth between the origin and destination country. As a consequence, they were relatively more inclined to repatriate: in 1974–1975, some 235,000 Italian migrants returned home from the countries of Central and Northern Europe – a number decidedly larger than those for the other nationalities (Lebon and Falchi 1980, 545). Towards the end of this phase of reduced labour mobility in 1985, around 1,200,000 Community workers were resident in another member state (Molle and Van Mourik 1988, 326). But the emphasis on migrant workers typical of the statistical surveys and sociological analyses of that period is misleading. As Western economies restructured themselves and as employment declined, migration became less strictly labour-oriented. Family reunifications grew more frequent, especially for citizens of third countries, and other forms of mobility – for instance, by students and pensioners – emerged. They were facilitated by the support for not purely work-oriented free movement systematically provided for by the ECJ (see Chapter 1). Only a minimal part of the citizens of the new member states who moved to other European countries fitted with the *Gastarbeiter* model of migration, now superseded economically by the decline of Fordism and legally by the evolution of free movement rights.

2. How many movers are there? Slow progress and a leap forward

Whilst there is a large body of literature on policies and legislation concerning mobility within the EU (and its earlier incarnations), as we saw in Chapter 2, surprisingly little is known about the demographic and sociological characteristics of the protagonists of these migratory flows. This is firstly because migration statistics, despite substantial improvements compared with some decades ago, lag behind when it comes to tracking cross-border flows of European citizens. It is likewise due to the scant harmonization of national bureaucracies and their statistical systems: some countries have municipal registers, others do not, and even where they exist, there are not always sufficient incentives to declare residency (Poulain et al. 2006). Moreover, a significant part of intra-EU migration has an 'incomplete' or 'liquid' character, marked by short-term or circulatory cross-border projects (Okolski 2001; Engbersen et al. 2010). Linked to this, there is a widespread reluctance of mobile Europeans to register as residents – after all, the sheer notion of EU citizenship-backed mobility has been dubbed by lawyers as 'the right *not* to encounter the administrative authorities of a member state' (Guild 2006, 15). This last limitation casts serious doubts on every estimate of entry and exit flows, except for the special cases of citizens who must possess a specific permit – particularly, so-called 'posted workers'.[3] Consequently, in this chapter, I shall almost exclusively examine data on stocks: that is, the figures on legally resident EU citizens. Moreover, because of a radical difference characterizing intra-European mobility at the turn of the twenty-first century, I shall distinguish the mobile population into two macro-categories: 'old' European citizens (that is, of the EU15 member states) and 'new' European citizens (that is, of the states which joined the EU in the first decade of the 2000s).[4]

Figure 3.1 shows the evolution of the stocks of Europeans resident in a member state different from the one of which they are citizens between 1990 and 2012. It also shows the incidence in the total number of presences in the five largest EU countries – Germany, France, the UK, Italy and Spain. In this time span, the mobile European population more than doubled: from 5,400,000 to 13,600,000 people. The growth, however, was fuelled more by political events than by socioeconomic changes or in-built migration dynamics (such as network-based flows). The change of pace happened, in fact, with the eastward enlargements of 2004 and 2007. It was during the 2000s, and before the actual enlargements, that intracontinental migration massively increased, fuelled by a sort of 'announcement effect'. By contrast, another significant political event – the introduction of EU citizenship in 1993, which strengthened

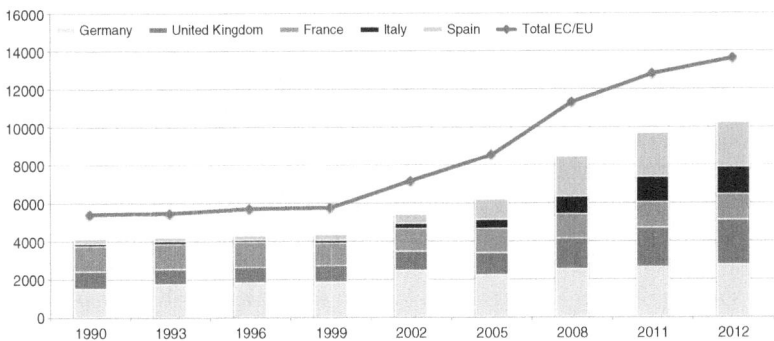

Figure 3.1 European citizens residing in a member state different from their own, 1990–2012 (in thousands)

Source: Eurostat Statistics Database, Population and Social Conditions (http://epp.eurostat.ec.europa.eu/portal/page/portal/statistics/search_database, consulted between 2002 and 2013).

Note: Data on France for 1993, 1996 and 2005 are not available and have been replaced with the closest available year.

the right to free movement, at least symbolically – had almost no impact on the mobility practices of neo-European citizens. The 1990s saw a very modest rise (around 6 per cent) in the stock of mobile Europeans. Half of them resided in Germany (around 30 per cent) and France (around 20 per cent). Spain and Italy, in fact, hosted only a very small number of movers: the two countries jointly accounted for 10 per cent of the total number of foreign EU residents. In 2002, as said, mainly but not solely because of the removal of the visa requirement for entry into Western Europe by citizens of the countries about to join the EU, movers (including the latter) abruptly increased to more than seven million in number. Almost two and a half million of them lived in Germany; numbers started to become substantial in Spain – close to half a million. The growth of the mobile population continued, and indeed accelerated, after the enlargement to Romania and Bulgaria. Spain's appeal increased further. The presence of intra-EU migrants on Spanish territory rose fourfold in six years, reaching two million in 2008 – that is, only 400,000 less than Germany (a gap that was reduced even slightly further in 2012, in spite of the euro crisis in Spain). After enlargements, the quota of EU movers in Great Britain exceeded that of France, which in turn was attained by Italy where large flows came from Eastern Europe. Moreover, despite the economic crisis, the number of mobile Europeans continued to increase between 2008 and 2012, rising to almost 14 million persons. I shall return to this point – mobility and the euro crisis – in the conclusion of this chapter.

The demographic evolution of mobility should be framed in the overall context of migration in Europe. After around 15 years of 'zero immigration' – during which entries in fact continued but at a slower pace and primarily for the purposes of family reunification, applications for asylum and irregular stay – at the end of the 1980s there began a new migratory cycle in which Western Europe played a leading global role (Castles and Miller 2003, 79 ff.). Between 1990 and 2012, as shown by Figure 3.2, the number of foreign citizens legally resident in the EU more than doubled from 15 to 34 million.[5] Part of this trend depends on the growth of intra-EU migration. We can thus distinguish three phases.

The first phase covers the whole of the 1990s. Growth was prevailingly fed by immigration of third-country nationals, from Africa and the former communist countries of Central-Eastern Europe. Some migrants from the latter area would become European citizens over the next ten years, experiencing a legal and status upgrade which was, however, not always straightforward (Favell and Nebe 2009). In terms of

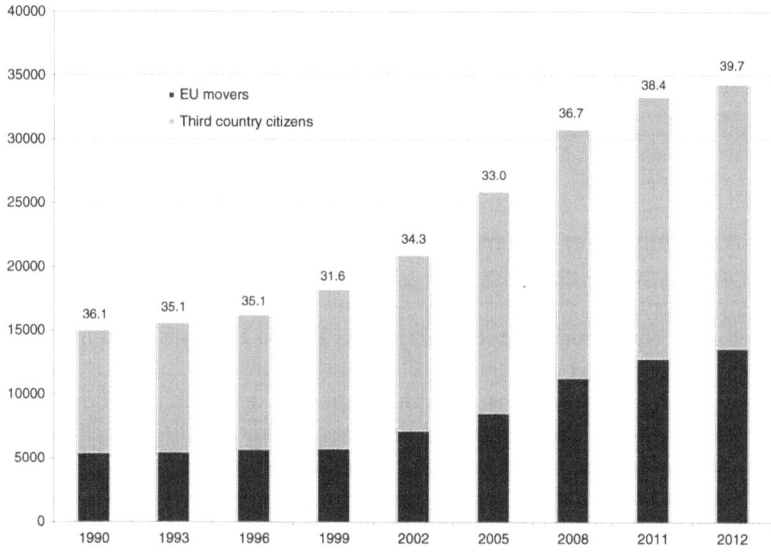

Figure 3.2 EU movers and third-country citizens residing in the EU, 1990–2012 (in thousands)

Sources: Eurostat Statistics Database, Population and Social Conditions (http://epp.eurostat.ec.europa.eu/portal/page/portal/statistics/search_database, consulted between 2002 and 2013; cf. also Recchi et al. 2003; Recchi 2008).

Note: Values on top of the bars stand for the proportion of EU movers on the total of foreigners in member states.

flows, Eurostat estimates that in the second half of the 1990s just over 1 in 1,000 EU residents moved from one member state to another each year (Thorogood and Winqvist 2003, 2). Another estimate reports that European citizens represented barely 19 per cent of immigrant workers in the EU member states between 1995 and 2000 (Bailly et al. 2004, 39). This explains why, during this phase, the contribution of intra-EU mobility to the stock of migrants declined from 36.1 per cent in 1990 to 31.6 per cent at the end of the decade (as indicated by the percentages above the bars in Figure 3.2).

The second phase spanned the first half of the 2000s. This was the 'golden' period of migration in Europe: the arrival of citizens from both third countries and EU member states (or about to become such) increased. At the turn of the century, the EU assumed a prominent role in the scenario of global migrations. Between 1995 and 2000, net migration in the EU was 600,000 per year – that is, around half the rate recorded in the USA. Between 2000 and 2005, however, this value doubled to exceed the American rate – also because, after 11 September 2001, the USA adopted more restrictive immigration policies. The peak came in 2003, when net migration in the EU reached two million (Eurostat 2009, 54). These entry flows were distributed asymmetrically. The highest absolute values were recorded by Spain, Germany, the UK and Italy. In relative terms, immigration was extraordinarily robust in Spain, Ireland, Luxembourg and Cyprus, where every year there were 15 to 20 more foreign residents per thousand inhabitants (Herm 2008, 2). To a large extent, the boom was driven by the *expectation* of the enlargements of 2004 and 2007. The prospective EU citizens took advantage of the lifting in 2001 of the visa requirement for entry into the EU15, confident that they would soon enjoy the benefits of European citizenship. For example, 40 per cent of immigrants from Central-Eastern Europe applying for a work permit in the UK in 2004 – immediately after the enlargement – were already UK residents (European Commission 2008, 11). The phenomenon would recur for Bulgarians and Romanians on the eve of their countries' accession into the EU in 2007.

The enlargement of May 2004, however, initiated a third phase, during which the number of immigrants in Europe continued to increase but did so mainly because of intra-EU migrations, particularly those originating from the new member states. The number of EU movers increased by almost 50 per cent in six years, while that of third-country nationals did so 'only' by 18 per cent. Hence in the 2005–2012 period, the proportion of EU citizens in the total number of immigrants in the EU rose from 33 per cent to 39.7 per cent. By the end of the period, mobile European citizens formed 2.7 per cent of the European population, while third-country citizens represented 4.1 per cent. Given the concentration of both categories in the 'old' Europe, in the EU15 these proportions were, respectively, 3.2 per cent and 4.9 per cent.

Contrary to several demographic projections,[6] the increase in the number of citizens of the new member states resident in the EU15 in the second half of the decade was vigorous and persistent (Table 3.1). Overall, almost 5,500,000 Central-Eastern Europeans were resident in Western Europe in 2012. At the beginning of the century they had numbered around one million. In particular, Romanians (2,380,000) were more than ten times more numerous than they had been in 2000. Poles, the second most numerous nationality (over 1,600,000), more than tripled. In relative terms, also remarkable is the increase in the presence of Lithuanians (almost nine times more than in 2000) and Slovaks (almost eight times). Even the countries least involved in East–West mobility, namely Slovenia and Hungary, recorded a remarkable growth in the number of their citizens resident abroad in the Union – by 58 per cent and 83 per cent, respectively. The peak years for these flows were those immediately following the two enlargements. Between 2004 and 2007, around 350,000 new EU citizens per year left their countries (in large part Poles). Then, in 2007 and 2008, around one million Romanians and Bulgarians per year established their residences in Western Europe (European Commission 2011a, 248). Movements after the second enlargement were immediately much larger: already at the end of 2007, the number of Romanian and Bulgarian movers was equal to that of movers from the new member states of 2004.

Five years after their country's accession to the EU, 10.8 per cent of Romanians had chosen to live in another European country and likewise 6.6 per cent of Lithuanians, 5.9 per cent of Bulgarians and 4.1 per cent of Poles.[7] It should then be borne in mind that these figures are rounded down, because they do not include seasonal migrants, commuters or temporary workers, who are nearly impossible to track statistically.

The age profile of Central-Eastern European movers matches that of traditional economic migrants: young people aged under 35 represent 70 per cent of the working-age citizens (between 15 and 64 years old) who have moved to the EU15 from the new member states of 2004, and 62 per cent of migrants from Romania and Bulgaria. Just 34 per cent of the labour force of the receiving countries is in the same age range (European Commission 2011a, 265). In terms of gender, an overrepresentation of women is recorded among migrants from Romania and Bulgaria, probably because of the demand for domestic workers in

Table 3.1 The rise of Central-Eastern Europeans residing in other EU member states, 2000–2011 (2000 = 100)

	2000	2001	2002	2003	2004	2005	2006	2007	2008	2009	2010	2011	N (2011)
Czech Rep.	100	125	137	168	148	168	215	246	196	205	210	204	86,587
Estonia	100	113	123	145	145	166	178	199	199	218	235	260	48,027
Hungary	100	112	116	111	108	120	125	156	144	158	164	179	152,435
Latvia	100	89	102	113	111	152	194	196	217	225	221	248	53,756
Lithuania	100	151	172	222	218	353	473	531	557	576	845	876	211,671
Poland	100	112	114	121	127	159	208	272	292	313	309	332	1,580,193
Slovakia	100	147	155	174	208	324	363	525	652	751	753	766	193,053
Slovenia*	100	129	131	150	136	146	144	151	153	156	156	158	37,700
EU10 Total	100	115	120	129	132	167	210	266	281	302	311	330	2,363,422
Bulgaria**	100	144	197	233	285	307	357	381	469	522	543	602	430,048
Romania	100	131	179	254	333	405	493	714	781	911	982	1056	2,298,834
EU2 Total	100	134	183	249	321	380	459	645	704	815	873	944	2,728,882
Total	100	120	138	164	187	228	282	375	403	450	472	506	5,092,304

Source: Eurostat Statistics Database, Population and Social Conditions (http://epp.eurostat.ec.europa.eu/portal/page/portal/statistics/search_database, consulted between 2010 and 2013).

Note: *UK data missing; **UK data refer to 2005.

Western Europe. Finally to be considered are educational qualifications. Some Central-Eastern European countries initially feared that because free movement would facilitate access by their graduates to better-paid jobs in the West, it might provoke a 'brain drain', especially in the health care sector (Kaczmarczyk and Okolski 2008; Kaczmarczyk 2010). In fact, however, migrants from those countries have been mainly individuals with upper-secondary diplomas (61 per cent of the contingent from the 2004 new member states and 50 per cent from the 2007 ones), while graduates (22 per cent and 14 per cent, respectively) are proportionally less numerous among movers than among stayers in the countries of origin (25 per cent and 19 per cent) and destination (29 per cent) (European Commission 2011a, 271–2). In spite of their young age, on the whole the Eastern European citizens who moved across the EU do not have particularly high educational qualifications, although they are overqualified for the manual occupations in which most of them find employment (see Chapter 4). By contrast, the mobile citizens from the EU15 are characterized by education levels markedly above the nationals averages of both the country of origin and the country of destination (49 per cent are graduates) (ibid.) and, as we shall see, they move – albeit in much smaller numbers – to much more prestigious and well-paid jobs.

3. Where are the movers? Channelled mobility and diffused mobility

In this section, I shall examine the statistics on the presence of mobile European citizens in each country of the EU at the beginning of the first and second decade of the twenty-first century – that is, in 2001 and 2012. These two reference dates each occurred eight years after the two most important events in the history of free movement: the entry into effect of the Maastricht Treaty (November 1993) and the enlargement of May 2004. As we saw in the previous section, 2001 marked the turning point between the phases of stagnation and expansion of intra-EU migration. The main question which I shall seek to answer is the following: where do mobile Europeans go when they decide to settle in another country of the EU?

Not surprisingly, the largest countries also host the largest contingents of EU movers. Germany held over 2,400,000 of them in 2001, and more than 2,700,000 eleven years later. The UK has seen an even more substantial increase in EU citizens living on its soil (from about one million to over 2,300,000). However, Spain has experienced such a strong immigration inflow that it has become the country with the second largest number of intra-EU migrants (2,354,000). Finally, in proportion to the number of residents, Ireland has recorded the greatest demographic change: EU movers (primarily from Eastern Europe) formed 8.4 per cent of its population in 2012, more than twice the number at the beginning of the 2000s. But who 'hosts' whom (see Tables 3.2 and 3.3)? At the start of the century, the distribution of EU movers across the continental space was substantially driven by two principles: ethnic–geographical proximity and historical continuity. In accordance with the first principle, in 2001, 73.2 per cent of the migrant community in Ireland consisted of British nationals, and in the UK 35.7 per cent were Irish; in Finland 26.2 per cent were Swedish and in Sweden 48 per cent were Finnish; in Cyprus 53.6 per cent were Greek and in Greece 18 per cent were Cypriot; in Austria 39.1 per cent were German and in Germany (where there had also been large-scale immigration by other nationalities) 7.5 per cent were Austrian. The second principle is the result of consolidated migratory traditions, and the capacity of immigrant communities to resist naturalization (which, incidentally, European citizenship makes easier). Thus, in France and Luxembourg, the Portuguese predominated (44.6 per cent and 41.7 per cent of EU movers); in Germany, the Italians (31.6 per cent); in Spain, the Britons (22.7 per cent) and the Germans (18.6 per cent). However, these patterns were disrupted by the flows subsequent to enlargement, with some first signs of change already apparent in 2001.[8] In 2012, Romanians and Poles formed the largest communities of mobile Europeans in a broad array of countries. Romanians numbered 1,072,000 in Italy where they thus represented 74.5 per cent of EU movers, while they reached 38 per cent in Spain and 35.7 per cent in Portugal. Poles predominated in Ireland (33.1 per cent), the UK (28.4 per cent) and Denmark (19 per cent), with a very large presence also in Germany (20.5 per cent), the Netherlands (21.8 per cent) and Sweden (16.4 per cent). Also sizeable were the communities of Lithuanians in Ireland (9.9 per cent) and Estonians in Finland (51.6 per cent).

The same data can also be viewed from the perspective of the countries of origin – that is, in terms of the national diasporas and their changing geography (Tables 3.4 and 3.5). One can thus plot a map of the routes followed by intra-European mobility during the first decade of this century.

Unsurprisingly, all nationalities share a marked preference for mobility to Western Europe. In 2012, there were only two contingents of mobile European citizens recording more than 10 per cent of presences outside the EU15: the Slovaks and the Czechs. But these anomalies resulted more from changes in political borders than from changes in migratory processes – that is, they were produced by a movement of

Table 3.2 EU movers in 2001: % of each nationality by country of residence

Country of residence	AT	BE	DK	FI	FR	DE	EL	IE	IT	LU	NL	PT	UK	ES	SE	CY	EE	LV	LT	MT	PL	CZ	SK	SI	HU	BG	RO	Total
Austria		0.5	0.4	0.5	2.2	39.1	1.1	0.3	5.4	0.2	2.1	0.5	2.9	0.8	1.4	0.0	0.1	0.1	0.1	0.0	11.8	4.0	4.2	3.7	6.9	2.3	9.4	100
Belgium	0.4		0.6		19.1	6.0	3.1	0.6	33.3	0.6	15.9	4.5	4.6	7.8	0.6	0.0	0.0	0.0	0.0	0.0	1.4	0.1	0.1	0.0	0.2	0.2	0.4	100
Denmark	1.2	0.8		3.3	4.2	19.9	0.9	1.7	4.4	0.0	7.1	0.9	19.8	2.7	17.0	0.0	0.7	1.2	1.9	0.0	8.7	0.4	0.2	0.1	0.6	0.6	1.7	100
Finland	0.7	0.3	1.9		2.9	7.3	0.9	0.6	2.6	0.0	2.0	0.4	7.3	1.8	26.1	0.1	36.0	0.8	0.7	0.0	2.3	0.3	0.2	0.1	2.2	1.0	1.6	100
France	0.3	5.4	0.4	0.2		6.1	0.5	0.3	16.1	0.3	2.0	44.6	6.1	12.8	0.6	0.0	0.0	0.0	0.0	0.0	2.7	0.1	0.1	0.1	0.2	0.3	0.8	100
Germany	7.5	1.5	0.8	0.4	4.2		14.5	0.6	30.6	0.3	4.8	6.0	3.9	5.7	0.7	0.0	0.2	0.4	0.5	0.0	7.8	1.7	0.7	0.6	1.8	1.4	3.4	100
Greece	1.1	1.0	0.4	0.4	3.8	8.8		0.3	4.2	0.0	1.8	0.2	9.8	0.6	1.5	12.9	0.1	0.0	0.1	0.0	9.5	0.4	0.2	0.1	0.4	26.1	16.3	100
Ireland	0.4	0.6	0.4	0.6	4.5	5.1	0.2		2.7	0.0	2.2	0.5	73.2	3.1	0.9	0.0	0.2	1.2	1.5	0.1	1.5	0.7	0.1	0.0	0.3	0.0	0.0	100
Italy	2.9	2.6	0.7	0.7	13.6	16.3	2.8	0.6		0.1	2.7	1.3	9.0	5.8	1.0	0.1	0.1	0.1	0.1	0.2	12.5	1.5	0.9	1.3	1.4	2.5	19.2	100
Luxembourg	0.4	10.4	1.3	0.5	14.1	7.1	0.8	0.6	13.4		2.6	41.7	3.1	2.0	0.8	0.0	0.0	0.1	0.0	0.0	0.5	0.1	0.1	0.0	0.1	0.1	0.3	100
Netherlands	1.5	12.1	1.2	0.9	6.2	26.0	2.6	1.8	8.5	0.2		4.5	19.5	8.0	1.4	0.1	0.1	0.1	0.2	0.0	2.7	0.4	0.2	0.1	0.6	0.3	0.8	100
Portugal	0.5	2.8	0.7	0.5	30.1	16.4	0.2	0.7	3.4	0.8	5.4		16.2	17.6	1.0	0.0	0.3	0.1	0.3	0.0	0.4	0.1	0.1	0.1	0.3	0.9	1.1	100
UK	1.3	1.3	1.1	0.7	6.3	17.6	2.2	35.6	7.0	0.1	2.6	2.4		3.5	1.4	5.1	0.1	0.3	0.3	2.0	4.0	0.8	0.4	2.1	0.9	0.5	0.4	100
Spain	0.9	3.7	1.2	1.0	11.1	18.5	0.2	1.0	8.7	0.1	4.4	9.7	22.7		2.1	0.0	0.1	0.1	1.0	0.0	3.8	0.4	0.3	0.0	0.2	2.4	6.4	100
Sweden	1.1	0.3	12.3	48.0	2.3	7.9	2.0	0.6	2.1	0.0	1.8	0.6	6.3	1.5		0.1	0.7	0.3	0.3	0.0	8.0	0.2	0.2	0.3	1.4	0.5	1.2	100
EU15	2.7	2.5	1.1	1.8	6.1	9.5	6.1	8.1	17.4	0.1	4.2	12.0	7.2	6.0	1.1	1.3	0.1	0.1	0.1	0.3	5.4	0.8	0.2	0.5	1.0	1.3	3.0	100

Cyprus	0.4	0.3	0.2	0.6	1.2	2.5	53.6	0.8	0.6	0.0	0.6	0.1	36.5	0.1	1.2	0.0		0.1	0.2	0.1	0.0	0.4	0.2	0.1	0.0	0.2	0.0	0.0	100
Estonia	0.2	0.1	1.0	23.1	0.5	3.7	0.1	0.2	0.5	0.0	0.6	0.0	1.4	0.3	3.3	0.0		35.1	27.5	0.0	0.0	1.9	0.0	0.0	0.0	0.2	0.3	0.0	100
Latvia	0.5	0.3	2.6	2.5	1.3	6.7	0.2	0.3	0.8	0.0	1.0	0.0	4.1	0.3	4.2	0.0	15.2		53.5	0.1	4.5	0.2	0.0	0.0	0.4	0.9	0.2	100	
Lithuania	0.3	0.4	3.3	2.5	2.9	12.9	0.2	0.2	1.4	0.0	1.2	0.1	2.2	0.3	1.8	0.0	3.3	23.2		0.0	41.4	0.4	0.0	0.0	0.4	1.2	0.4	100	
Malta	0.7	0.6	0.5	0.2	2.1	8.4	0.3	1.1	8.1	0.0	2.8	0.1	67.5	0.3	1.1	0.1	0.0	0.0	0.2		0.8	0.4	0.6	0.2	0.2	3.3	0.4	100	
Poland	2.3	1.2	0.6	0.2	4.9	52.2	4.1	0.1	4.2	0.0	2.4	0.1	4.4	1.3	2.7	0.1	0.1	0.3	3.2	0.0		4.3	2.2	0.1	2.6	5.2	1.2	100	
Czech Rep	1.8	0.3	0.1	0.1	1.5	6.3	1.6	0.2	1.4	0.0	0.8	0.1	2.3	0.3	0.4	0.1	0.0	0.1	0.2	0.0	24.6		45.0	0.2	0.7	7.6	4.3	100	
Slovakia	1.4	0.3	0.1	0.0	0.6	3.2	0.6	0.0	0.9	0.0	0.3	0.1	0.6	0.1	0.1	0.1	0.0	0.0	0.1	0.0	13.2	47.8		0.5	11.0	5.7	13.3	100	
Slovenia	14.9	1.3	0.0	0.0	5.9	27.3	0.0	0.0	24.5	0.0	2.8	0.0	5.4	3.4	1.0	0.1	0.0	0.0	0.0	0.0	2.5	4.2	2.8		4.0			100	
Hungary	1.8	0.2	0.1	0.4	1.1	9.1	0.7	0.1	0.9	0.0	0.5	0.0	1.2	0.1	0.4	0.1	0.1	0.0	0.1	0.0	3.0	0.4	6.8	0.1		1.9	70.9	100	
NMS 2004	1.5	0.3	0.3	0.8	1.5	10.2	10.4	0.2	1.4	0.0	0.8	0.1	8.0	0.2	0.8	0.1	0.1	0.3	1.0	1.7	0.0	9.7	4.2	15.4	0.2	1.4	3.9	25.6	100
Bulgaria	1.0	0.5	0.4	0.3	2.4	0.2	48.5	0.2	4.4	0.0	0.5	0.1	2.2	0.6	0.6	3.9	0.1	0.3	0.2	0.1	16.4	6.3	2.4	0.3	2.6		5.5	100	
Romania	2.2	1.6	0.3	0.1	10.0	0.3	30.6	0.3	34.2	0.0	2.6	0.3	6.2	1.4	1.4	0.0	0.0	0.0	0.0	0.0	1.0	0.2	0.4	0.2	3.1	3.6		100	
NMS 2007	1.7	1.1	0.3	0.2	6.9	0.2	37.9	0.3	22.1	0.0	1.7	0.2	4.5	1.1	1.0	1.5	0.1	0.2	0.1	0.0	7.3	2.6	1.2	0.3	3.0	2.2	2.3	100	

Source: Eurostat Statistics Database, Population and Social Conditions (http://epp.eurostat.ec.europa.eu/portal/page/portal/statistics/search_database, consulted between 2002 and 2012).

Table 3.3 EU movers in 2012: % of each nationality by country of residence

Country of residence	AT	BE	DK	FI	FR	DE	EL	IE	IT	LU	NL	PT	ES	SE	UK	CY	CZ	EE	HU	LV	LT	MT	PL	SK	SI	BG	RO	Total
Austria		0.5	0.3	0.3	1.9	39.3	0.8	0.3	4.3	0.2	2.0	0.5	0.8	0.9	2.5	0.0	2.7	0.1	0.1	0.2	0.1	11.1	11.1	5.4	2.2	2.7	9.7	100
Belgium	0.6		0.6	0.7	0.0	8.9	0.3	0.9	3.6	0.1	27.5	8.0	11.4	1.0	5.5	0.1	0.7	0.2	1.1	0.1	0.4	0.1	12.5	1.3	0.2	4.6	9.6	100
Denmark	1.0	0.7		1.8	4.2	17.1	0.9	1.1	3.9	0.0	0.5	1.0	3.1	10.3	11.6	0.0	0.7	0.9	1.7	3.0	6.0	0.0	19.1	0.8	0.2	3.1	7.3	100
Finland	0.6	0.5	1.0		2.6	5.8	0.9	0.7	2.6	0.0	1.5	0.6	2.2	12.8	5.6	0.1	0.6	51.6	2.3	1.8	1.4	0.0	0.4	0.4	0.1	1.6	2.3	100
France	0.4	6.5	0.4	0.2		7.2	0.5	0.6	14.1	0.4	2.8	39.0	10.7	0.6	10.6	0.0	0.2	0.0	0.2	0.1	0.1	0.0	2.9	0.2	0.1	0.3	1.9	100
Germany	0.8	1.0	0.9	0.7	5.1		12.0	0.4	21.1	0.6	5.8	4.9	0.5	0.8	3.9	0.0	1.9	0.3	3.2	0.9	1.4	0.0	20.5	1.4	0.8	4.1	7.0	100
Greece																												
Ireland	0.2	0.3	0.2	0.2	0.2	2.9	0.1		2.0	0.0	0.0	0.7	1.8	0.4	30.4	0.0	1.5	0.1	2.2	5.6	9.9	0.0	33.1	2.9	0.1	0.5	4.7	100
Italy	0.5	0.4	0.1	0.1	2.4	3.0	0.1	0.2		0.0	0.6	0.3	1.5	0.3	2.1	0.0	0.4	0.1	0.6	0.0	0.3	0.1	7.7	0.7	0.2	3.8	74.5	100
Luxembourg	0.4	9.3	1.2	0.6	15.0	6.6	0.8	0.7	10.8		2.1	43.4	1.8	0.9	2.8	0.0	0.3	0.2	0.4	0.2	0.2	0.1	1.1	0.3	0.2	0.1	0.5	100
Netherlands	1.3	9.3	0.9	0.8	6.0	24.4	0.0	1.6	0.8	0.1		0.6	6.8	1.3	13.9	0.1	1.0	0.3	2.6	0.1	1.2	0.1	21.7	1.2	0.2	0.6	3.1	100
Portugal	0.5	1.7	0.4	0.4	5.0	8.7	0.2	0.8	4.9	0.1	4.5		8.6	0.8	16.7	0.0	0.2	0.1	0.4	0.4	0.6	0.0	1.2	0.2	0.1	7.9	35.6	100
Spain	0.5	1.5	0.5	0.5	5.3	8.1	0.2	0.8	8.4	0.0	2.2	5.9		1.0	16.4	0.0	0.4	0.1	0.4	0.2	1.0	0.0	0.4	0.4	0.1	7.7	38.0	100
Sweden	1.2	0.5	15.6	26.1	2.6	10.7	0.2	0.7	2.5	0.0	2.5	0.7	2.0		7.0	0.1	0.5	1.5	2.0	1.5	3.0	0.0	16.4	0.5	0.2	1.6	0.4	100
UK	1.0	0.6	0.9	0.5	6.2	6.6	0.7	18.6	5.7	0.0	2.4	5.4	3.5	1.3		0.5	0.3	2.5	0.3	2.8	5.0	0.3	29.3	1.3	0.0	0.4	3.9	100
EU15	0.6	1.8	0.9	1.1	4.0	6.7	2.8	3.6	9.3	0.2	3.7	8.4	2.9	1.0	7.6	0.1	0.8	0.9	1.2	1.0	1.9	0.4	13.9	1.0	0.3	3.4	20.5	100

Cyprus	2.2	0.4	0.2	1.8	10.5	0.6	0.4	2.0	0.0	0.2	0.1	0.5	0.4	3.3	0.1		0.1	0.6	0.2	0.3	0.0	12.8	54.6	0.2	5.0	3.3 100
Czech Rep	6.9	1.3	0.4	0.7	3.8	36.8	0.9	0.7	3.4	0.0	2.0	0.4	1.3	1.8	4.4	0.3	0.7	0.2		0.2	0.2	0.1	4.7	13.6	0.4	2.3	12.5 100
Estonia	0.9	0.6	2.5	2.4	2.9	11.9	0.2	0.8	2.6	0.0	1.4	0.6	1.9	4.5	4.2	0.1	1.2	9.6	0.3		38.2	0.1	5.2	0.6	0.1	6.0	1.2 100
Hungary	1.0	1.2	6.1	3.3	9.7	17.2	1.6	1.1	4.9	0.0	2.2	0.3	2.1	3.3	4.8	0.0	0.7	3.1	0.2	15.9		0.1	19.3	0.4	0.2	0.8	0.5 100
Latvia	1.5	0.7	1.4	0.6	5.7	5.5	1.7	2.0	19.3	0.0	2.2	0.2	0.6	4.3	44.4	0.0	0.7	0.0	1.2	0.1	0.2		1.5	1.0	0.3	2.2	2.7 100
Lithuania	3.7	1.4	1.9	0.3	6.7	28.8	3.7	1.6	8.1	0.1	2.2	0.5	2.9	3.3	8.6	0.1	4.9	0.1	2.5	0.8	4.8	0.1		2.9	0.3	5.9	3.8 100
Malta	4.3	0.8	0.5	0.2	2.9	8.0	0.6	0.4	3.9	0.0	0.6	0.3	1.1	0.5	3.4	0.1	27.2	0.1	17.3	0.3	0.3	0.0	12.8		0.4	3.4	10.6 100
Poland	6.9	1.0	0.4	0.5	3.1	13.6	0.3	0.7	16.2	0.0	1.6	0.4	1.1	1.1	6.7	0.0	2.7	0.3	2.8	0.4	0.5	0.0	3.2	7.2		24.9	4.3 100
Slovenia	3.6	0.7	0.6	0.4	2.9	16.3	0.9	0.6	3.8	0.0	0.9	0.3	1.0	1.2	5.2	0.1	5.3	0.4	3.5	0.4	1.8	0.0	9.8	29.3	0.3	4.5	6.2 100
NMS 2004																											
Bulgaria	2.3	1.5	0.6	0.5	3.7	10.9	16.2	0.8	6.1	0.1	0.1	0.5	1.9	0.8	29.4	1.1	3.7	0.5	1.5	0.7	0.6	0.1	9.4	1.9	0.4		4.7 100
Romania	2.2	1.7	0.3	0.1	8.3	11.3	23.9	0.3	31.7	0.1	1.9	0.3	1.6	1.4	5.5	0.1	0.2	0.0	4.0	0.0	0.0	0.0	1.4	0.6	0.1	3.0	100
NMS 2007	2.2	1.6	0.5	0.3	5.4	11.1	19.2	0.6	15.9	0.1	0.8	0.4	1.7	1.0	20.3	0.7	2.4	0.3	2.5	0.5	0.4	0.0	6.3	1.4	0.3	1.2	2.9 100

Source: Eurostat Statistics Database, Population and Social Conditions (http://epp.eurostat.ec.europa.eu/portal/page/portal/statistics/search_database, consulted 20 July 2012).

Note: Data for Austria, France, Luxembourg, Lithuania, Malta, Romania and the UK refer to the latest available year (between 2005 and 2010).

Table 3.4 EU movers in 2001: % of countries of residence by nationality

Country of residence	AT	BE	DK	FI	FR	DE	EL	IE	IT	LU	NL	PT	UK	ES	SE	CY	CZ	EE	HU	LV	LT	PL	SK	SI	BG	RO
Austria		0.5	1.0	0.7	0.9	10.2	0.4	0.1	0.8	3.3	1.3	0.1	1.0	0.3	2.9	0.1	10.0	0.3	15.9	0.8	0.8	5.3	12.0	11.0	3.8	6.4
Belgium	1.1		4.0	2.0	24.7	4.9	3.8	0.6	15.3	37.5	29.9	3.0	4.9	10.5	4.7	0.1	0.8	0.4	1.6	0.8	0.5	2.0	0.8	0.3	1.0	0.9
Denmark	0.4	0.3		1.5	0.7	1.8	0.1	0.1	0.2	0.2	1.5	0.1	2.4	0.4	12.1	0.0	0.3	2.4	0.5	3.8	4.5	1.3	0.2	0.1	0.4	0.4
Finland	0.1	0.1	0.7		0.2	0.3	0.1	0.0	0.1	0.1	0.2	0.0	0.4	0.1	8.7	0.0	0.2	57.1	0.8	1.2	0.7	0.2	0.1	0.0	0.4	0.2
France	2.1	35.6	5.4	2	10.9		1.2	1.0	16.0	31.9	8.2	64.8	14.1	37.3	7.9	0.3	2.4	1.1	3.7	1.4	2.0	8.3	1.7	1.2	3.0	3.9
Germany	75.6	16.1	18.6	5.9	19.4		77.7	2.1	51.5		31.9	14.4	18.6	26.9	15.5	0.1	47.9	19.2	45.2	40.8	34.6	43.6	22.8	30.1	29.8	33.2
Greece	0.7	0.7	1.0	0.5	1.2	1.7		0.1	0.5	0.3	0.8	0.0	2.5	0.2	2.4	18.1	0.9	0.3	0.7	0.2	0.4	3.1	0.5	0.1	31.8	8.1
Ireland	0.3	0.4	0.8	0.6	1.4	1.0	0.1		0.3	0.1	1.0	0.1	19.3	1.0	1.4	0.0	1.5	0.3	0.5	9.3	7.7	0.5	0.5	0.1	0.0	0.0
Italy	3.1	3.1	2.0	1.0	6.6	5.0	1.4	0.3		3.5	2.0	0.4	3.8	2.9	2.8	0.1	4.9	1.1	4.0	2.1	1.3	6.6	3.2	4.9	5.2	15.3
Luxembourg	0.3	7.9	2.3	0.5	4.5	1.4	0.2	0.2	1.5		1.2	6.8	0.8	0.7	1.2	0.0	0.1	0.1	0.2	0.0	0.1	0.2	0.1	0.1	0.1	0.1
Netherlands	1.7	13.8	3.1	1.4	3.0	7.8	1.2	0.7	1.5	2.8		1.1	7.7	4.0	3.5	0.0	1.4	0.6	1.9	0.9	1.3	1.4	1.1	0.3	0.8	0.6
Portugal	0.1	0.8	0.4	0.2	3.4	1.2	0.0	0.1	0.1	4.2	0.9		1.6	2.1	0.5	0.0	0.1	0.1	0.2	0.3	0.5	0.1	0.0	0.0	0.4	0.2
Spain	1.9	8.5	6.5	3.5	10.5	11.1	0.2	0.7	2.9	2.7	6.1	4.7	17.7		9.6	0.1	2.2	0.5	1.2	2.3	15.7	4.0	1.8	0.2	9.2	9.9
Sweden	1.4	0.3	30.9	70.8	1.1	2.3	1.0	0.2	0.4	0.2	1.2	0.2	2.4	0.8		0.1	0.6	8.2	3.7	3.6	2.1	4.1	0.5	1.0	0.9	1.1
UK	9.6	11.5	22.6	8.1	21.6	37.7	7.6	93.8	8.6	13.1	13.3	4.3		12.7	24.9	80.7	15.5	5.0	16.4	22.1	15.9	14.8	9.5	50.0	6.6	2.0
EU15	98.4	99.6	99.3	98.7	99.2	97.3	95.0	100.0	99.7	99.9	99.5	100.0	97.2	99.9	98.1	99.7	88.8	96.7	96.5	89.6	88.1	95.5	54.8	99.4	93.4	82.3

Cyprus	0.1	0.1	0.1	0.1	0.1	3.9	0.0	0.0	0.1	0.0	2.2	0.0	0.4		0.1	0.0	0.1	0.3	0.1	0.0	0.1	0.0	0.0
Czech Rep	0.5	0.1	0.1	0.2	0.5	0.2	0	0.1	0.2	0	0.2	0.0	0.3	0.1		0.1	0.5	0.2	0.3	3.2	37.7	0.3	3.7
Estonia	0.0	0.0	0.1	0.7	0.0	0.0	0.0	0.0	0.0	0.0	0.0	0.0	0.2	0.0	0.0		0.0	7.3	4.0	0.0	0.0	0.0	0.0
Hungary	0.5	0.1	0.1	0.2	0.8	0.1	0.1	0.0	0.1	0.0	0.2	0.0	0.3	0.1	0.4	0.2		0.1	0.2	0.5	6.5	0.2	1.1	15.9
Latvia	0.0	0.0	0.1	0.1	0.0	0.0	0.0	0.0	0.0	0.0	0.0	0.0	0.1	0.1	0.0	2.6	0.0		5.4	0.0	0.0	0.0	0.0	0.0
Lithuania	0.0	0.0	0.1	0.1	0.0	0.0	0.0	0.0	0.0	0.0	0.0	0.0	0.0	0.0	0.0	0.3	0.0	2.1		0.2	0.0	0.0	0.0	0.0
Malta																								
Poland	0.2	0.1	0.1	0.0	0.2	1.1	0.1	0.0	0.1	0.1	0.0	0.1	0.1	0.5	0.0	0.9	0.1	0.5	0.3	1.8		0.5	0	0.7	0.1
Slovakia	0.1	0.0	0.1	0.0	0.0	0.0	0.0	0.0	0.0	0.0	0.0	0.0	0.0	0.0	0.0	9.4	0.0	2.0	0.0	0.0	0.5		0.1	0.8	0.7
Slovenia	0.1	0.0	0.0	0.0	0.0	0.0	0.0	0.0	0.0	0.0	0.0	0.0	0.0	0.0	0.0	0.1	0.0	0.1	0.0	0.0	0.0	0.1		0.1	0.0
NMS 2004	1.5	0.4	0.7	1.3	0.7	2.7	4.3	0.2	0.1	0.5	0.1	2.7	0.1	1.8	0.2	10.9	3.3	3.2	10.3	11.8	4.4	44.9	0.6	6.4	17.6
Bulgaria	0.0	0.0	0.0	0.0	0.0	0.0	0.4	0.0	0.0	0.0	0.0	0.0	0.0	0.0	0.1	0.3	0.0	0.1	0.1	0.1	0.1	0.2	0.0		0.1
Romania	0.1	0.0	0.0	0.0	0.1	0.0	0.3	0.1	0.0	0.0	0.1	0.0	0.1	0.0	0.0	0.0	0.0	0.2	0.0	0.0	0.0	0.1	0.0	0.2	
NMS 2007	0.1	0.0	0.0	0.0	0.1	0.0	0.7	0.0	0.1	0.0	0.1	0.0	0.1	0.1	0.0	0.3	0.3	0.1	0.1	0.1	0.1	0.3	0.0	0.2	0.1
Total	100	100	100	100	100	100	100	100	100	100	100	100	100	100	100	100	100	100	100	100	100	100	100	100	100

Source: Eurostat Statistics Database, Population and Social Conditions (http://epp.eurostat.ec.europa.eu/portal/page/portal/statistics/search_database, consulted between 2002 and 2012).

Table 3.5 EU movers in 2012: % of countries of residence by nationality

Country of residence	AT	BE	DK	FI	FR	DE	EL	IE	IT	LU	NL	PT	ES	SE	UK	CY	CZ	EE	HU	LV	LT	PL	SK	SI	BG	RO
Austria		0.7	0.9	0.9	1.0	15.8	0.8	0.2	1.3	2.5	1.6	0.2	0.8	2.4	0.9	0.9	8.1	0.2	0.3	0.6	0.0	2.3	8.6	18.3	2.2	1.4
Belgium	3.1		2.6	2.4	24.3	4.8	0.4	0.9	1.5	2.1	28.7	3.7	14.9	3.6	2.8	2.6	2.8	0.9	3.3	0.1	0.9	3.5	2.7	2.3	5.1	1.8
Denmark	1.4	0.4		1.9	1.0	2.7	0.4	0.3	0.5	0.2	0.1	0.1	1.2	10.8	1.7	0.3	0.9	1.2	1.5	3.4	3.3	1.5	0.5	0.6	1.0	0.4
Finland	0.5	0.1	0.6		0.3	0.5	0.2	0.1	0.2	0.1	0.2	0.0	0.4	7.0	0.4	0.3	0.3	33.8	1.0	1.0	0.4	0.0	0.1	0.2	0.3	0.1
France	5.6	38.2	5.2	2.4		11.0	1.7	1.9	16.4	22.5	8.3	50.3	39.4	6.5	14.9	1.9	2.4	0.5	2.0	0.6	0.5	2.3	0.9	2.1	0.8	1.1
Germany	22.0	11.9	20	13.6	19.6		88.3	2.6	47.5	62.6	32.9	12.2	3.5	16.5	10.8	7.6	41.3	6.1	53.6	18.7	15.2	31.4	16.2	57.2	24.7	7.2
Greece																										
Ireland	0.8	0.5	0.7	0.7	1.5	1.3	0.1		0.7	0.2	0.0	0.3	1.9	1.4	12.7	0.6	4.9	0.3	5.5	18.5	16.4	7.7	5.2	0.5	0.4	0.7
Italy	8.1	3.1	0.2	1.5	5.5	5.2	0.2	0.8		1.4	1.9	0.6	6.2	3.0	3.4	1.4	5.6	1.2	5.4	0.2	2.2	6.9	4.5	8.6	13.7	45.1
Luxembourg	0.9	7.7	2.0	0.9		1.3	0.4	0.3	1.8		0.9	7.8	0.9	1.4	0.6	0.2	0.4	0.3	0.5	0.3	0.1	0.1	0.2	0.8	0.0	0.0
Netherlands	4.6	12.9	2.5	1.9	3.0	8.8	0.1	1.1	0.2	1.7		0.2	5.9	3.0	4.5	1.8	2.6	0.8	5.3	0.2	1.6	4.0	1.7	1.7	0.4	0.4
Portugal	0.6	0.9	0.4	0.3	0.9	1.1	0.0	0.2	0.5	0.6	1.1		2.6	0.7	1.9	0.1	0.2	0.1	0.3	0.3	0.3	0.1	0.1	0.2	2.0	1.5
Spain	12.4	16.2	11.3	10.1	16.4	22.4	1.4	4.4	17.4	3.1	11.5	13.7		19.4	41.3	1.7	8.5	1.8	6.6	3.8	10.3	0.5	4.0	3.6	43.0	36.4
Sweden	3.6	0.6	36.9	54.6	1.1	3.4	0.2	0.5	0.5	0.2	1.6	0.2	1.6		2.0	1.5	1.1	3.8	3.5	3.6	3.4	2.7	0.6	1.6	1.0	0.0
UK	23.0	5.7	15.0	7.8	23.6	15.5	4.0	86.2	10.1	2.5	10.6	10.7	19.7	21.1		75.7	5.9	47.8	3.5	47.7	42.9	35.1	11.8	0.0	1.8	3.2
EU15	86.6	98.9	98.3	99.0	98.2	93.8	98.2	99.5	98.6	99.7	99.4	100.0	99.0	96.8	97.9	96.6	85.0	98.8	92.3	99.0	97.5	98.1	57.1	97.7	96.4	99.3

Cyprus	3.8	0.2	0.3	0.2	0.4	1.9	0.3	0.2	0.3	0.1	0.0	0.2	0.5	0.5	0.7	0.1	0.6	0.2	0.2	1.2	38.5	0.8	1.8	0.2
Czech Rep																									
Estonia																									
Hungary	4.8	0.4	0.2	0.3	0.3	2.6	0.2	0.1	0.2	0.1	0.3	0.0	0.2	0.9	0.3	1.4	0.5	0.1		0.1	0.2	3.8	0.6	0.3	0.3
Latvia	0.1	0.0	0.2	0.2	0.1	0.1	0.0	0.0	0.0	0.0	0.0	0.0	0.1	0.4	0.0	0.0	0.1	0.9		1.7	0.0	0.0	0.0	0.1	0.0
Lithuania	0.0	0.0	0.2	0.2	0.1	0.1	0.0	0.0	0.0	0.0	0.0	0.0	0.0	0.1	0.0	0.0	0.0	0.1	0.4		0.0	0.0	0.0	0.0	0.0
Malta	0.2	0.0	0.1	0.0	0.1	0.1	0.0	0.0	0.0	0.0	0.0	0.0	0.0	0.3	0.5	0.0	0.1	0.0	0.0	0.0	0.0	0.0	0.1	0.1	0.0
Poland	0.8	0.1	0.3	0.0	0.1	0.1	0.0	0.2	0.1	0.1	0.1	0.0	0.2	0.5	0.2	0.2	0.8	0.0	0.3	0.1	0.4	0.3	0.1	0.3	0.0
Slovakia	2.7	0.2	0.3	0.1	0.3	0.6	0.2	0.1	0.1	0.0	0.1	0.0	0.2	0.2	0.2	0.2	13.0	0.0	6.3	0.1	0.4		0.6	0.5	0.2
Slovenia	0.5	0.0	0.0	0.0	0.1	0.1	0.0	0.0	0.1	0.0	0.0	0.0	0.0	0.1	0.0	0.0	0.1	0.0	0.1	0.0	0.0	0.2		0.4	0.0
NMS 2004	12.9	0.9	1.6	1.0	1.6	6.0	0.8	0.5	1.1	0.3	0.6	0.0	0.9	3.0	1.7	2.5	14.6	1.2	7.4	0.9	2.5	1.8	42.8	2.2	3.5	0.7
Bulgaria	0.3	0.1	0.1	0.0	0.1	0.1	0.5	0.0	0.1	0.0	0.0	0.0	0.1	0.1	0.4	0.9	0.4	0.0	0.1	0.1	0.0	0.1	0.1	0.1	0.0
Romania	0.2	0.1	0.0	0.0	0.1	0.1	0.5	0.0	0.2	0.0	0.0	0.0	0.0	0.1	0.0	0.0	0.0	0.0	0.2	0.0	0.0	0.0	0.0	0.1	
NMS 2007	0.5	0.2	0.1	0.0	0.2	0.2	1.0	0.0	0.3	0.0	0.0	0.0	0.1	0.2	0.4	0.9	0.4	0.0	0.3	0.1	0.0	0.1	0.1	0.1	0.0
Total	100	100	100	100	100	100	100	100	100	100	100	100	100	100	100	100	100	100	100	100	100	100	100	100	100

Source: Eurostat Statistics Database, Population and Social Conditions (http://epp.eurostat.ec.europa.eu/portal/page/portal/statistics/search_database, consulted 28 November 2012).

frontiers rather than by a movement of people. The 38.5 per cent of Slovaks resident in the Czech Republic and the 13.0 per cent of Czechs in Slovakia were probably in large part tied to their country of residence by affective or occupational relations which preceded the peaceful division of Czechoslovakia.

Theoretically, two polar patterns can be imagined in the geographical dispersion of migrations: a *channelled* mobility, whereby migrants settle in one country only; and a *diffused* mobility, whereby migrants distribute uniformly among all possible destinations. The first pattern is consistent with traditional migration, in which migration chains induce movers to turn to destinations predefined by the experiences of relatives, friends and neighbours, who act as precursors and then facilitate integration into the host societies. The second pattern instead fits with a form of individualized mobility, in which the choice of destination is less socially structured, or responds to a highly diversified range of motivations and life projects.

A second dimension of analysis has to do with variations over time. A comparison between the situations in 2001 and 2012 then makes it possible to determine the *stability* of the above-described migration patterns.

In order to measure the degree of dispersion of national diasporas in Europe more systematically, I apply the index proposed by Lieberson (1969). The index varies from 0 (maximum concentration) to 1 (maximum dispersion). It assumes higher values the more the communities of mobile citizens are equally distributed among the possible destination countries (Table 3.6). As a rule of thumb, one may assume that the nationalities which record indices equal to or greater than 0.75 have *diffused* mobility, while those with lower indices have *channelled* mobility. Empirically, this means that national diasporas are considered to be concentrated if at least one-third of migrants live in a single foreign country. Nationalities then differ by the continuity of their mobility pattern when comparing the 2012 situation with 2001. Applying these classification criteria yields the scheme set out in Table 3.7.

Overall, this classification shows that intra-EU geographical mobility in 2012 is prevailingly and increasingly channelled. In part, this is due to the persistence of long-established migration routes of traditional diasporas – mostly but not exclusively from Southern Europe, as they include the Irish, Finns, Estonians and Slovenians, who constantly tend to move to neighbouring countries. Mobile citizens from new member states – Poland, Lithuania, Latvia, Romania and Bulgaria – also follow a similar pattern, concentrating on specific destinations after EU enlargements. Traditional mechanisms of labour migration chains are most

Table 3.6 Dispersion of intra-EU mobility by nationality in 2001 and 2012 (Lieberson index)

	2001	2012
Austria	0.43	0.82
Belgium	0.83	0.74
Denmark	0.84	0.74
Finland	0.51	0.62
France	0.87	0.75
Germany	0.84	0.85
Greece	0.40	0.17
Ireland	0.12	0.21
Italy	0.71	0.66
Luxembourg	0.77	0.51
Netherlands	0.81	0.73
Portugal	0.57	0.65
UK	0.90	0.73
Spain	0.79	0.73
Sweden	0.91	0.82
Cyprus	0.33	0.38
Estonia	0.55	0.61
Latvia	0.80	0.66
Lithuania	0.85	0.71
Poland	0.80	0.72
Czech Republic	0.75	0.75
Slovakia	0.81	0.76
Slovenia	0.67	0.62
Hungary	0.77	0.65
Bulgaria	0.82	0.69
Romania	0.85	0.61

Note: Indexes have been computed on the basis of data included in Tables 3.4 and 3.5 with the following formula of population diversity (Lieberson 1969):

$$\frac{1 - \sum x_i^2}{1 - \frac{1}{K}}.$$

likely structuring their flows. However, and more surprisingly, a similar process of concentration of mobility patterns is found among a number of Western European nationalities as well. In some cases, this change is emphasized by the arbitrary cut-off point used (such as for the Spanish), as the increase in concentration between 2001 and 2012 is modest; in others, noticeably for Britons, the process is in fact quite substantial, with their growing focus on Spain and France as mobility targets. This change

Table 3.7 National patterns of geographical mobility in the EU between 2001 and 2012

		Stability of migration pattern (2001–2012)	
		Yes	No
Dispersion of flows in 2012	Low (channelled mobility)	Finns, Greeks, Irish, Italians, Portuguese, Cypriots, Estonians, Slovenians	Belgians, Danish, Luxemburgish, Dutch, British, Spanish, Latvians, Lithuanians, Poles, Hungarians, Bulgarians, Romanians
	High (diffused mobility)	French, Germans, Swedes, Czechs, Slovaks	Austrians

mirrors a shift in the reasons for migration (from work to a better quality of life) and the consolidation of Northern European ethnic enclaves in rural and coastal areas of the receiving countries (see Chapter 4).

The most diffused diasporas are those of the Germans, Swedes, French, Czechs, Slovaks and Austrians. Only the Austrians have considerably changed their mobility pattern, which used to hinge on Germany as the dominant destination (75 per cent lived there in 2001), but has more recently opened up to a larger canvas of countries and ended up featuring the UK as its relatively preferred settlement. In all cases, the spread of movers from the same nationality across different EU countries is a testimony to individualized mobility projects and trajectories.

4. What do they do? The 'new' movers in the labour market of the 'old' Europe

As we have seen, the 2004 and 2007 enlargements of the EU increased the population of European citizens and, more proportionally, that of EU movers. Differences of income with respect to the 'old' Europe, in fact, stimulated a revival of economic migration within the borders of the continent unequalled since the 1960s (and which, in some specific cases, was even more intense).[9] The new EU movers of the former communist countries primarily found work in the construction industry, manufacturing, tourism (hotels and restaurants) and domestic and cleaning services, where they eventually formed a considerable part of the labour force. The European Commission (2011a, 270) estimated that 17 in every 1,000 jobs in 'elementary occupations'[10] in Western Europe were held by citizens of the 2007 enlargement countries, and 16 by citizens of the member states of the 2004 enlargement, who emigrated to the West after acquiring European citizenship. Table 3.8 provides a picture of the occupational positions of European citizens in 2007 and 2010. The table distinguishes among three categories of nationalities: EU15 citizens, the citizens of the new member states of 2004 (EU10) and the citizens of the new member states of 2007 (EU2). Within each of these categories, it is possible to compare the occupational positions of stayer and mover workers. The most evident finding is the marked difference between the occupations of Western and Eastern European movers. The former find jobs abroad which are better than those of their counterparts in the home country. For example, 27.6 per cent of them work as free professionals in another EU member state: almost double the proportion of those in the home countries (14.8 per cent). A further

Table 3.8 Mobility and work during the crisis: occupational positions of 'stayers' and 'movers' from the EU15 and from new member states (NMS) of the first and second enlargements, 2007 and 2010 (as % of workers per occupational category)

Occupational group (ISCO-88)	EU15				EU10				EU2			
	Stayers		Movers		Stayers		Movers		Stayers		Movers	
	2007	2010	2007	2010	2007	2010	2007	2010	2007	2010	2007	2010
Managers	8.8	9.0	11.7	12.6	6.8	6.9	2.6	4.8	3.9	3.4	nd	1.5
Professionals	13.9	14.8	26.6	27.6	14.0	15.2	4.3	6.6	10.6	11.8	3.1	2.5
Technicians and associate professionals	17.4	17.6	16.8	16.8	14.1	14.9	5.2	5.2	9.8	9.7	2.4	3.3
Clerical support workers	11.9	11.7	9.0	7.8	7.5	7.6	4.4	4.7	5.3	5.6	2.0	2.5
Service and sales workers	13.9	14.6	11.9	14.4	12.6	13.0	17.6	16.9	12.3	13.3	16.0	15.9
Skilled agricultural and fishery workers	2.5	2.5	na	1.4	7.6	6.9	na	1.1	17.2	17.1	2.9	2.5
Craft and related trades workers	13.6	12.4	8.3	8.1	17.3	15.9	16.0	15.6	17.0	15.7	28.3	24.0
Plant and machine operators, and assemblers	8.1	7.3	5.5	4.1	12.2	11.7	18.0	14.5	12.3	11.7	4.4	6.0
Elementary occupations	9.9	10.0	9.9	7.3	7.9	7.8	31.0	30.5	11.8	11.8	39.1	40.4

Source: European Commission (2008, 130; 2011a, 271); estimates based on LFS data.

12.6 per cent are in managerial positions, which are held by no more than 11.7 per cent of their fellow countrymen at home. The reverse holds for the lowest-level job categories, in which Western movers are underrepresented compared with Western stayers. In short, intra-EU mobility is a top-notch option for workers in the 'old Europe'.

Matters are quite the contrary for the mobile citizens of the new member states. For these movers, resettling in another country of the Union means, potentially, working in jobs that are less prestigious than those offered by the national labour market. Some 45 per cent of Poles and other new EU citizens of 2004 who work abroad are blue collars: a position occupied by only 19.5 per cent of their compatriots at home. The discrepancy is even more marked for Romanians and Bulgarians. Among those working in Western Europe in 2010, 46.4 per cent were manual labourers (mostly unskilled), as opposed to 23.5 per cent at home. As a mirror image, the reverse is true at the apex of the occupational pyramid. Among the movers of the first enlargement, 11.4 per cent have become managers or professionals (22.1 per cent in the home country) and 4 per cent (compared with 15.2 per cent in the home country) among those of the second enlargement.

At least in the early years after the enlargements of the 2000s, the new EU mobile citizens faced a trajectory of downward social mobility (Anderson et al. 2006; Barrett and Duffy 2008; Clark and Drinkwater 2008). The European Commission (2011a, 272) estimates that this was the experience of around 30 per cent of migrants from Central-Eastern Europe. Perhaps even more than in other migratory systems, an increase in income in the destination country is offset by a decrease in the social prestige of the occupation entered. But in this case, the political dimension also comes into play, owing to the immediate acquisition of citizenship rights – which are usually more generous in terms of social protection than those of the country of origin. From the point of view of the migrants, this unusual combination of an upgrade in citizenship and the simultaneous loss of social status has often produced frustration and disenchantment – as if European integration were only a half-kept promise. In response to this apparent contradiction, the experience of mobility is therefore deprived of its political significance and subjectively reduced to a utilitarian strategy for income maximization – as was typical among traditional migrants (Anghel 2008a; Morawska 2008; Csedő 2008).

On top of this, movers from the new member states enter the West European labour markets not only from the lowest ranks of the occupational structure but also with an extraordinary contractual flexibility which often borders on irregularity (Rea 2013). Paradoxically, the guarantees furnished by European citizenship enable them to accept jobs in the informal economy more than can third-country migrants, who are exposed to the risk of expulsion if discovered. According to the official figures, it is particularly Romanians and Bulgarians who find jobs with fixed-term contracts. One-third of those who migrated to Western Europe after 2007 obtained a contract of this type, whereas the average among natives was 14 per cent (European Commission 2011a, 273). By contrast, the situation of the citizens of the member states of the first enlargement has gradually approached that of natives, in terms of both job security (no more than 15 per cent of workers have fixed-term contracts) and the match between their jobs and educations (particularly in the UK; Bachan and Sheehan 2011).[11] But it is also true that their initial experiences in the West European labour markets have been marked by hyper-flexibility, with frequent changes in jobs and tasks. A 'migration industry' (Garapich 2008) of temporary work agencies – often acting as recruitment channels directly in Central-Eastern Europe – has controlled the entry into employment of a large proportion of new EU citizens: around one Central-Eastern European in every three found his/her first job through such agencies in the UK (Meardi 2009, 109). Not surprisingly, qualitative surveys have often recorded feelings of insecurity and scant forward planning amid such precarious conditions (Cyrus 2006; Düvell 2006; Cook et al. 2011). The situation of working women from Eastern Europe seems to be less flexible, at least in terms of occupational outcomes: the majority are absorbed by domestic work and cleaning services. However, qualitative studies report an emancipation pathway which leads from full-time domestic work, through part-time domestic work, to jobs with cleaning firms, which are preferred because of the greater welfare and job security that they offer (Metz-Göckel et al. 2008; Catanzaro and Colombo 2009).

As often happens among migrants, upward social mobility is achieved through self-employment. In this case, it should be borne in mind that setting up on one's own was often a stratagem to circumvent the restrictions on dependent employment imposed by the transitional regimes of the years immediately following the enlargement. Nevertheless, some studies on the matter point out that mobile Central-Eastern European entrepreneurship stems from longer and more stable settlement in the host society (Eade et al. 2006; Pajares 2007, 197–9; Barberis 2008; Viruela Martinez 2009, 84). In Germany and the UK, Polish firms have a marked ethnic connotation and cater mainly to co-national immigrants (Miera 2008; Ram and Jones 2008; Rabikowksa and Burrell 2009). In Italy,

74 *Mobile Europe*

however, the extraordinary penetration of the Romanian diaspora has generated more businesses than has the Polish diaspora, especially in the construction industry (Caritas-Migrantes 2009, 277 ff.).

Before concluding, it is necessary to consider a critical aspect of the phenomenon under scrutiny: how has the recession of the late 2000s impacted intra-European mobility? Figure 3.1, at the beginning of this chapter, shows that the stock of mobile European citizens has not stopped growing in the years of the crisis covered by the available data. More specifically, net migration from both Western and Eastern Europe has remained positive year on year, with a deceleration in the *pace of growth* between 2006 and 2009, though then followed by a subsequent upturn. The decrease has been more substantial among the citizens of the 2004 enlargement countries, who increased by only 18,000 units in 2009 (compared with the 77,000 from the EU15 and the 186,000 from the new member states of 2007) (European Commission 2011a, 254). But the trend of intra-EU mobility contrasts, above all, with the progressive decline in the number of foreigners from third countries: in 2010, the latter increased in the EU by no more than 160,000 compared with 667,000 new EU movers (ibid.). During the crisis, therefore, the internal component of mobility has outstripped the external one, confirming that the European migratory system as a whole has changed since the enlargements.

Besides the strictly demographic scenario, have mobile Europeans been affected by the crisis? Eurostat data show that, in 2010, European citizens resident in another state of the EU had maintained levels of employment higher than those in the countries of origin (ibid., 265).[12] The data in Table 3.8 afford more detailed understanding of the impact of the crisis on the labour-market achievements of mobile Europeans. Two rather obvious conclusions can be drawn. The first is the continuing ability of Western European movers to attain better jobs than their co-national stayers. The EU15 movers working abroad as blue collars represented 15.4 per cent of the total in 2007 and 11.4 per cent three years later. The gap between them and co-national stayers even widened. The second conclusion concerns the difference in occupational outcomes between Poles, Lithuanians and other EU10 movers, on the one hand, and Romanians and Bulgarians on the other. The presence of the former increased in free professions and senior management, and decreased in manual jobs. Instead, the latter were even more confined to blue-collar jobs, in which more than half of them were employed (the figure had been 43.5 per cent three years previously). Perhaps because of their time advantage in accessing European citizenship, the position on West European labour markets of the 2004 new-EU citizens was approaching, albeit timidly, that of the native population. Some studies on the behaviour of mobile citizens of the new member states during the crisis suggest that a 'wait-and-see' attitude has prevailed (Baczynska 2009; Cingolani 2009; Schneider and Holman 2009; Blanchflower and Lawton 2010). Subjectively, movers have reframed their migration biographies with an enhanced emphasis on 'self-development' rather than economic returns (Flipo 2013; Krings et al. 2013). Romanians and Bulgarians especially have accepted lower wages and reduced working hours rather than lose their jobs. On the other hand, whilst the economic situation has deteriorated in the host societies, it seems to be even worse in Romania (unlike in Poland, which has therefore recorded more returns). Finally, as we have seen, Romanian migration has been channelled to Italy and Spain. In those countries, ethnic communities have formed which are able to provide support networks during times of difficulty, and on which Europeans who have undertaken more individualized mobility paths cannot rely. Relatively speaking, the crisis has hit some categories of mobile Western Europeans even harder: for example, the British retirees resident on Spain's coasts who used their savings to purchase properties at the height of the Spanish construction bubble (Campbell 2011). Despite free movement, the economic conjuncture traps them in their *buen retiro*. With the resale value of a Spanish house purchased at the beginning of the century, it is difficult to find an equally commodious property back in the UK. The reversibility of the migration option – which forms the innermost core of the right to free movement in Europe – has been cancelled under the pitiless assault of the recession.

5. Conclusion: diversification, expansion, normalization?

How many EU movers are there, where are they and what do they do? This chapter has sought to answer these questions in a long-term perspective. Overall, since its 'pre-history' in the 1950s and 1960s, intra-European migration has progressively diversified in the last decades of the twentieth century – from a Fordist labour-related phenomenon to a more individualized and also geographically more dispersed practice. The first decade of the new millennium was in fact marked by a robust expansion of flows, mainly due to the 2004 and 2007 enlargements. Interestingly, the economic recession that ended the decade, and hit some of the prominent receiving countries (particularly Spain and Italy), smoothed but did not terminate West- and South-bound movements.

At the same time, it did not prompt as large South-to-North flows as expected. The *neuen Gastarbeiter* narrative of the European popular press (for example, Der Spiegel 2013), presenting anecdotal evidence on Spanish accountants and newly graduated Italians fleeing to Germany, was not matched by official statistics. The objection that these guestworkers remain undercover is unconvincing, given their job-driven mobility and the tight labour laws in the host countries.

Proportionally, between 2006 and 2012, the population of EU movers has grown less in Germany than in Belgium and Ireland (which experienced some ups and downs over the period), much less than in the UK and Spain and a modest 11 per cent more than in Portugal (Table 3.9). Quite surprisingly, the country with the strongest rise in this period is Italy, where the number of resident EU movers grew by a factor of 2.7 – mostly due to immigration from Romania. Compared to 2007, the non-national EU citizens living in Greece have diminished by 4 per cent only.

More fine-grained evidence about the composition of the EU mover population in the single most important and thriving national economy of the Union – that is, Germany – shows that the stock of Southern European and Irish nationals remained quite stable from before the crisis to 2012 (Statistische Bundesamt 2013, tables 3a and 3b). Rises in migration inflows of Greeks, Spanish and Italians – much publicized in the media – have thus been compensated by outflows of people from the same nationalities. People come and go, as is typical of the mobility regime of the EU. In contrast, the numbers of Poles and especially Romanians and Bulgarians settling in Germany have soared: the latter two nationalities approximately tripled in six years.[13]

Table 3.9 Stocks of EU movers in selected EU countries: growth rate (2006 = 100)

	2006	2007	2008	2009	2010	2011	2012
Belgium	100	103	107	112	116	122	127
Germany	100	109	111	112	113	116	124
UK		100	111	123	132	141	161
Greece		100	100	103	103	97	96
Spain	100	132	159	155	155	155	157
Italy	100	113	173	210	230	248	269
Portugal		100	121	89	98	108	113
Ireland	100	126	133	91	86	95	131

Source: Eurostat online database (consulted 12 November 2013). Reference year: 2007 for UK, Greece and Portugal.

The bottom line is that, even during the euro crisis, the proportionally larger contingent of movers was not formed by Southern Europeans, but still by Central-Eastern Europeans and citizens of the Baltic states. At the same time, flows out of the richer EU member states did not taper off. All this may point to some normalization of intra-EU movements, with some changes determined by economic cycles, but also by a sort of in-built inertia and channelling of migration routes which attest to the structural nature of cross-state mobility in European societies.

Part II
Practising Free Movement: Sociological Perspectives

4
'Old' and 'New' EU Movers: Integration Pathways Compared

1. Western Europeans on the move: a scattered literature

As a sociological category, mobile European citizens have been relatively little studied within the broad universe of migrants. Yet they possess several features of interest to those who wish to identify non-traditional patterns of migration (King 2002) and to focus on concrete processes of transnational social integration (Favell and Guiraudon 2011). Intra-European migrants occupy the increasingly blurred – owing to the multiplication of mobility practices, the reconfiguration of national borders and the proliferation of international agreements – boundary area between international and internal migration in which it is possible to grasp novelties in migration (King and Skeldon 2010).

The first studies on this population concentrated on particular subsets of mobile people and lacked full awareness of the political and legal factors that give specificity to mobility in Western Europe. Prompted by an anthropological interest in the formation of 'circular territories', Tarrius (1992) tracked the everyday itineraries of frequent travellers to London, Paris and Brussels. Although he did not have a systematic sample, he concluded that 'the occupants of high professional positions rarely travel, and then only briefly, to sign a contract or to conclude a transaction, [but they do not form] a "circulating European elite"'. In the end-of-century world of European businesses, movers 'are the holders of intermediate positions, novice or just-confirmed middle managers [. . .] to be "broken in" [or to be] "got out of the way" if too hungry for power' (ibid., 94–5).

Elsewhere in the continent, and in largely the same years, King et al. (1998, 2000) analysed the migratory paths and integration into host societies of British retirement migrants to certain areas of Southern Europe. Their pioneering studies evidenced that the choice of destination by this category of migrants was strongly conditioned by individual economic and cultural capital; for example, upper-class British retirement migrants preferred Tuscany, while middle-class ones favoured the Costa del Sol and the Algarve. In light of demographic changes and political integration in the continent, King et al. predicted the probable expansion of this type of migration to the European shores of the Mediterranean. Yet Northern Europe retirees represent only the tip of the iceberg of what has been subsequently called 'lifestyle migration' and which finds a wide range of examples among mobile Europeans (Hoggart and Buller 1994; Barou and Prado 1995; Waldren 1996; O'Reilly 2000; Mulé and Galassi 2003; Huber 2004; Aledo Tur 2005; Casado Díaz 2006; Kesselring 2006; Bousiou 2008; Drake and Collard 2008; Benson and O'Reilly 2009). Notwithstanding the variety of their trajectories and life-worlds (from a 'return to nature' in the French provinces to 'liminality' on the Greek and Spanish coasts), lifestyle movers seem united by a desire to escape the standard models of life-course organization. On this reading, the right to free movement is exercised as 'agency' over 'structure', especially by migrants originating from unrewarding, if not repressive, contexts of origin.

Other niche studies have analysed the intra-European mobility of specific social categories. Ackers (1998) has examined female migration and the obstacles it faces, showing how EU citizenship rights can open opportunities for working women otherwise prevented from advancing in occupations where gender discrimination still persists. As Morokvasic (2004) notes with regard to Eastern European societies, the EU mobility regime can be even more empowering for women than traditional migration. In later works, Ackers (2005) also considered the mobility of scientists and researchers, and the tangle of legal and social problems surrounding the free movement right of minors – especially the children of separated parents living in different member states (Ackers and Stalford 2004). Although they deal with a provisional and brief type of sojourn abroad, mention should also be made of studies on university students enjoying mobility thanks to the Socrates-Erasmus Programme or EU post-graduate grants (Teichler 2002; King and Ruiz-Gelices 2003; Bettin Lattes and Bontempi 2008; Kennedy 2010; Mitchell 2012; van Mol and Timmerman 2014; from a broader perspective, Cicchelli 2012). The majority of these studies stress the avant-garde Europeanized culture of the students examined, but the most recent – and also more sophisticated – analyses reverse the cause–effect relationship between

Erasmus mobility and European identification: Erasmus students are more enthusiastic than others about European integration because it is the most Europhile (and affluent) students that participate in the Erasmus Programme (Sigalas 2010; Wilson 2011; Kuhn 2012; but see also Mitchell 2012, 2014; van Mol 2013).

The research project on so-called 'Eurostars' – that is, high-skilled workers who move among European capitals (London, Amsterdam, Brussels) – is perhaps the most acute and widely known ethnographic investigation of mobile Western Europeans (Favell 2004, 2006, 2008a; see also Scott 2006). The penetrating in-depth interviews on which Favell's work is based highlight the subtlety and obstinacy of cultural barriers to successful integration, despite the apparent cosmopolitanism of the settlement contexts considered. The boundary between emancipation and isolation is ambiguous and mutable in the experience of transnational living. Rather than in Europe as such, 'Eurostars' tend to anchor their life-worlds in the urban dimension, as incarnated in the highly specific settings they choose.

A European capital – Berlin – also forms the backdrop of the study by Verwiebe and Eder (2006) on the performances of French, British, Italian, Danish and Polish migrants in the local labour market. This analysis emphasizes both the shared features common to European movers in Berlin and the stratification within this microcosm of intra-EU mobility. These nationalities of mobile Europeans are relatively privileged in terms of education and socioeconomic status. Nevertheless, the French and British are better able than the Italians and Poles to gain economic returns from their mobility strategy, whilst, sociostructural conditions remaining equal, Danes manage to earn incomes even higher than those of native German workers.

Differences in EU movers' income may stem not only from contextual features and individual assets, but also from variations in migration projects. Built on the combination of the free movement regime and the extended network of EU-wide low-cost flights, transnational commuting is less unusual among mobile Europeans than in other categories of migrants. A qualitative study of the 'Euro-commuting' Irish details three social types with distinct strategies: the 'select', whose dual residency reflects a lifestyle choice relatively unconcerned with economic returns; the 'strivers', who aspire to upward social mobility but intend to keep their family life and other possible prospects in the home country and the 'survivors', who get downwardly mobile occupations abroad but manage to 'save face' at home by commuting (Ralph 2014).

The most extensive comparative analysis on the population of mobile European citizens was undertaken as part of the Pioneur Project conducted by an international team between 2002 and 2006. In 2004, a survey was carried out on a sample of 5,000 mobile Europeans (EIMSS: *European Internal Movers' Social Survey*).[1] The interviews were conducted in France, Germany, the UK, Italy and Spain – the demographically largest countries of the then EU15 – with intra-European migrants of French, German, British, Italian and Spanish origin (that is, interviewed in each country were citizens of the four other nationalities under scrutiny). Recchi and Favell (2009) provide an overview of the results of this composite research project. Put briefly, it depicts a population which is unique but not homogeneous. Braun and Arsene (2009) distinguish four clusters of mobile Western Europeans: 'Eurostars', who match the profile drawn in qualitative terms by Favell (see above); 'late traditional migrants', with features similar to those of classic economic migrants in terms of education, employment and privileged relationships with co-nationals; 'retirement migrants', who follow the North–South route to the climatically more agreeable areas of Southern Europe, but also with a large presence in the French provinces; and the 'pre-retirement commuters', usually professionals who still have jobs but are able to manage them at a distance or with frequent movements, and who share features with Eurostars and retired migrants. One of the main discoveries of the research concerns the prevalence of migratory projects *not* undertaken for economic reasons (see also Hadler 2006; Koikkalainen 2013, 173). The affective dimension seems to be behind the majority of the mobility experiences of EU movers who want to reside with a partner of another nationality or, in a sizeable number of cases, to live their homosexuality without the social control of the home environment (Santacreu et al. 2009). Consistently, it appears that upward social mobility is not a particularly frequent outcome; but, on the other hand, geographical mobility is not excessively penalizing in terms of socioeconomic status in the country of settlement. In fact, mobile Western European citizens tend to be middle to upper class and are able to avoid the occupational downward mobility typical of migrants, at least in the first phases of their experiences abroad. Moreover, movers of lower social origins are better able to ascend the social scale in the European labour market than are their counterparts at home – showing that free movement to some extent fuels meritocracy (Recchi 2009; Favell and Recchi 2011).

Again with support from the European Commission, in 2007 another comparative project was conducted on mobile Europeans in Belgium, France, Germany, Poland, Spain and Switzerland, but this time with an emphasis solely on job-related mobility (Schneider and Meil 2008). This project revealed that around half of workers aged between 25 and 54 had experienced some form of job-related spatial mobility. Overall, the most interesting finding was that the differences in this regard had more to do with individual characteristics than with contextual and national ones: in particular, this form of intra-EU mobility turned out to be much more common among young men. Moreover, confirming the Pioneur results (Recchi 2009), job-related geographical mobility was not so much a means to acquire better chances of upward social mobility as to avert the risk of downward mobility (Meil 2008, 313). On the basis of residential choices, and of the distance, duration and regularity of movements, this team of researchers drew up a typology of mobile European workers: on the one hand, the 'residentially mobile', and on the other, the 'commuters'. This latter group further divides among 'long-distance commuters', 'overnighters', 'shuttles' and 'vari-mobiles' who often change their patterns of movement (Limmer and Schneider 2008).

2. How EU movers integrate: a multi-dimensional picture

Transnationalism is a phenomenon that has attracted considerable attention among migration scholars since the 1990s. In an age of increasing globalization, the concept has entered the current lexicon of analyses on migratory phenomena from social and cultural anthropology. It denotes 'the processes by which immigrants build social fields that link together their country of origin and their country of settlement' (Glick Schiller et al. 1992, 1; see also Portes et al. 1999, 210; Vertovec 1999). As often happens, the success of the notion has led to its overuse and sometimes to its abuse as an umbrella term for activities of very different kinds. On balance, theoretical debate on the theme has prevailed over empirical analysis – especially in Europe (Fibbi and D'Amato 2008, 7). Nevertheless, it is difficult to deny that the fluidification of national borders and belongings to which transnationalism refers is ideally embodied by Western European movers. With few exceptions, their personal networks consist of a balanced mix of co-nationals, citizens of the host country and of other countries (Alaminos and Santacreu 2009). Likewise, in their access to information and their cultural consumption, they tend to combine media of the home and host countries, rather than privileging nostalgic, or conversely, assimilative choices (Tambini and Rother 2009). Must one therefore conclude that free movement in Europe elides specificities due to the country of origin (henceforth CoO) and country of residence (henceforth CoR) to generate a homogeneous space of social and cultural integration on the basis of a common and shared package of legal rights – that is, EU citizenship? This section will seek to give an empirical answer to this question, which has gone relatively unaddressed by the broad-gauge analyses on migratory pathways, social practices and attitudes presented thus far.[2]

To address the question, it is necessary to determine whether there are significant differences which depend on the CoO and the CoR of migrants – and in particular on the combination of these two features. Doing so systematically, however, would require page after page of tables comparing different indicators and how these are simultaneously associated with diverse independent variables (among them, the CoO/CoR interaction). In this section, I instead intend to draw a general overview on the matter without going into excessive detail. For this purpose, I shall analyse EIMSS data on British, German, French, Spanish and Italian EU movers (in 2004) and Moveact data on Polish, Romanian, British and German EU movers (in 2012) using multiple correspondence analysis (MCA). The aim of this well-known multi-variate technique is to identify the dimensions underlying the structure of the data. It therefore summarizes the relations of interdependence among the original variables and furnishes a graphic representation which facilitates interpretation by identifying 'latent variables' that function as axes of the original variables projected in a Cartesian system (Greenacre and Blasius 1994).[3] Although a more complex representation might be better suited to some of the data, I shall use the more standard two-dimensional representation consisting of orthogonal axes which intersect to create a point of origin on the plane. In these graphs, distance from the centre and position with respect to the axes efficaciously capture the discriminatory power of variables (or their modalities) and their reciprocal relations of greater or lesser association in the data. As regards associations, the distances in the bidimensional space should be interpreted with care. If the modality of a variable is located close to the centre, all of its associations with the modalities of another variable will be low – that is, its distribution resembles the marginal distribution. The closest associations are among the modalities distant from the centre and located in the same direction. The meaning of the axes themselves must also be appropriately interpreted: it is suggested by the modalities located at the two poles.[4]

I shall now conduct a first analysis which considers, alongside the demographic characteristics of the sample, a number of variables concerning the 'structural' integration of migrants: their social class position, employment status, education level and previous experiences of mobility. The same operation will then be repeated, but using variables instead related to 'sociocultural' integration, and then again with those variables that have to do with 'identificational' integration (with the CoO, with the CoR, Europe and the place of residence). I shall finally develop a model that uses only the variables that have proved significant in each of the preceding analyses.

My strategy of analysis starts with examination of the structural characteristics shared by EU movers. Therefore considered are the CoO/CoR combinations and sociodemographic variables (gender, the period of migration, age at time of migration, education level, social class,[5] previous experiences of life and work abroad). In this graphic representation (Figure 4.1), the vertical axis quite sharply shows the differences in *social status*: a higher education and a higher social class are both in the uppermost part of the figure. The horizontal axis relates to the time dimension: migration at a young age and further in the past is located to the left, while migration in adulthood and in more recent years is located to the right. However, the horizontal axis also shows a difference in terms of labour-market integration, and may consequently be interpreted in terms of *structural integration* (with maximum integration to the left).[6] All social classes are located in the left-hand part of the graph, with the exception of unclassified individuals – mainly students and housewives (retirees are classified according to last occupation) – who are in fact to be found in the right-hand part. Moreover, respondents who had previous work experiences in the CoR are on the left, those who did not on the right. The groups with previous experience of living abroad or in the CoR (before the final decision to migrate) are all located close to the centre. This, therefore, is a variable that does not contribute much to interpretation of the meaning of the Cartesian axes. Nor does gender discriminate, at least in terms of structural integration patterns among mobile Western Europeans.

Where do the CoO/CoR combinations fit in in this scheme? Germans and Britons in Spain and France, but also the French in Spain – all groups with prevailingly middle-class status – are close to the pole of low structural integration (to the right in the graph). This also applies to Italians in Spain and Germans in Italy, albeit to a less marked extent. By contrast, French and Italian migrants in Great Britain, and Britons in Germany, appear to be well integrated. French and German migrants in Britain also enjoy higher status. These groups perhaps qualify as a sort of 'migrant elite', to use the concept of superstratification introduced by Verwiebe and Eder (2006), so that their entry into national labour markets may have 'stretched' pre-existing

88 Mobile Europe

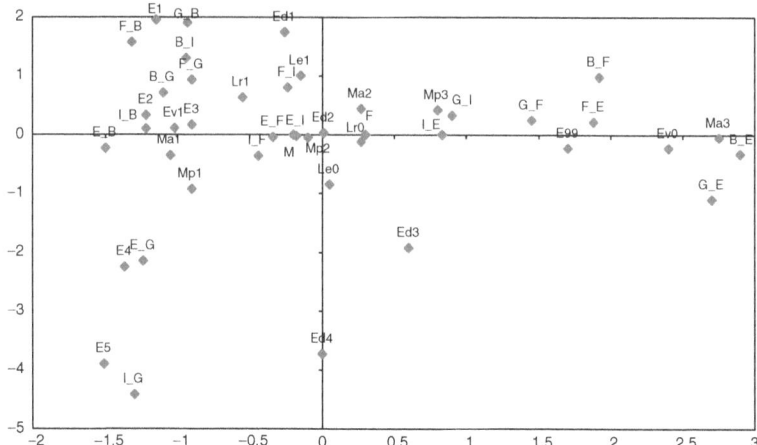

Figure 4.1 Structural characteristics of Western EU movers in France, Germany, Great Britain, Italy and Spain (2004): multiple correspondence analysis

Source: EIMSS, N = 4,919.

Notes:

Variables	Label	Codes
Demographic variables		
Gender		M = man, F = woman
Migration period	Mp	1 = 1974–1983, 2 = 1984–1993, 3 = 1994–2003
Age at migration	Ma	1 = 18–29, 2 = 30–49, 3 = 50 or more
Education	Ed	1 = tertiary, 2 = upper-secondary, 3 = lower-secondary, 4 = primary or no educational qualification
Social class	E	1 = EGP I–II, 2 = EGP III, 3 = EGP IV, 4 = EGP V–VI, 5 = EGP VII, 99 = not classified
Employed in CoR before	Ev	1 = yes, 0 = no
Lived in CoR before	Lr	1 = yes, 0 = no
Lived in another foreign country before	Le	1 = yes, 0 = no
Context variables		
CoO–CoR combinations		First letter = CoO, second letter = CoR; F = France, G = Germany, B = Great Britain, I = Italy, E = Spain

social hierarchies upwards – for instance, by inflating housing prices (the case of London is well known).[7] Conversely, high structural integration is combined with lower status among Italian and, to a lesser extent, Spanish migrants in Germany.

I now move to the second analysis. Here I add to the CoO/CoR combination a series of variables concerning sociocultural integration (language knowledge at the time of migration and of the interview, nationality of friends and of the partner).[8] In this case, MCA yields an almost one-dimensional pattern. Interpretation of the horizontal axis – the one on which the greatest variations are recorded – seems clear in terms of 'intercultural competence' (Padilla 1980). Situated at the extreme right of this axis are interviewees with a scant knowledge of the host country's language, both on arrival and at the time of the interview, without friends from the CoR, with numerous friends from the CoO and frequently with a partner from the CoO. Located at the opposite pole, to the left side of the graph, are interviewees with better language skills, numerous friends from the CoR and often with a partner from the CoR. Those with a partner from a third country or who were single lie close to the centre.

How are the CoO/CoR combinations arranged? Located at the right-hand side – that of low intercultural competence – are Germans and Britons in Spain and, for presumably different reasons, Italians in Germany. The latter seem to have greater familiarity with the language of the host country, but they are characterized above all by a marked tendency to marry persons of the same nationality and to maintain close ties with co-nationals. Lying on the left-hand side – that of strong intercultural competence – are all the groups of migrants residing in Britain (but especially German and French) and the majority of those who live in Italy. Of course, this condition may have been achieved through very different trajectories – above all in the labour market. Previous analyses have shown that, during the years of the survey, the unemployment risk of European movers in Italy was almost double that of their counterparts in the UK (Recchi et al. 2006). This perhaps helps to explain the different positions of residents in Italy and in Britain on the vertical axis, also bearing in mind that in Figure 4.2 EU movers in Italy are distinguished by a lack of friends among persons of the same nationality and EU movers in Britain show an uncommonly advanced knowledge of the host country's language. In the former case, the emphasis is on social relations with natives, that is, on an 'expressive' form of intercultural competence; in the latter, on employability, that is, on an 'instrumental' declination of intercultural competence. The distance on the vertical axis, therefore, perhaps reflects differences in terms of subjective strategies of structural integration which, however, remain somewhat in the background because of the combination of variables used in this analysis.

I now examine identitarian integration – which is the aspect of integration that most closely concerns attachment to the host country. I shall first consider the sense of territorial belonging. I shall then determine whether the reasons for migration significantly differ according to the various combinations of CoO and CoR – distinguishing in particular between instrumental reasons (work, study) and expressive ones

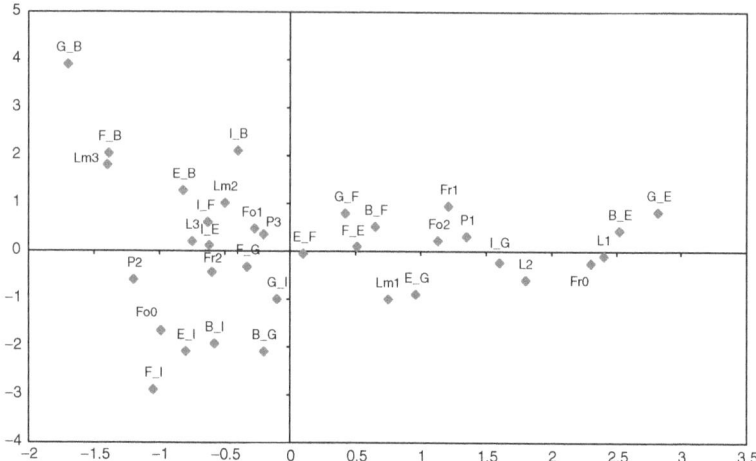

Figure 4.2 Sociocultural characteristics of Western EU movers in France, Germany, Great Britain, Italy and Spain (2004): multiple correspondence analysis

Source: EIMSS, N = 4,919.

Notes:

Variable	Label	Codes
Sociocultural variables		
CoR language knowledge at migration	Lm	1 = low, 2 = medium, 3 = high
CoR language knowledge at interview	L	1 = low, 2 = medium, 3 = high
Friends from CoO	Fo	0 = none, 1 = few, 2 = many
Friends from CoR	Fr	0 = none, 1 = few, 2 = many
Nationality of partner	P	1 = CoO, 2 = CoR, 3 = third country or no partner
Context variables		
CoO-CoR combinations		First letter = CoO, second letter = CoR; F = France, G = Germany, B = Great Britain, I = Italy, E = Spain

(love, quality of life). In this regard, equally important is the migrant's intention to remain abroad, to return to the CoO, or to move to a third country. Finally, significant as well among this set of symbolic–communicative factors is the preference for the CoR's or for the CoO's mass media (especially television channels).

The resulting graph (not shown) is much more complex than the previous ones – indeed, it would require a third axis for better spatial representation – and not all the variables considered seem to have an unambiguous impact. The horizontal axis is clearly interpretable: those who migrate in search of a better quality of life lie to the right-hand side, while those who do so for reasons of work, study or love lie to the left. The former group includes individuals who have deliberately selected their destinations; the latter group includes interviewees whose decision to move to a foreign country has been prompted by a specific factor (a job, university enrolment, a partner), but who are less attracted by the CoR in itself. The latter are consequently more likely to return to the CoO – a likelihood virtually absent among those who have moved abroad to enjoy a better quality of life.

Quality-of-life migration is connected with a strong sense of belonging to the CoR, but without implying large use of that country's media. For the other types of motivation, the contrary appears to be the case: movers for work, study or family reasons do not feel attached to the CoR, but they watch its television channels. Some CoO/CoR combinations tell specific stories. Germans and Britons in Spain are characterized by their low use of the local media. German and French movers in Great Britain make large use of the British media – a possible 'BBC effect'? As regards identification, French and Italian movers in Spain, but also Germans in Italy and Britons in France, show strong attachment to the CoR, rather than to the CoO. Low attachment to the CoR is recorded by Spanish movers in all the countries considered, and by Italians in Germany and Britain. Overall, attachment to the EU is not discriminatory: European identification appears to be a culturally distinct dimension which responds to a logic independent from the combinations of nationality and place of residence. In other words, it is not the nationality/residence association which determines variations in EU identification, but rather individual factors – a not irrelevant finding.

Finally, as said, I will analyse a composite set of variables which includes the structural, sociocultural and identitarian characteristics that have proved most discriminatory in the analyses illustrated thus far (Figure 4.3). In other words, I omit those variables that have not contributed significantly to defining the semantic space in the previous graphs: age, gender, past experience of living in the CoR or a third country, intentions of return to the CoO, language knowledge at the time of migration, past experience of work in the CoR and the number of friends from the CoO. As regards the variable measuring attachment to CoR, its modalities have been reduced so as to produce a smaller number of points on the Cartesian plane.

The principal dimensions that emerge from this analysis are, once again, referable to *socioeconomic status* (vertical axis) and *intercultural competence* (horizontal axis). As in Figure 4.1, status is sharply defined by education and social class. Overall, intercultural competence is

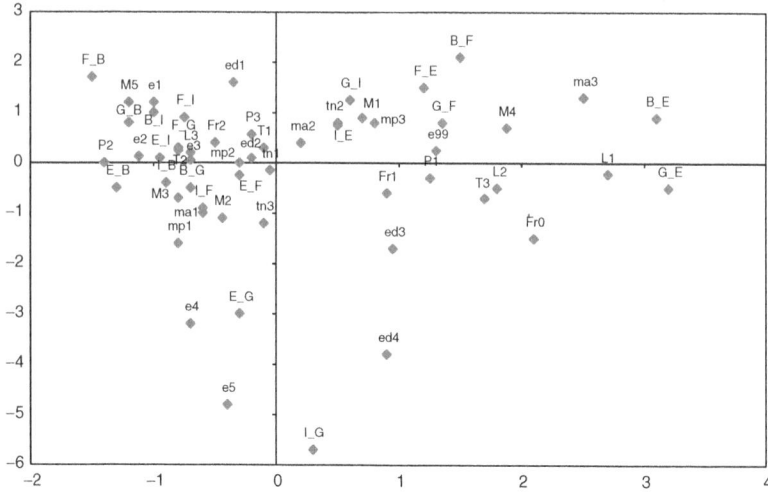

Figure 4.3 Structural, sociocultural and identitarian characteristics of Western EU movers in France, Germany, Great Britain, Italy and Spain (2004): multiple correspondence analysis

Source: EIMSS, N = 4,919.

Notes:

Variable	Label	Codes
Demographic variables		
Migration period	Mp	1 = 1974–1983, 2 = 1984–1993, 3 = 1994–2003
Age at migration	Ma	1 = 18–29, 2 = 30–49, 3 = 50 or more
Education	Ed	1 = tertiary, 2 = upper-secondary, 3 = lower-secondary, 4 = primary or no educational qualification
Social class	E	1 = EGP I–II, 2 = EGP III, 3 = EGP IV, 4 = EGP V–VI, 5 = EGP VII, 99 = not classified
Sociocultural variables		
CoR language knowledge at interview	L	1 = low, 2 = medium, 3 = high
Friends from CoR	Fr	0 = none, 1 = few, 2 = many
Nationality of partner	P	1 = CoO, 2 = CoR, 3 = third country or no partner
Identitarian variables		
Migration motives	M	1 = various, 2 = work, 3 = family/love, 4 = quality of life, 5 = study
TV use	T	1 = no TV, neither or both CoO and CoR channels, 2 = only or more CoO channels, 3 = only or more CoR channels
National identification	tn	1 = equally close to CoO and CoR, 2 = closer to CoR, 3 = closer to CoO
Context variables		
CoO–CoR combinations		First letter = CoO, second letter = CoR; F = France, G = Germany, B = Great Britain, I = Italy, E = Spain

more salient than status, thus demonstrating its greater discriminatory power. By contrast, the identitarian dimension seems to be almost irrelevant.

Some of the CoO/CoR combinations stand out. In particular, whilst Italian movers (and to a lesser extent Spanish ones) in Germany have low status but average intercultural competence, Britons and Germans in Spain occupy a medium to high position in terms of status but possess low intercultural competence.

To conclude, with the aid of MCA, I have sought to determine the existence and nature of significant differences tied to nationality and the context of residence – the CoO/CoR combination – of intra-EU movers. Not only do these differences exist, but they are aligned along two key dimensions: socioeconomic status and intercultural competence.[9] There are striking cases in which nationality and residence constrain integration. The first concerns Italian and Spanish movers (but among the latter, only those who migrated in the late 1970s and early 1980s) living in Germany. They constitute a coda of Fordist migration and are personified by the classic *Gastarbeiter*, with very low status and an intermediate level of sociocultural integration. Whilst low-skilled workers pertain to an outdated scenario as regards migrants in Western Europe – unless the economic crisis in the Euro-zone dramatically deteriorates – this type of migration is now undertaken by Central-Eastern Europeans. The second outstanding case concerns Britons and Germans living in France and especially Spain, whose intercultural competence in the destination societies tends to be markedly lower than that of the rest of Western EU movers.

3. Central-Eastern European movers: from the Berlin Wall to European citizenship

As already noted in Chapter 2, at the time of their accession into the EU, Romania and Bulgaria had average incomes equal to around one-tenth of the EU15 average. The discrepancy was less marked (around one-quarter) in the 2004 enlargement countries, but it was considerable nonetheless. It is not possible to analyse the development of intra-European migratory projects along the East–West axis without considering these economic figures, because they summarize a plethora of hardships inherited from the communist regimes and which, in many cases, were further exacerbated by the political, economic and cultural turmoil of the immediately subsequent years (see Judt 2005, ch. 21). The numerous ethnographic studies conducted on migrants from Central-Eastern

Europe have shown that objective economic difficulties (unemployment and underemployment, decline in industrial output, deregulation, disintegration of welfare systems) have been subjectively filtered until they induce the decision to migrate (Triandafyllidou 2006; Woolfson 2007; Metz-Göckel et al. 2008; Catanzaro and Colombo 2009; Cingolani 2009; Favell and Nebe 2009; Meardi 2009).

In general, the economic motivations of migration can be arranged along a continuum extending from the need to earn a living, at one extreme, to a desire to increase purchasing power or investment capacity (for instance, to buy a house or to start a business) at the other. An intermediate, very common, motivation is to pay for children's schooling or enable them to attend higher education. Whatever their personal reasons may be, potential migrants from Central-Eastern Europe have also had to reckon with the political and economic evolution of their countries, the reconfiguration of EU law and the demand for immigrant labour in Western Europe. On the basis of the intersection among these factors, four phases of East–West mobility in Europe since the 1980s can be distinguished.

The first phase spanned the years prior to the collapse of the communist regimes. The pioneers were the political refugees who perilously found asylum beyond the Iron Curtain from the 1950s onwards. Part of this contingent of migrants used free Europe – as their predecessors had done in the immediate post-war period – as a springboard for subsequent migration to the USA and Canada. Often, however, they created informal networks which provided assistance in crossing frontiers to an increasing, though still relatively small, number of migrants who combined political and economic motives with affective ones (for instance, because they had married Western students and researchers sent to universities beyond the Iron Curtain) (Morawska 2002). During the years of the Cold War, Western states enacted legislation which allowed immigration by refugees from the former communist countries, so that their status was entirely regular.

The second period began in 1990 with the demise of the communist regimes, and it concluded with the abolition in 2001 of EU entry visas for citizens of the future member states. In this phase, migration patterns diverged across nationalities. Poles and Romanians immediately began to move to Western Europe, whilst emigration from Bulgaria instead grew towards the end of the decade, following the severe economic crisis that hit the country in 1997 (Okolski 2001). During the 1990s, the majority of Central-Eastern European migrants crossed frontiers on tourist visas (which they then let expire) or by irregular means (Koryś 2003). Considerable use was made of forged documents and immigrant-trafficking organizations. Border crossings between Bulgaria and Greece and between Slovenia and Italy were particularly frequent. However, a state of semi-clandestinity was common to these arduous movements characterized by long journeys, changes in means of transport, wearisome border controls and bribes to border guards (Jordan and Düvell 2002; Potot 2007; Anghel 2008b).

During this phase, expectations of regularization in the immigration countries were sometimes satisfied by amnesties or, more often, by loopholes in administrative regulations. For example, in the UK, many exploited the opportunity to convert a tourist visa into a business visa – as recounted by a Polish migrant couple interviewed by Düvell (2006, 72):

> Before our first six month visa expired we found out [about a possibility of getting a business visa] from a mate Darius worked with at a building site. When you apply for a business visa you need to have a valid tourist visa, so, because ours were about to expire we went to France and back. We also started contacting people who could help in submitting visa applications. It took us four months to get all the papers together and apply for that visa. Firstly we talked to a man who presented our possibilities to us. He was an [Polish] accountant.

In Italy, Spain and Greece – which were proving attractive destinations for East–West mobility because of their relatively lax controls on irregular immigration – there developed the practice of enacting periodic amnesties for paperless immigrants. According to some scholars, however, the contention that such regularizations were the main reason for Southern Europe's attractiveness to citizens of the former communist countries is an over-simplification, given that bureaucratic obstacles and the drawbacks due to the complexity, and also the discretionality, of certain regularizations were perceived by migrants as signals intended to discourage further inflows (Triandafyllidou and Kosic 2006).

On the other hand, countries like Germany and the Netherlands, which did not regularize immigrants without residence permits – in part since in those years they had generously granted political refugee status to hundreds of thousands of fugitives from the former Yugoslavia – were not particularly welcoming. As a consequence, Polish migrants to Germany (especially those who by ancestry had been able to obtain a German passport) became commuters and seasonal workers with precarious, underpaid and largely informal jobs (Koryś 2003; Cyrus and Vogel 2006). But even the UK, which, as said, allowed entry by migrants from Central-Eastern Europe – among other reasons, because they were better suited to a highly flexible and deregulated labour market (particularly through private employment agencies which deliberately drew on this reservoir of cheap labour) – was by no means an El Dorado (Grabowska 2003; Eade 2007). The dilemma between settlement and return typical of the migration experience was a recurrent refrain in interviews conducted with young Polish movers at that time:

> I haven't got a visa any more. So if I get caught, I get caught. They will send me to Poland, and what can I do? If I get caught . . . Firstly, I don't carry my passport with me. If I get caught with some dodgy passport and they checked it on their computer or if I bought an Italian passport . . . and was asked a question in Italian then I'm done anyway. If I'm caught at work it'll not matter if I have a visa or not. I never know about any possibility of legally extending my visa. I will stay here till December. In December I will take First Certificate exam. And then I'll go back, 'cause I'm slowly having enough of getting up at 5:40 am. I'm a person who graduated from University. I cannot keep hovering till the rest of my life. Cleaners are the lowest layer, the lowest caste of working people. [. . .] After going back I'll have a rest for three months and then I'll get myself a ticket to England. No, no I'm joking. It's a joke. But that's what people do. They go back to Poland saying they would never come back. Stay there for a month, spend the money they've saved here. That's what people do very often. (Düvell 2006, 67)

The third phase began in 2001, when citizens of EU candidate countries were no longer required to possess entry visas to the Schengen area, and it concluded with the enlargements of 2004 (ten new member states, eight of them in former communist Europe) and 2007 (Romania and Bulgaria). Consequently, irregular immigrant status effectively ceased for all citizens of these countries present in Western Europe. A residence permit for work purposes was still necessary, but greater ease of entry and the prospect of an imminent upgrade with the granting of citizenship upon enlargement were major incentives for migration. The consequent flows targeted the informal labour market and therefore headed for those countries – especially Italy, Spain and Greece – in which jobs in the underground economy were more readily available (Reyneri et al. 1997; Reyneri 1998; Baldwin-Edwards and Arango 1999; Reyneri 2004; Ribas-Mateos 2004). The weight of the informal economy and the spread of labour-intensive occupations (that is, demand-side factors) explain the greater attractiveness of Southern European countries compared with Central-Northern ones – even if the latter were more affluent – for potential migrants from the new EU member states. The importance of this southward migratory axis was only partly mitigated by the attractiveness of the British Isles after 2004.

The final phase started with the enlargements of 2004 and 2007, when the citizens of the new member states automatically became European citizens. As already stated, in order to stem possible mass migration to certain countries (Germany and Austria above all, for reasons of geographical and historical proximity), the EU introduced a complex set of transitional rules which did not restrict the right to free movement but discriminated against the new European citizens in their access to dependent employment in the 'old' Europe. Exceptions were the UK, Ireland and Sweden, which, given their buoyant economies, dispensed with the transitional rules from the start. The UK and Ireland – but not Sweden, because of language and an industrial relations system less amenable to an immigrant labour supply – thus formed the other 'magnet', together with Southern Europe, for East–West mobility, at least until the economic crisis of the late 2000s (Kępińska 2007). Besides ease of entry into employment, the English-speaking countries could offer the appeal of their language and their role as avant-garde centres of youth culture (Krings et al. 2009; Wickham et al. 2009), thus adding an emancipatory undertone to migration choices (Flipo 2013). Obtaining European citizenship meant, above all, immediate regularization of stay for the large number of Central-Eastern Europeans who had previously profited from the visa exemption to settle in those countries. But, owing to the transitional measures, it did not mean the regularization of work. Consequently, the ambiguity persisted whereby EU citizens from the former communist countries – precisely because of the legality of their stay – were better candidates for irregular jobs than were third-country immigrants – for whom regularity of the work contract was instead essential to keep a residence permit. Nevertheless, EU citizenship gave Eastern Europeans a trump card to play in asserting their rights in negotiations with employers. It freed them from the more or less explicit blackmail to which they had been typically subject when their residence itself was irregular (for an exemplary case, see Krings et al. 2011). Moreover, the possibility of easy communication with the home country, when a parallel infrastructural network developed (particularly the low-cost flights which proliferated between the British Isles and Eastern Europe: see Williams and Baláž 2009), spurred shuttle migration especially suited to irregular employment (Sandu 2006). As a qualitative study summarizes, under these circumstances 'migrants gradually turn into circulating citizens' (Marcu 2013, 45). Concomitantly, this enhanced mobility reconfigures family relations into a transnational form (Moskal 2011).

The occupational situation of mobile Eastern Europeans in Western Europe has progressively changed over three decades of transformation in every part of the continent. Besides temporal differences due to radical political changes (from the fall of the Berlin Wall, through the introduction of European citizenship, to the admission into the EU of the former communist countries), likewise to be considered is the high variability of the national and subnational contexts in which migratory flows have taken place (see Favell 2008b). This section has distinguished four phases in such flows between the 1980s and the early 2000s. In the first phase, the enormous difficulty of leaving the countries of origin was matched by straightforward integration into the receiving countries. However, the flows were modest in size. In the second phase, once the barriers to exit had fallen, citizens of the former communist countries usually experienced more or less tolerated situations of irregularity, but with significant differences among countries connected in part to national economic and political cycles. Opportunities for work were largely concentrated in the informal economy: the construction industry, agriculture and manual labour for men, domestic and tourism services for women. In Southern Europe, in particular, emergence from irregularity to legal status seems to have been more tortuous and episodic, with relapses into illegality following job loss and the consequent impossibility of renewing residence permits. The first decade of the century, nevertheless, saw first the announcement and then the granting of European citizenship to the majority of East European citizens living in the EU15, by virtue of entry into the Union of their countries of origin, and a further inflow of new EU movers. The latter did not have the same interest as their predecessors in the regular jobs necessary to enjoy citizenship rights and, also, to move freely between the receiving and the sending country. Paradoxically, therefore, their citizenship was often an incentive for unlawful employment. Rather than generating full-fledged integration, it fostered a perception of free intra-EU mobility from the countries of Central-Eastern Europe as accessory to flexible employment. Hence, albeit in the new form of rapid geographical movement, the extension of European citizenship to migrants from the former communist countries led to the 'resurrection of guest workers' (Castles 2006) as the protagonists of migratory flows in Europe.

'Old' and 'New' EU Movers 99

4. How Central-Eastern European movers integrate: between continuity and specificity

To complete the foregoing qualitative overview on the integration of Central-Eastern European movers in the EU15 countries, in this section I shall present an analysis analogous to the one illustrated in section 2 relative to mobile Western Europeans. That is to say, I shall use almost the same indicators to synthesize the differences in patterns of integration between Poles and Romanians – the two most numerous nationalities among the new European citizens resident in EU15 – using MCA.

The analysis is based on data from the Moveact survey carried out between November 2011 and February 2012 (Recchi et al. 2012). This survey was to a large extent a replica of the EIMSS, but it was conducted on a smaller scale in terms of the nationalities and countries involved, as well as the size of the sample, which consisted of 2,000 Britons, Germans, Poles and Romanians resident in Greece, France, Italy and Spain (see the Methodological Appendix). I shall focus in particular on the data relative to European movers originating from two countries of the 'new' Europe – Poland and Romania – my purpose being to examine their specific patterns of integration with respect to the mobile citizens of the countries of the 'old' Europe (as surveyed in 2004 and illustrated in the analysis above, and as emerged from the 2011–2012 survey, though only in regard to Britons and Germans).

Figure 4.4 shows the graphic result of the joint MCA of the structural, cultural and identitarian dimensions considered in Figure 4.3. Before I comment on its contents, however, I should point out some differences from the previous analyses in regard to the variables used. Given the smaller size of the sample, I conflated the modalities of the variables relative to education level, language knowledge and reasons for migration. Rather than a specific question on the use of television, the Moveact survey included a question on the nationality of the media which the interviewees chose when they wanted to obtain important news (whether they used information media of the CoO, the CoR or both). Given the emphasis on the option between CoO or CoR in the relationship with mass media, this is evidently a proxy variable. Finally, there are differences as regards the coding of social class. In the Moveact survey, the questions on occupation – from which the class position is inferred – were only put to respondents in employment. Retirees, students and other inactive interviewees were therefore included in a residual category, which thus comprised individuals of diverse socioeconomic status.

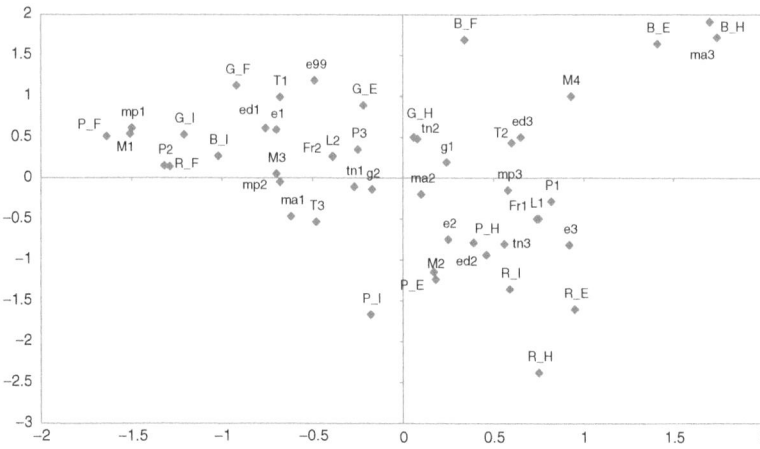

Figure 4.4 Structural, sociocultural and identitarian characteristics of EU movers in France, Italy, Spain and Greece (2012): multiple correspondence analysis

Source: Moveact, N = 2,020.

Notes:

Variables	Labels	Codes
Demographic variables		
Migration period	Mp	1 = 1974–1983, 2 = 1984–1993, 3 = 1994–2003
Age at migration	Ma	1 = 18–29, 2 = 30–49, 3 = 50 or more
Education	Ed	1 = tertiary, 2 = upper-secondary, 3 = lower-secondary, primary or no qualification
Social class	E	1 = EGP I–II, 2 = EGP III–IV 3 = EGP V–VI–VII, 99 = not classified
Sociocultural variables		
CoR language knowledge at interview	L	1 = low-medium, 2 = high
Friends from CoR	Fr	1 = none-few, 2 = many
Nationality of partner	P	1 = CoO, 2 = CoR, 3 = third country or no partner
Identitarian variables		
Migration motives	M	1 = study/other, 2 = work, 3 = family/love, 4 = quality of life
Mass media preference to access important news	T	1 = indifferent, 2 = CoO media, 3 = CoR media
National identification	tn	1 = equally close to CoO and CoR, 2 = closer to CoR, 3 = closer to CoO
Context variables		
CoO–CoR combinations		First letter = CoO, second letter = CoR; F = France, I = Italy, E = Spain, H = Greece, G = Germany, B = Great Britain, P = Poland, R = Romania

Despite these limitations, the results of the analysis are very similar to those of 2004. The horizontal axis, at first sight, reflects temporal differences. Largely located to the left are those interviewees who had migrated in more distant decades and at a young age; vice versa to the right. Associated with these differences, however, are aspects of greater significance for the organization of social relations: 'knowledge of the CoR's language' (high to the left, low to the right); 'partner's nationality' (of the CoR to the left, of the CoO to the right); 'presence of CoR citizens in one's friendship network' (prevalent to the left, limited or non-existent to the right). As in the preceding analyses, therefore, the horizontal axis incorporates differences in the degree of *intercultural competence* in the host society – high on the left-hand side and low on the right-hand side of the graph. Interpretation of the vertical axis is less straightforward. Several variables define it, but none of them does so decisively. The two modalities most clearly located at the two extremes of the axis are 'migration for quality of life' (M4, high) and 'migration for work' (M2, low). The modalities of the class position also range from high ('upper class', e1) to low ('middle class', e2, and 'working class', e3), but not in a manner precisely orthogonal to the horizontal axis, and with the residual class of 'not in employment' (e99, in which retirees predominate) occupying a position even higher than that of the upper class. In fact, we know that the majority of the interviewees in this category were relatively well-off German and British pensioners, so that the finding supports – as in the previous analysis of 2004 – an interpretation of the axis as expressing a latent factor tied to *socioeconomic status*. This is also borne out by the distribution of the modalities of the variable 'education level', which reflects the distribution of class differences. However, it registers the anomaly of a higher value for interviewees with low school credentials, perhaps because it is affected by the generational component (German and British movers are much older than Romanian and Polish ones; consequently, a larger proportion of them have elementary or lower-secondary educations). Finally, as found in 2004, gender differences are very small and lie close to the centre of the graph. This means that markedly different integration patterns are not associated with the two genders – at least not on the basis of the factors analysed.

Given this interpretation of the axes defining the relationship between the modalities of the variables considered, what is of most interest is the position of the different nationalities – according to the CoO/CoR combination – in the Cartesian space. Once again, the similarities with the 2004 results are striking.[10] It should be recalled that the categories most distant from the centre are those that diverge most from an average profile. Lying in the upper-right quadrant are the Britons settled in Greece and Spain and, somewhat closer to the centre, their co-nationals living in France. Their distinctive features are high status and low sociocultural integration in the countries of residence. In 2004, the Britons in Spain had a status relatively closer to the average, but they were also conspicuous for their few contacts with the host society. The Britons in France are instead in the same position they occupied in the survey of eight years before. Likewise, the Germans in France and Italy occupy a portion of the graph similar to that recorded in 2004 in terms of status, but with a higher level of intercultural competence than in the previous survey.

The position of the new mobile European citizens – Poles and Romanians – harbours some surprises. Three clusters of combinations of CoO and CoR are apparent. The first and most clearly characterized consists of Romanians resident in Greece, Spain and Italy. Their shared features are low status and a low intercultural competence (but, nevertheless, higher than that of the Britons in Spain and Greece). Besides their condition as migrant workers, which not infrequently likens them to immigrants from less-developed countries when gaining entry to the labour market, in terms of sociocultural integration Romanians are also penalized by their more recent arrival in the host societies. The Poles who live in Greece, Spain and Italy are not distant from them, but they, nevertheless, have greater intercultural competence and a higher status (although in Italy Poles have the same level of status as Romanians). Finally, the situation of Poles and Romanians in France is very different. In this case, their status is close to the average of the whole sample, but they score decidedly higher on the axis of intercultural competence. This result stems from an almost century-long history of migration from these two countries to France, rather than to the other countries of Southern Europe and, simultaneously, from the relatively modest inflow of Poles and Romanians in France after the enlargements.

5. Some concluding remarks

European movers form a composite population which, moreover, is not always perceived, nor perceives itself, as part of the universe of migrants. Studies on this population have been hampered by the heterogeneity of its social features – status, age, motives for migration and, obviously, nationality. As a consequence, until a few years ago, such studies were relatively rare in the huge body of research on migration. They were highly fragmented in that they concentrated on specific categories of European citizens resident in foreign countries: from retirees to Erasmus students, from the urban 'creative class' to 'neo-ruralists', from 'international commuters' to the new *Gastarbeiter*. Each of these facets is only one part of the kaleidoscope, and it is objectively difficult to synthesize such diversity into a single schema. Yet one can try to plot the coordinates within which such differences are located. This was the overall aim of two surveys (taken from the Pioneur and the Moveact research projects) conducted in 2004 and 2011–2012 on European movers resident in Italy, France, Spain, Greece, Germany and Great Britain. Drawing on data from those surveys, in this chapter I have sought to outline some fundamental features which characterize the social integration experiences of European movers.

MCA was applied symmetrically to both samples and yielded a parsimonious reconstruction of the principal cleavages cutting across the population of mobile Europeans. In brief, the analysis has shown that the integration of EU movers in other EU member states hinges to a large extent on two macro-factors: socioeconomic status and intercultural competence. The case of Britons in Spain, Greece and France is typical of a 'gilded cage' kind of integration in which enjoyment of a privileged socioeconomic condition is combined with a marked distance from the host society. By contrast, the Western Europeans who move to Britain, whatever their nationality, are strongly acculturated, as are the Britons and Germans who live in Italy. For these combinations of CoO and CoR, the data for 2004 and 2011–2012 are extremely similar. Instead, the situation of Germans in Spain has changed, as in the most recent survey they record a level of intercultural competence higher than in the past. Finally, the situation of the 'new' Europeans is not uniform. Romanians in Southern Europe have a lower status and a below-average level of intercultural competence compared to the rest of the EU movers inquired. They thus constitute a typical case of 'segregated' immigration, similar to the Italians resident in Germany in the 2004 analysis (the majority of whom had migrated in the guestworker era). The situation of Poles is less extreme, though qualitatively similar. An exception is the integration of Romanians and Poles in France, for whom many indicators signal a robust acculturation into the receiving society.

A caveat is in order before concluding. It would be wrong to believe that a sociological configuration persists entirely unchanged over time. The analysis of the different migration periods has shown, for instance, that the levels of status and integration of the Spanish who migrated to Germany in the 1990s are considerably different from those of their predecessors of the 1970s. One may expect the profiles of EU movers by CoO and CoR to change with further migratory waves and shifts in social and economic scenarios, as well as with the simple passage of time, which usually works in favour of greater integration. Added to these factors are technological transformations – in particular the advent of low-cost airlines which link most peripheral areas of the continent and intensify flows to the largest urban areas. This complex fresco may be marked by emerging inequalities as long as EU citizenship is an instrument of social closure (Paul 2013; Faist 2014) and free movement a possible accelerator of change at different levels – individual, national and transnational.

5
A Sterile Citizenship? Intra-European Mobility and Political Participation

1. More Europe, fewer Europeans: political participation and the EU's legitimacy

The democratic deficit of the EU has been well known and much discussed for decades (Lindberg and Scheingold 1970; Scharpf 1999; Siedentop 2001; Moravcsik 2002; Schmitter 2003; Déloye 2005; Føllesdal and Hix 2006). But time does not seem to have remedied it. European integration has been carried forward by elites (Haller 2008), with the distant and overall passive support of ordinary citizens, notwithstanding the increasing Europeanization of crucial political issues. The expectation that the 'permissive consensus' expressed by a silent public would progressively change into explicit consensus by virtue of the advantages deriving from 'an ever closer Union' – the so-called 'output legitimacy' (Scharpf 1999; see also Schmidt 2013) – has proved to be misplaced. The indifference of the majority of citizens towards the EU has not changed into active support as EU policies have penetrated more deeply into the regulation of almost every aspect of social life. Quite the opposite; in fact, Euroscepticism has gained ground in public opinion, especially among the less educated, in conjunction with the post-2009 euro crisis and recession (Hakhverdian et al. 2013). This hostility towards the EU started to become apparent in the referendums of 2005 which halted ratification of the European constitution in countries traditionally considered pro-Europe, like France and the Netherlands, and of the Lisbon Treaty by the 2008 referendum in Ireland. The majority of those countries' citizens rejected the integration project – at least in the form that it was taking at the time – and demanded a return to the full sovereignty of nation states. 'Permissive consensus' began to turn into a 'constraining dissensus' (Hooghe and Marks 2009). The widespread, spectacular rise of neo-nationalist and anti-EU parties thereafter was only the next logical step of this trend.

A significant indicator of disaffection for European integration is the progressive decline in turnouts for elections to the European Parliament. The turning point came in 1999. In that year, the percentage of non-voters (50.5 per cent compared with 43.3 per cent in the previous elections) slightly exceeded that of voters (49.5 per cent). In 2004 (45.5 per cent), 2009 (43 per cent) and 2014 (42.5 per cent), turnouts diminished further. In 2014, the lowest voter participation rate was recorded in Central-Eastern Europe, particularly in Slovakia (13 per cent), the Czech Republic (18.2 per cent), and Poland (23.8 per cent).[1] This slump in electoral participation unequivocally highlights the critical distance between citizens and European institutions.

Downturn in voter participation mirrors declining trust in the EU. This, according to Eurobarometer data, fell drastically between the spring of 2007, when it reached its all-time peak (57 per cent), and the spring of 2013 (26 per cent).[2] Even more striking is another Eurobarometer finding: a sharp decline in Europeans with a positive image of the EU (from 52 per cent in 2007 to 30 per cent in 2013). A radically negative judgement was passed on the EU by 15 per cent of the interviewees in 2007 and by 28 per cent in 2012, when the proportion of respondents expressing a neutral opinion (39 per cent compared with 31 per cent in 2007) by far exceeded the proportion of those expressing a positive one.

There is no doubt that the post-2008 euro crisis must be factored in. Whilst in past decades European integration developed in a context of overall economic growth, the recession of the late 2000s has exacerbated anti-Europeanism and rekindled nationalist sentiments. Because the crisis was symbolically linked with the single currency, it heightened perception of the limits and contradictions of the integration process. Perhaps for the first time, European integration faces not a temporary impasse but may indeed go into reverse, as testified by the debate in many countries on whether to leave the euro system, the Schengen area or indeed the EU in its entirety.

However, the economic crisis has only exposed the structural weakness of EU legitimacy, for which sociologists and political scientists have proposed two general interpretations.[3] The first is what I would call the 'persistent nationalism' reading: national identities are so deeply embedded that they maintain a solid grip on political socialization processes, thus hampering the development of concern about, and commitment to, supranational causes. Indeed, as has often been pointed out, European electoral campaigns do not cease to be structured and contested around domestic political issues (Perrineau 2005; Schmidt 2006). In the view of the political class and public opinion, they are 'second-order elections' whose main purpose is to judge national governments (Reif and Schmitt 1980; Van der Eijk and Franklin 1996; Marsh 1998; Schmitt 2005). The euro crisis came to reinforce the centrality of national identities, especially when national interests were pitted against each other in popular discourses – Southern European publics denouncing stifling Northern austerity, and their Northern European counterparts claiming to be dragged down by Southern profligacy.

The second, broad reading of the weakness of EU legitimacy imputes it to 'citizenship light' – a notion I borrow from Joppke (2010b) and that I use as an umbrella term for a number of different critical remarks on the EU's incapacity to make its citizenship politically consequential. The EU 'input legitimacy' deficit hinges on the feebleness of supranational political practices among European citizens. According to many, citizens' absence from EU-level politics also stems from the insufficient development of a 'European public sphere' – that is, a participated arena where common issues are debated to channel and structure common governance (Koopmans and Erbe 2004; Eriksen 2005; Koopmans 2007). The transnationalization of the decision-making process has not been accompanied by a parallel transnationalization of political participation writ large. The EU's legitimacy deficit is therefore primarily a reflex of poor political participation – also contingent on the lack of appropriate fora and institutional mechanisms – in its various forms.[4]

The two interpretations outlined above – 'persistent nationalism' and 'citizenship light' – are not mutually exclusive, but rather touch upon two distinct political dimensions of citizenship: the sense of belonging to a community (the *identity* dimension) and involvement in collective decision-making (the *participation* dimension). How do they fit into EU movers' attitudes and practices? Given the centrality of European citizenship in their life choices, are EU movers unaffected by the identity and participation issues that trouble the continent? These questions substantially entail the following *a fortiori* inference: if those who 'live' a united Europe do not feel European and are not politically active at the EU level, who else can? In perspective, these questions may be particularly revealing of possible developments in European integration 'from below' linked to an increase of mobility in Europe. In this and the following chapter I shall tackle these issues, starting from the second one – participation.

2. Are EU movers active European citizens?

Studying the political participation of mobile Europeans makes it possible to address the topic of European citizenship differently from traditional analyses. Should we expect the relationship of EU movers to politics to resemble that of the rest of the population? Or does their cross-border experience make them more aware of their status as European citizens, and of the relevance of the supranational scope of the political process? Do EU movers show evidence that their citizenship is being reformulated in post-national terms?

In order to answer the above questions, in this chapter I shall use data from four surveys: the 2004 Eurobarometer (EB) and the 2010 European Social Survey (ESS) (relative to Germany, the UK, Italy, France, Spain, Poland and Romania) as regards the settled population, and the EIMSS and the Moveact survey as regards EU movers (see Methodological Appendix). From this last survey I shall draw on data relative to mobile Europeans originating from two countries of the 'new' Europe – Poland and Romania – and compare them with the data relative to the mobile citizens of the countries of the 'old' Europe.

More precisely, the aim of the analysis is (a) to show whether and how the political participation of EU movers differs from that of the general population, and (b) whether the differences found are due to the sociodemographic composition and socioeconomic characteristics of movers. In regard to the latter, a huge body of research reports that political participation is essentially a function of education level and socioeconomic status – what some authors call the 'social centrality thesis' (Milbrath and Goel 1977, 86 ff.). Are these factors also decisive in defining the conditions of participation among mobile Europeans, or do their effects diminish when migrating? I shall then seek to determine the influence of national political cultures. Do mobile Europeans have political attitudes and behaviours similar to those of their settled co-nationals, or do they exhibit a specific pattern of participation alien to the imprinting of nationality? Does exercise of the right to free movement foster transnational political behaviours?

The necessary, though not sufficient, condition for political participation is interest in political affairs. In the sample of mobile Europeans interviewed in 2004, those who declared themselves interested in politics outnumbered their compatriots in the home country. With minimal differences of nationality and country of residence, 56 per cent said that they were 'interested' in political events in the country of origin, and 24.3 per cent 'very interested' (compared with an 11.7 per cent average in the respective countries). In 2011, similar results were recorded among the Western European movers surveyed by Moveact: 50.5 per cent of the British respondents and 70.9 per cent of the German respondents declared that they were 'interested' in politics. The mobile Europeans from Eastern Europe interviewed in 2011 also expressed an interest in politics greater than that of their co-nationals resident in the country of origin. In particular, 56.4 per cent of mobile Poles were interested in politics compared with 39 per cent of their compatriots resident in Poland. Among Romanians, the two percentages were almost the same (42.8 per cent and 43.1 per cent).[5] Moreover, the mobile Poles declared that they 'often' discussed political events with family members (23.8 per cent) and friends (27.3 per cent), whilst the mobile Romanians were very close to their co-nationals at home, expressing a much lower propensity to talk about politics with family and friends (16.8 per cent and 14.5 per cent, respectively).[6]

However, if we consider a series of indicators of political involvement (Table 5.1), we find that only a minority of EU movers convert abstract political interest into concrete action – that is, change from being spectators to active participants in political life. This means that, although mobility involves citizens on average slightly more interested in politics than the general population, it fosters – at least initially – a process of withdrawal from active political engagement. This can be explained by a joint process of detachment from political issues in the home country and a progressive involvement in those of the residence country. The clearest signal of this shift of focus is provided by analysis of participation in elections in the home country. In 2004, the participation rate among mobile Europeans from the 'old' Europe was half that of voters in their home countries; and in 2011, it was only one-third among EU movers from the 'new' Europe. To a certain extent, this discrepancy may be due to legal and logistic factors, such as the possibility to vote by post or at consulates; but these are probably not enough to explain such low rates.

Before beginning analysis of participation in elections, it is worthwhile examining more ordinary political activities undertaken in everyday life. One such activity consists in searching for direct contact with political representatives. Mobile Europeans engage in this form of participation (towards politicians in both the CoO and the CoR) to a greater extent than their settled co-nationals. The difference with respect to the latter is particularly marked among EU movers from Central-Eastern Europe, who perhaps more insistently seek protection in the host society's political system so that they can cope with the difficulties of a migratory experience which often makes them more economically vulnerable than Western European movers.

Table 5.1 The political participation of EU movers and stayers: components of the politicization index (%)

	EU15 movers (EIMSS) 2004	Polish and Romanian movers (Moveact) 2011	Population (Italy, Spain, France, Great Britain, Germany) 2004	Population (Poland and Romania) 2010
1. Interest in politics: very much*	24.2	18.5	11.7	7.1
2. Contacted politician	19.0	20.1	14.7	9.3
3. Signed petition, sent political email**	19.2	5.7	30.0	5.1
4. Took part in lawful political demonstration	15.3	6.6	11.8	2.8
5. Trade union membership	8.1	5.9	3.2	15.0#/33.0##
6. Political party membership	3.0	1.5	2.1	3.8
7. Voted in last general elections	40.1	21.5	80.8	66.8
N	4,855	994	9,076	3,897

Sources: For Italian, Spanish, French, British and German citizens: EIMSS and ESS 2004; for Polish and Romanian citizens: Moveact and ESS 2010 (Poland) and ESS 2008 (Romania).
Notes: *For EU movers: 'Interest in politics in country of origin'. **EIMSS: 'signing a petition'; Moveact: 'signing or sending an email with political content'. #From CBOs survey of 2010, ICTWSS database (http://www.uva-aias.net/208, consulted 18 August 2012). ##Estimate in http://www.worker-participation.eu/National-Industrial-Relations/Countries/Romania (consulted 18 August 2012).

One method very frequently used to make one's voice heard on political issues is to sign a petition. Since the advent of the Internet, this form of participation has assumed ever greater importance, with the development of virtual communities which make systematic use of it as device for democratic involvement, not infrequently on issues of a transnational nature – from the moratorium on whale hunting to laws on censorship in third countries. Given the diffusion of the Internet, in the 2011 survey the 'petition' item was updated to 'signed or sent an email with political content'. However, mobile Europeans are not in the forefront in this regard, either in the traditional practice of signing

A Sterile Citizenship? 111

petitions (less common among Western European movers than among the general population in 2004) or in its virtual mode (which in the year prior to the interview had been used by only 5 per cent of mobile Poles and Romanians, the same proportion as among their co-nationals at home).

Forms of political participation are also distinguished by their differing economic, psychological and social costs. Sending an email can take only a few seconds in spontaneous reaction to a visual prompt or a slogan. Joining a street protest is more demanding. Yet participation in authorized political demonstrations involved a percentage of mobile Europeans larger than that of the respective national populations, both in 2004 (15.3 per cent) and in 2011 (6.6 per cent). In this case too, however, Eastern European movers were more reluctant to mobilize compared with the British (15.3 per cent) and German (12.7 per cent) movers interviewed in 2011. For that matter, participating in demonstrations, even if authorized, is extremely rare in the home countries, given that only 3 per cent of Polish and Romanian citizens do so. It is likely that mobility frees East European movers from the inhibition and apathy of the home countries, considering that more than three-quarters of those who joined street protests declared that they did so in the host country.

Even more costly in terms of time – and often also socially costly because of the visibility that it gives to one's political preferences – is enrolment with a trade union or a political party. In the countries of origin, both kinds of membership are highly unusual: they concerned less than 4 per cent of the population in both 2004 and 2011. Once again, Western European movers (including the British and German ones interviewed in 2011) are more active than their co-nationals. But this is not the case with Poles and Romanians. There is no doubt that the characteristics of their inclusion in the labour force in countries of destination – mainly through flexible and atypical jobs – restricts their unionization, which is instead very widespread in Poland and Romania (although the figures on 'trade union density' are not entirely reliable, especially for Romania; see the note to Table 5.1). Before joining a political party – which is decidedly less frequent than in the home country – migrants need to gain confidence and find their bearings in the political culture of the host country. As the representative of a Romanian association interviewed within the Moveact project put it:

> In terms of politics in Romania, I feel myself closer to the right. In Italy I don't feel close to the right at all [. . .]. Strange things happen: for

example, Romanians who vote on the left but in Italy support Fini [a right-wing political leader]. Or the opposite: voters on the right in Romania feel themselves closer to the leftist political parties in Italy. (Romanian resident in Italy, man, 43 years old). (Recchi et al. 2012, 25)

3. Determinants of the politicization of EU movers

The data examined thus far show that, compared with the populations of the seven countries considered in the surveys of 2004 and 2011, mobile Europeans have an above-average interest in politics. Nevertheless, this interest does not translate into more active involvement on all fronts. The West European movers interviewed in 2004 were more reluctant than their co-nationals to sign petitions, while the East European movers interviewed in 2011 were loath to join trade unions and political parties. But above all, both groups were even more averse to going to the polls. Voting – the core of active citizenship – fits badly with the experience of mobility.

For a concise analysis of the relationship with politics of mobile Europeans, Muxel (2009) has constructed an additive politicization index based on the seven variables of political interest and conventional participation illustrated in Table 5.1.[7] Overall, the distribution of the politicization index is very unbalanced. On a 0–7 scale, only 41.2 per cent of the 2004 sample and 18.4 per cent of Poles and Romanians in 2011 record a score of more than one point. Among Western Europeans, Spanish and German movers record the highest values, with British movers at the other extreme. Romanians' and Poles' average scores are very low: 0.83 and 0.87, respectively. But to what extent do these results reflect characteristics of the political cultures of origin, and to what extent the sociological composition of the sample?

To answer this question, examination of the regression models set out in Table 5.2 is necessary. Such analysis makes distinguishing the influence exerted by individual and contextual variables on the level of politicization of mobile Europeans possible. The social centrality hypothesis, according to which politics is of more interest to people with greater socioeconomic resources, is borne out. In both samples, the politicization of EU movers with university education is clearly greater. In the 2011 sample, however, social class makes no difference. The variables 'age' and 'length of residence in the host country' also lose statistical significance; in the first survey, it was the more elderly and more recent migrants who recorded higher levels of politicization. Apparently, the post-enlargement migratory waves have mitigated these

Table 5.2 Determinants of political involvement of EU movers in 2004 (EIMSS) and 2011 (Moveact): OLS regressions of the politicization index

	EIMSS	Moveact
Age	0.184**	0.159
Age (squared)	−0.147	−0.216
Gender (=woman)	0.004	−0.019
Education (ref: Primary–secondary)		
Tertiary	0.155**	0.148**
Social class (ref: EGP VI–VII)[#]		
EGP I–II	0.104**	0.039
EGP III	0.028	
EGP IV	0.026	0.004
EGP V	0.003	
Years in country of residence	−0.065*	0.019
Country of origin (ref: Germany)		
Spain	0.020	
France	−0.064**	
Great Britain	−0.125**	−0.046
Italy	−0.093**	
Poland		−0.107**
Romania		−0.108**
Country of residence (ref: Italy)		
Spain	−0.123**	0.026
France	−0.030	0.001
Great Britain	−0.088**	
Germany	−0.144**	
Greece		0.097**
Ideological position (ref: Centre)		
More left-wing	0.182**	0.155**
More right-wing	0.020	0.046
DK, no answer	−0.085**	−0.007
Attachment to the EU (scale 1–4)	0.122**	0.005

Sources: EIMSS, $N = 4,756$; df = 21; $R^2 = 0.19$; $F = 52,571$. Moveact, $N = 1,862$, df = 17; $R^2 = 0.07$; $F = 8,694$.

Notes: $*p < 0.05$, $**p < 0.01$. [#]In Moveact a simplified version of the Erikson-Goldthorpe-Portocarero (EGP) social class schema was used: bourgeoisie, middle class and working class (reference). Coefficients are standardized.

effects. The same dynamic may also explain an unexpected finding: the disappearance of the association between attachment to the EU and political involvement. The most politicized movers in 2011 were not necessarily those who felt themselves most European. This may be indicative of the loss of salience of European citizenship – or better, its symbolic dimension – as a driver of political participation. It may also reflect a rising mobilization, even among mobile Europeans, around the anti-EU discourse. Confirmed instead are the marked differences of nationality which – net of composition effects (that is, of the individual characteristics considered thus far) – relate to the persisting influence of political socialization models. Politicization is constantly and significantly higher among German movers, while that of English movers, who ranked lowest in 2004, has been superseded by the even lower politicization of Poles and Romanians. Differences due to the country of residence have instead diminished. Overall, migrants in Greece are slightly more inclined to participate than are those resident in Italy, the country for which the highest politicization was recorded in 2004. This perhaps reflects a historical juncture at which Greece found itself in the eye of the hurricane of the financial crisis. Finally, the analysis confirms the more marked political involvement of the mobile Europeans who place themselves on the centre-left of the political spectrum – a finding which replicates those of several classic studies on political participation, especially when non-conventional forms of participation are also considered (Klingemann 1979, 286; Mayer and Perrineau 1992, 139; Boy and Mayer 1997, 364).

4. EU movers at the polls

Construction of a European public sphere requires the full recognition and exercise of EU citizenship as a political entitlement, and therefore as a premise for participation. The first step in this direction cannot but consist in exercise of the right to vote for the European Parliament. Do mobile European citizens participate in these elections more or less than the rest of the population? And how do they behave when elections are held in their countries of origin?

As said, it is electoral participation which evidences the widest differences in political behaviours between EU movers and the rest of the population. According to the 2004 EIMSS data, the majority of mobile Western Europeans (60 per cent) did not vote in the last parliamentary elections of the countries of which they were citizens, whilst abstentionism in those countries (Italy, Spain, France, the UK and Germany) was less than 30 per cent. By contrast, participation by EU movers in the 2004 European Parliament elections was higher than that of stayers in their home countries (56 per cent against 49 per cent). This indicates that movers regard European elections as more important than national ones, despite the difficulties of registration that may inhibit their voting as resident foreigners. The 2011 Moveact data confirm the results on German and British mobile citizens, but above all they help reconstruct voting patterns by mobile citizens from two Central-Eastern European countries, Poland and Romania. These latter are less inclined than their compatriots in the home country to vote for the Brussels Parliament. Nevertheless, also in their case, the rate of participation in European elections is higher than that for general elections in the CoO.

Voting behaviour is a litmus test of individuals' political priorities. For most EU movers, overall, the European arena matters more than that of the home country. They thus seem to be interpreters of a post-nationalization of political citizenship. But, if we compare the results of 2004 and 2011, it is a 'downwards' post-nationalization: the outcome more of a decline of interest in national politics than of greater enthusiasm for the European dimension.

A number of differences by nationality and CoR in this overall picture warrant comment. Turnouts for national general elections (Figure 5.1) among mobile Western Europeans of 2004 were highest among Spanish (51 per cent) and German (47 per cent) residents abroad. National traditions matter for these voters, given that above-average rates of electoral participation are recorded in Germany and Spain (81.4 per cent and 68.7 per cent, respectively). At the opposite extreme stand British expatriates, among whom only 25 per cent voted (compared with 59.4 per cent of the electorate in the UK). In 2011, turnouts for national parliamentary elections by German and British residents abroad were substantially lower than in 2004. The decrease was proportionally greater than that recorded in the general population. This divergence may be partly due to the different composition of the sample, which comprised only mobile citizens resident in the countries of Southern Europe, where there is a smaller presence of professionals and a larger one of retirees and inactive persons who may have 'pulled the plug' on politics at home.

On the other hand, Romanian and Polish mobile citizens, whose migration is more recent, participate even less in the general elections of the CoO: only 19.5 per cent and 23.6 per cent of them went to the polls in the last national parliamentary elections, respectively.[8] Their abstention matches the electoral behaviour of their fellow countrymen in the home country. The electoral participation rates in Romania (39.2 per cent in the elections of 2008) and Poland (49.8 per cent in the elections of 2011) are lower than those recorded in the UK (65.1 per cent in 2010) and Germany (70.8 per cent in 2009).

116 *Mobile Europe*

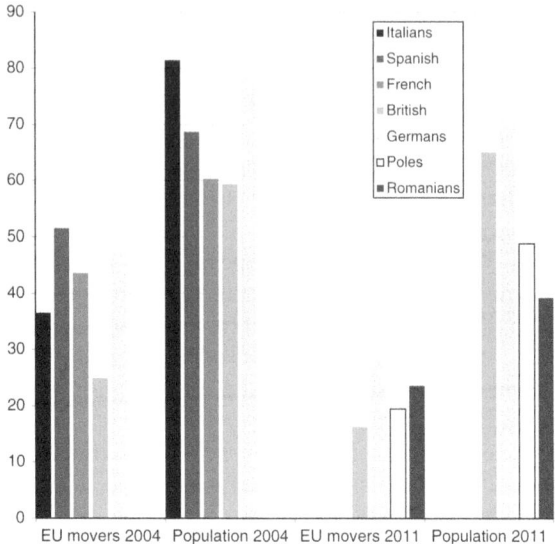

Figure 5.1 EU movers at the polls for national general elections: turnout rates (%)
Source: EIMSS, N = 4,855; Moveact, N = 1,997. Figures on national elections are taken from http://www.idea.int (consulted 16 August 2012). They refer to 2000 in Spain, 2001 in Italy, 2002 and 2009 in Germany, 2001 and 2010 in Great Britain, 2008 in Romania and 2011 in Poland.

Some more detailed comment is also required on participation in elections for the European Parliament. It should be borne in mind that, according to the provisions of the Maastricht Treaty, all EU citizens have passive and active voting rights in local and European elections. Nevertheless, how those rights can be exercised is regulated differently by each member state. Some states allow their citizens to vote independently of residence in European elections by post or at consulates on candidate lists presented in national constituencies (Strudel 2003). This scant harmonization has conditioned practices in exercising the right to vote. In 2009, only 11.6 per cent of voting-age European citizens resident in another country of the EU were enrolled on the electoral registers of their countries of residence (European Commission 2010, 6): a modest result, which halts the upward trend recorded from 1994 (6 per cent), through 1999 (9 per cent), to 2004 (12–15 per cent) (Strudel 2005, 2009) – very probably because of recent arrivals from the new member states. Differently from administrative elections, however, EU mobile citizens can choose to vote for the

A Sterile Citizenship? 117

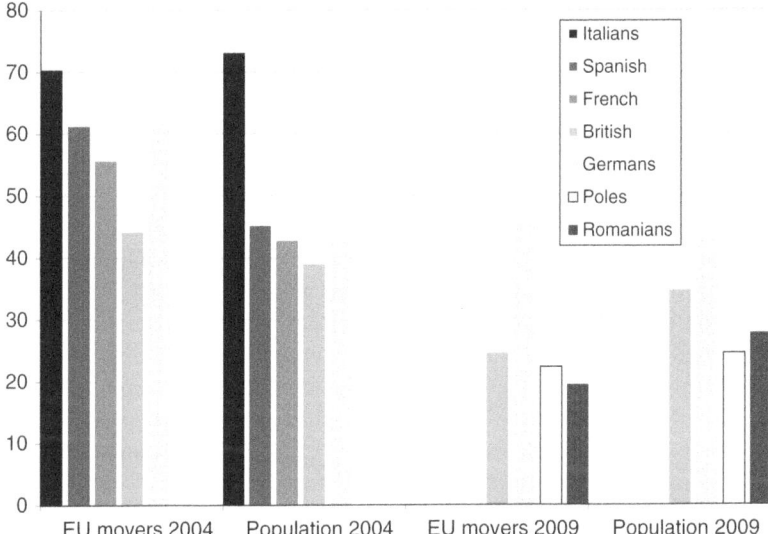

Figure 5.2 EU movers at the polls for the European Parliament: turnout rates (%)
Sources: EIMSS, N = 4,713; Moveact, N = 1,953. Turnouts for the European Parliament are taken from http://www.europarl.europa.eu/aboutparliament/en/000cdcd9d4/Turnout-%281979-2009%29.html (consulted 16 August 2012).

European elections in their countries of origin, which enables them to express their preference for candidates of the same nationality.[9]

In 2004, it was Italians and Germans abroad who were most conscientious in turning out to vote for the European Parliament: 70.4 per cent and 61.9 per cent, respectively (Figure 5.2).[10] German movers, indeed, had a rate of participation in European elections substantially higher than that of German stayers (+19 percentage points), while participation by mobile Italians was only slightly lower than that of the general population in Italy. Also Spanish and French movers voted to a proportionally greater extent than their co-nationals (+16 and +13 percentage points), while British expatriates highlighted the scant propensity of UK citizens to go to the polls (only 38.9 per cent declared that they had voted in the European elections: −5 points with respect to the UK resident population). The 2011 survey recorded even lower participation by the British respondents (24.5 per cent) and confirmed, albeit to a less striking extent, the greater electoral assiduousness of Germans (45.4 per cent). Once again evident was the abstentionism of Polish and Romanian mobile citizens: only 21.3 per cent and 19.4 per cent voted. Overall, even if the only partial comparability of the data (due to differences of CoO and CoR) is taken into account, the propensity of mobile citizens to participate in European elections to a greater extent than the general population recorded in 2004 seems to have almost entirely vanished by the time the next elections were held. Only the Germans abroad were still more active than their compatriots at home – though by only two percentage points – when electing their European representatives.

Table 5.3 enables us to focus on what most influenced participation by EU movers in the European Parliament elections of 2004 and 2011. To some extent, voters were induced to participate in the European Parliament elections by the same factors which engender more robust politicization. Principal among them is ideological position on the political spectrum: people unable or unwilling to place themselves on the right–left axis tend – quite logically – to be abstentionist. In the 2004 sample, participation rates in the European elections were higher among leftist EU movers. In 2011, however, this difference disappeared, probably because of the above-noted opacity of the right–left distinction among new EU citizens from former Communist countries. Likewise, the influence of social class on electoral participation waned, offset by the already significant effect of higher education. In this case, it is likely that the finding reflects the downward occupational trajectory of the mobile citizens of new member states, whose migration to the 'old' Europe has forced them to accept jobs of lower status, so that their current class position no longer reflects their human and cultural capital. Other factors prompting the decision to turn out for the European Parliament elections instead persist: primarily, longer residence in the country of immigration and a greater sense of belonging to Europe. But specific national features, notwithstanding differences in the composition of the two samples, also show marked continuity. On the one hand, German citizens are still the most assiduous voters, *ceteris paribus*, while the British continue to stay away from the polls in large numbers, regardless of their personal characteristics. Among the new EU citizens, Polish migrants are more reluctant to vote than Romanians, and likewise their co-nationals in Poland. On the other hand, the CoR is a variable which is anything but incidental insofar as it defines the structure of the political opportunities for non-national citizens – as several comparative studies on the topic have already shown (for example, Ireland 1994; Morales and Giugni 2011; on the electoral behaviour of Poles abroad, Fidrmuc and Doyle 2006). In our case, whatever their nationality, migrants in Italy were significantly more likely to vote in European elections, both

Table 5.3 Determinants of voting for the European Parliament among EU movers in 2004 and 2011: logit regressions

	EIMSS	Moveact
Age	0.039	0.074*
Age (squared)	0.000	−0.000
Gender (=woman)	0.131	0.196
Education (ref: Primary–secondary)		
Tertiary	0.135**	0.433**
Social class (ref: EGP VI–VII)[#]		
EGP I–II	0.363**	0.040
EGP III	0.168	
EGP IV	0.198	0.057
EGP V	0.009	
Years in country of residence	0.033**	0.031**
Country of origin (ref: Germany)		
Spain	0.129	
France	−0.309*	
Great Britain	−0.833**	−0.652**
Italy	0.331*	
Poland		−0.811**
Romania		−0.148
Country of residence (ref: Italy)		
Spain	−0.801**	−0.472**
France	−0.694**	−0.463**
Great Britain	−0.359*	
Germany	−1.060**	
Greece		−0.300
Ideological position (ref: Centre)		
More left-wing	0.461**	−0.040
More right-wing	0.090	−0.131
DK, no answer	−0.288*	−0.712**
Attachment to the EU (scale 1–4)	0.363**	0.395**

Sources: EIMSS: $N = 4{,}913$; df = 21; chi-square = 571,514; Nagelkerke $R^2 = 0.16$. Moveact: $N = 1{,}804$; df = 17; chi-square = 294,537; Nagelkerke $R^2 = 0.22$.

Notes: *$p < 0.05$, **$p < 0.01$. [#]In Moveact a simplified version of the Erikson-Goldthorpe-Portocarero (EGP) social class schema was used: bourgeoisie, middle class and working class (reference). Coefficients are odds ratios.

in 2004 and in 2011. It is not easy to explain this effect of the context of residence. The institutional conditions for electoral registration are not more straightforward in Italy than elsewhere. In fact, on the occasions of the elections of 6 and 7 June 2009, when European and municipal elections coincided, non-Italian EU citizens enrolled on electoral registers numbered 43,766 out of 1,241,348 official residents, equal to less than 4 per cent: a small percentage indeed, which had not increased to a significant extent since the previous elections – probably because of the preponderant weight of new EU citizens, particularly Romanian, of recent immigration. The incentive to electoral participation imparted by residence in Italy, therefore, can only be explained by cultural conditions of greater sensitization to elections, even if the vote is cast in the CoO, where candidates and parties are probably easier to understand.

5. Conclusions: a sterile citizenship?

As I have repeatedly stressed, the decision to move to another European country stems from a wide range of factors, from which derive, in turn, diverse patterns of integration. Mobile European citizens therefore form a decidedly heterogeneous population. What unites them is a choice (migration in Europe) and a legal status (European citizenship). But to what extent are these shared features sufficient to make their political behaviour uniform?

Not very much, all things considered. Differences in the composition of the population of EU movers affect the form and intensity of their relationship with politics – from simple interest to electoral participation. In one respect, they relate to politics according to the well-known pattern whereby individuals endowed with more economic and cultural resources participate to a greater extent in political affairs (the so-called 'social centrality model'). In another respect, they reflect persisting divergences in the political cultures of the countries of origin. Comparison between citizens of the 'new' and 'old' Europe highlights that the influence of the political socialization received in the CoO does not cease with geographical mobility. In particular, mobile citizens from the former communist countries considered here – Poland and Romania – reproduce in their destination countries the lack of interest in politics characteristic of their homelands. Their scant participation is probably due to profound disaffection with state institutions and a cynicism towards politics developed in the times of totalitarianism, when politicization was largely compulsory. Two decades of democracy seem not to have altered these underlying attitudes in the societies of origin (Neundorf 2010), not even in a section of the population – migrants – tendentially dynamic and open-minded. Indeed, the democratic experience has often disappointed the great expectations placed in it, thus producing a surplus of detachment (Matei 2002).

Moreover, different patterns of political socialization do not just give rise to different levels of politicization. Before they do so, they shape the cognitive schemas with which political phenomena are interpreted. For example, the opposing notions of 'right' and 'left' – which after all are still the dominant coordinates used to distinguish among the programmes of political parties in Europe – assume diverse meanings for individuals socialized into politics in different countries. The majority of mobile citizens from Central-Eastern Europe consider the right–left distinction ambiguous and in any case useless when deciding their political preferences. Integrating into different societies may make some sort of political re-socialization necessary. But this is particularly difficult and onerous for migrants with fewer cultural and material resources, and who already have little interest in political affairs.

To conclude, EU movers emit just one timid signal of Europeanized political involvement: slightly greater participation in elections for the European Parliament compared with those for national parliaments. In other words, mobile Europeans more frequently exercise their political rights as EU citizens than they do as citizens of their CoO (with the significant exception of Romanians). And, as we have seen, this is so the longer their experience of life away from the homeland is. But the signal is faint and, above all, it is weakening further. EU movers seem anything but immune to the contagion of abstentionism now sweeping the continent. Between 2004 and 2011, their participation in elections of every type considerably decreased. More importantly, this decline was most marked for European elections. Europe finds it difficult to mobilize even those individuals able to recast their life courses precisely by virtue of the process of European integration.

The low salience of European citizenship is further demonstrated by the scant knowledge among EU movers about the content of such citizenship. Among the Moveact interviewees, fewer than 30 per cent (29.6 per cent, and just 22.9 per cent among Poles) declared that they knew their rights as European citizens 'very well' or 'well': a percentage close to that recorded for the EU population as a whole (32 per cent: Eurobarometer 2010, 12). It is therefore not only the right to vote that is taken lightly by the majority of mobile citizens but also the entire package of rights that uphold free movement.

To conclude, the hypothesis of a pervasive 'citizenship light' syndrome outlined at the beginning of the chapter seems corroborated on the basis of the interpretation given by Europeans to their status as EU citizens. Exercise of the right to free movement within the EU does not create aware and active European citizens in and of itself. Mobility does not necessarily incubate fuller European citizenship. In this regard, EU movers are an exemplary case of the more general 'lightening of citizenship' apparent in contemporary democracies (Joppke 2010b). Although citizenship confers protections and rights without precedent in human history, those entitled to them seem little interested in becoming active and engaged citizens – not even when citizenship generates unprecedented rights like the international movement without state controls granted in the EU. Joppke's description of citizenship as 'light' seems somewhat euphemistic: rather, EU citizenship looks 'sterile' in its capacity to generate stronger democratic participation – at least through its conventional means.

Are we therefore to believe that free movement in Europe will result in the 'bowling alone' scenario pessimistically envisaged by Putnam (2000), who blamed the decline of civic participation among Americans on their high spatial mobility? In truth, this may be too grim a diagnosis even for the USA (see, among others, Paxton 1999; Wuthnow 2002; Fischer 2005). In the European case, militating against this diagnosis is the generally minor extent of mobility (see Conclusion). It is also gainsaid by the persisting identitarian strength (not without an ethnic dimension) of the national communities in Europe – which are immensely more significant and subjectively involving for movers than the state-based identities of the USA.

If anything, one must conclude on the basis of the data examined in this chapter that the right to free movement works as a device more for *exit* from the national societies in which individuals are born than for *voice* in the societies where they choose to live, and also in the nascent post-national European society. In the next chapter, I shall examine whether EU citizenship is accompanied by a new *loyalty* – that is, a supranational identification – able to breach the barriers of national belongings.

6
Intra-EU Mobility and European Identity: Towards a Sense of Shared Belonging

1. How can Europeans be 'made'?

Delving into the numerous predicaments of European integration almost inevitably lays bare the issue of collective identity.[1] Whether one considers the widespread resistance of the wealthier member states against creating common EU public debt, the timidity of the EU in dealing with language issues or the hesitation in transforming the Union into a full-fledged federal state, the crux of the problem is always the European population's weak sense of a shared belonging. Low identification with Europe means poor solidarity with other Europeans – who are only viewed as 'the others'. Poor solidarity translates into the low legitimacy of European institutions when they endeavour to impose redistributive policies or to pool member states' resources. An appeal to German taxpayers to pay off the Greeks' debts cannot leverage – as happened after reunification of the two Germanies – a strong bond between the two populations. There is no financial alchemy able to remedy this fundamental shortcoming.

What can make Europeans aware of their 'Europeanness'? What can bind them to a political–territorial community that extends beyond national frontiers? These questions are not only of academic importance. Forging, or at least strengthening, a shared collective identity among Europeans is an obvious concern of EU institutions, which have always been confronted with the supranational version of the D'Azeglio problem which followed Italian unification (Bellamy et al. 2006, 1) – once Italy was unified, Italians had to be 'made'. 'Making Europeans', indeed, but how?

When the nation states took up the challenge of nation-building, they typically used the instruments of compulsory conscription, mass education (in particular the teaching of history and geography), explicit propaganda (especially in times of crisis) and 'banal nationalism' expressed through widespread symbols and narratives (Billig 1995). Today, compulsory military service has been discontinued by almost all the EU member states, so that proposing it on a continental scale would not be feasible. As regards education, some attempts to reconstruct a history of Europe purged of nationalistic biases have been made by teams of historians from different countries. But these textbooks are scarcely used, and they have not received the necessary institutional support because of the sensitivities that still condition treatment of controversial personages and events in national cultural traditions (Immerfall et al. 2010, 345–7). The European Commission has promoted a wide range of media campaigns, especially on the occasion of key events such as introduction of the euro. Less episodically, it is this propagandistic purpose that lies behind policies such as the designation of the 'European Years'; for instance, 2013 was (with striking identitarian significance) the 'European Year of Citizens', which was associated with promotional activities and awareness-raising initiatives. Likewise, the declared purpose of the annual proclamation of a European capital of culture is to strengthen a sense of collective belonging (Sassatelli 2002; Tsaliki 2007).[2] Last but not least, there is 'banal Europeanism'. This entails a diversified array of tools. Some of them have a deliberate identitarian connotation: the European flag, the European anthem, Europe Day (on 9 May, anniversary of the Schuman Declaration). Others have been created for different purposes; for instance, the common currency and mobility support programmes (see Chapter 2). But have these policies had significant effects on building a European identity?

It is extremely difficult to measure the effectiveness of each of these drivers of European identity. Yet the task seems easier in the case of free movement. As we shall see in the second part of this chapter, the Pioneur and Moveact surveys make it possible to determine whether mobile citizens feel themselves more or less European compared with non-movers. It is true that cross-sectional survey data (that is, collected at one particular time) cannot be used to establish conclusively whether this possible difference is due directly to the experience of mobility or to other factors that preceded it. Only longitudinal information collected before and after migration would settle the question. But, to anticipate the discussion of findings, there are good reasons to believe that the experience of transnational mobility fosters supranational (European and cosmopolitan) identifications. Accordingly, in the next section I shall set out the theoretical presuppositions that suggest a causal relationship between cross-border spatial mobility and supranational sense of belonging. I will then present data analyses which compare the sense of belonging to Europe between movers and stayers. I shall finally extend the discussion to other practices which, together with mobility, define the features of 'social transnationalism', and I shall evaluate their effects on European identification.

2. Theoretical premises: two models of collective identity formation

Before dealing specifically with the European case, it is useful to briefly reconstruct the models of collective identity formation developed in social theory but not always made explicit by those who use them in empirical research. In very general terms, and drawing on different sociological traditions, there are two dominant explanations of how a widely shared political identity is acquired: one is 'culturalist'; the other is 'structuralist'. In this context, qualifying as 'culturalist' is an approach which ascribes the formation of a person's attitudes to the internalization of socially transmitted messages and cultural meanings, whereas the term 'structuralist' denotes an approach which 'emphasizes the causal force of the relations among elements in a system or of [their] emergent properties' (Schneider 2007, 4856). As regards collective identity formation, the key difference between the two models consists in conditioning factors: on the one hand, exposure to communicative content (discourses and symbols); on the other, involvement in spatially situated associative relationships (regardless of their specific content).[3]

The culturalist model links the development of collective identities to political socialization. This happens both in childhood, when it is talk by the parents that influences the person, and at a more advanced life stage, when teachers, friends and the media exercise a more marked influence. This analytical perspective springs mainly from sociological notions drawn from psychoanalysis and developmental psychology (Bettin Lattes 2011). In the 1950s and 1960s, American and European scholars came to the conclusion that an individual's attachment to political contents involves three levels: the community (for example, the nation), the regime (for example, democracy) and political actors (for example, parties) (Dawson and Prewitt 1969, 96 ff.). The attachment to each level develops in sequence, one after the other, from the first years of life onwards (Easton and Hess 1962; Greenstein 1965). Whilst the classics of political socialization concentrated on childhood and adolescence, the idea that people's political identities are shaped throughout their lifetimes arose only subsequently. It was prompted by the observation that if this were not so, political change would only be possible with generational change. In other words, political socialization can also be secondary socialization (Marsh 1971; Searing et al. 1976). It is not necessary to go into detail regarding this old-school literature on which researchers tend to rely whenever they open the 'black box' of political attitudes. What I wish to emphasize here is not its empirical findings but its theoretical premise: *symbols, often defined through verbal messages, shape collective identities*. In other words, collective identities are cultural phenomena generated, largely reproduced and transmitted by culture itself.

The structuralist model has more diversified origins. In the same years when political socialization was on the agenda of mainstream sociology and political science, social psychology concerned itself with identity formation processes using different methods, in large part experimental, and with strong emphasis on relational dynamics examined through the observation of interactions within small groups of people. Hundreds of experiments conducted both in the field and in the laboratory demonstrated the influence of the 'in-group', even when membership was temporary and forced.[4] Although these studies considered groups which were typically small in size, it is likely that the conclusion that they drew can be extended to broader spheres of belonging: *associative relations and shared spaces shape collective identities*.

However, I maintain that experimental social psychology has developed at the micro level a model of social identification already present in the works of two of sociology's founding fathers, Karl Marx and Georg Simmel. Marx's assumptions on collective identities are well known and require only brief mention (see Wright 1985, 243 ff.). His reference notion was social class. In Marxian theory, class consciousness is the only meaningful collective identity. However, it is not the contents of such identity that are of interest here, but rather the conditions which confer a sense of identitarian unity on social classes. Although Marx died before he could write the chapter on classes in *Capital*, some of his sociological interpreters have specified those conditions (particularly Elster 1986, 129 ff.). The first condition is *physical proximity* and *ease of meeting*, which – as Marx himself observed – intensifies in the workplace with transition from agrarian to industrial society. The second is the *understanding of shared interests through association* which generates forms of collective action. Despite the existence of accessory factors (especially for the rise of class action: Weber 1998, 184; see also Giddens 1973, 92–3), these are the main presuppositions of class identification – or consciousness, in Marx's lexicon. As has already been pointed out,[5] the model proposes an interpretation of the process of subjective identity formation which is transferable outside its original frame of reference. Broadly speaking, it can be applied to all cases in which a collective identity emerges: a ghetto, a colony, the unification of a nation or – as in our case – a supranational community.

Simmel's (2009) contribution to the structuralist model of collective identity formation centres on the spatial anchorage of social relations. In his essay on *Space and the Spatial Ordering of Society*, Simmel highlights the psychological salience of the places in which socially significant interactions occur. Co-presence in an emotionally charged location invests this same location with a special quality that marks a person's memory and identity. Moreover, Simmel (2009, 557) hints at the importance of spatial 'pivots' around which individuals fix a cohesive bond: 'The strengths that radiate from such an apparent centre' – he insists – 'also reawaken the consciousness of belonging' (ibid., 559).[6]

To summarize, the two models envisage different sources and mechanisms of collective identity formation. As to the sources, the culturalist model focuses on symbolic contents, whilst the structuralist model concentrates on social relations and their spatial contexts. Coming to the mechanisms, the former model considers the psychological dynamics of attachment and persuasion typical of primary and secondary socialization, whilst the latter assumes that identity derives from the *habitus* and/or the concert of interests which accompanies repeated social practices.[7] Finally to be stressed is that the two models, although propounded in alternative forms, are not mutually exclusive, and that the dynamics which they assume can operate jointly and give rise to a collective identity in different ways – unless one adopts a rigid 'structural determinism' or, conversely, a radical culturalism (Emirbayer and Goodwin 1994).

3. The culturalist and structuralist models put to the test: the case of European identification

Although rarely fully aware of doing so, sociological studies on European identification rely on one or the other of the two models of collective identity formation just outlined.[8] Most often, even if implicitly,[9] they rest on the culturalist model, which attributes acquisition of European identity to forms of symbolic transmission of meaningful contents. Belonging in this category are the numerous studies that have investigated the identitarian impact of exposure to the EU's flag and anthem (Bruter 2003), the use of the euro and the European passport (Risse 2002; Cram et al.

2011), organizational norms in the institutions of the EU (Beyers 2005; Hooghe 2005; Lewis 2005), civic education and the teaching of European history (Hinderliter Ortloff 2005; Schissler and Soysal 2005; Grundy and Jamieson 2007; Faas 2010), publicity strategies (Hüller 2007) and EC cultural policies (Sassatelli 2002). Less directly, studies on the Europeanization of national publics through the media coverage of EU policies (Stoeckel 2008) or of European issues raised by political parties (Hooghe 2007; De Vries and Edwards 2009) likewise envisage a link between exposure to messages with Europeanist contents and identification with Europe.

Furthermore, the culturalist model also underpins studies on European identity inspired by historical sociology and the history of ideas.[10] These studies are based on the assumption that the cultural 'building blocks' of 'Europe' survive over time because they are transmitted from one generation to the next, giving rise to a civilizational identity precisely by virtue of their persistence. In this research tradition, identities are scripts that are taught, learnt and enacted. They are sometimes described as cognitive traits, like Morin's (1987) 'doubtfulness', and other times as a moral stance, like Brague's (1992) 'secondariety'. Such identities reproduce themselves basically via socialization dynamics. Their 'emotional thickness' – on which, for instance, Eder (2009) insists – is key to guaranteeing their durability and success, like for any value transmitted through affective attachments.

A much smaller number of studies have adopted the structuralist model to explain the genesis and consolidation of identification with Europe. As a matter of fact, this approach first emerged in the pioneering years of European studies, when Karl W. Deutsch set out his 'transactionalist thesis' on European integration. Deutsch began his academic career as a scholar of nationalism. In his view, nation-building comes about mainly through the construction of 'infrastructures' which facilitate economic and social exchanges within territorial boundaries. Infrastructures create 'societies', while communication and culture create 'communities'. But the latter cannot exist without the former. The sense of belonging to a nation grows out of the intensification of social relations in conditions of 'complementarity'.[11] As a result of this process, 'each cluster of intensive social communication is a people' (Deutsch 1953, 188). Its members interact with each other more than they do with people external to the community, thereby strengthening their sense of solidarity and common destiny. Deutsch subsequently revised his theory of nationalism in light of processes of supranational integration.[12] As in the case of incipient nations, the expansion of economic, social and cultural exchanges across the boundaries of pre-existing polities is expected to lead to the formation of 'security communities' – one of which was the newborn European Economic Community, which Deutsch held could progressively endow itself with a collective identity through increased transnational interactions (Deutsch et al. 1957).[13]

These insights into the conditions for the 'bottom-up' growth of European integration and identity have only very recently been taken seriously by empirical research. The rediscovery of Deutsch in sociological studies on the EU was probably initiated by Jan Delhey, who, by taking the transactionalist thesis to its extreme, concluded that 'European social integration would be fully achieved if intergroup relations between the EU nationalities were mutually as frequent and cohesive as in-group relations within these nationalities – in this case, the component parts of the European social space would be dissolved because Europeans act (and think) like citizens of one single nation' (Delhey 2004, 20; see also Trenz 2011, 206–8; Delhey et al. 2014).[14] A reappraisal of Deutsch's legacy is also the basis of Fligstein's (2008) analysis of European integration. Examining in parallel Eurobarometer data relative to support for the EU and data relative to the transnational practices of Europeans (in particular, some preliminary results from the Pioneur Project: Rother and Nebe 2009), Fligstein notes that the same social categories – young people, more highly educated individuals and members of the upper social strata – figure among the most pro-Europe *and* transnational citizens. However, because Fligstein's analysis is conducted on separate data, it is unable to prove that the two phenomena are indeed associated. Even if they belong to the same social categories, what ensures that the supporters of European integration and the Europeans with the most experience of mobility are the same people? This question is addressed in the next section.

4. European through Mobility? EU movers' and stayers' identifications compared

EU movers form a small fraction of Europeans. As seen in Chapter 3, EU citizens resident in another member state hover around 3 per cent of the total population. This makes it impracticable to study their characteristics, behaviours and attitudes using data from sample surveys conducted with random criteria on the entire population: even in large-scale surveys, the absolute number of sampled cases would be rather modest. It would be difficult to compare those few cases with the large majority of 'stayers'. A solution is to combine data from population surveys with data

130 *Mobile Europe*

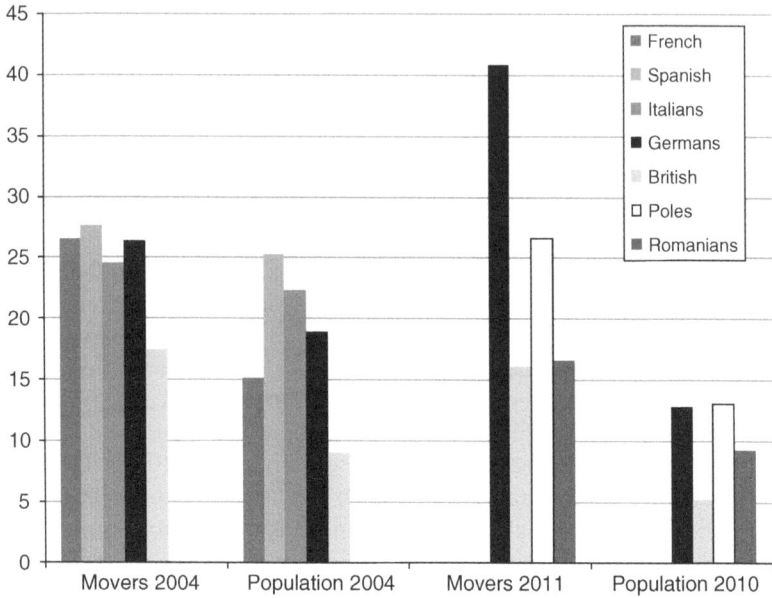

Figure 6.1 Feeling European: EU movers and stayers who declare themselves to be 'very attached' to Europe (2004 and 2010–2011) (%)

Sources: 2004: Eurobarometer 62 and EIMSS (*N* = 10,728); 2011: Eurobarometer 73 and Moveact (*N* = 6,852).

from *ad hoc* surveys on migrants that deal with the same phenomena using the same indicators. This is the strategy adopted in the following analyses. I merged Eurobarometer data with data from the EIMSS and Moveact surveys, which were designed to make this operation possible (see Methodological Appendix). More specifically, I constructed a first joint matrix relative to 2004 with data from Eurobarometer 62 and the EIMSS survey on German, British, French, Spanish and Italian nationals. The second matrix has 2010–2011 as its temporal reference, and pools data from Eurobarometer 73 of 2010 with data from the 2011 Moveact survey on citizens of German, British, Polish and Romanian nationality.[15] It is thus possible to compare – among other things – the sense of identification with Europe of the stayers and movers of different countries at two distant moments of time.

Both surveys show that the European citizens who feel 'very attached' to Europe are proportionally more numerous among those living in another member state than in the rest of the population (Figure 6.1). This is the case within each and every nationality examined, independently of its level of identification with Europe. In absolute terms, in 2004, the Spanish respondents, both stayers and movers, accounted for the largest proportion of convinced Europeans. In 2010–2011, across a different range of nationalities, the highest level of European identification was expressed by Germans among mobile citizens and Poles among non-mobile ones. Not surprisingly, in both 2004 and 2010–2011, British respondents recorded the lowest levels of attachment to Europe. In the more recent survey, the percentage of Romanians who expressed a strong attachment to Europe was almost equally low (16.7 per cent among movers and 9.3 per cent among stayers). But there are no exceptions to the rule that attachment to Europe is more widespread among mobile citizens. Moreover, among the nationalities for which it makes sense to conduct an intertemporal comparison – German and British – a decrease in the proportion of respondents strongly attached to Europe is apparent among stayers but not among movers. Indeed, in the sample of Germans resident abroad in 2011, 41 per cent of respondents were very attached to Europe.

This result is confirmed when a different measure is adopted: not the proportion of 'very attached' respondents but the average level of attachment calculated by attributing scores from 1 to 4 on the Likert scale for this questionnaire item ('not at all attached' = 1; 'not very attached' = 2; 'quite attached' = 3; 'very attached' = 4). For all the nationalities and in both waves of the survey, the average value recorded by the sample of mobile citizens was higher than that recorded by the rest the population, with a slightly wider gap in the second wave (2004: 1.76 vs 1.66; 2010–2011: 1.80 vs 1.43).

'Europeanness' can hardly be analysed without reference to national identities. Indeed, existing research on the relationship between European and national identifications emphasizes their compatibility. Both conceptually and in subjective experience, the former does not undermine the latter – just as European citizenship does not replace national citizenship, but instead flanks it. Scholars speak of 'nested identities' (Díez Medrano and Gutiérrez 2001) and 'mixed identities' (Risse 2004), with the respective metaphors of the 'matrioska' (where one identity is dominant) and the 'marble-cake' (where identities are blended in different ways in different social groups). But whatever the interpretative model adopted, the empirical evidence (though with some exceptions) tends to show that European identification correlates strongly not only with national identification but also with its regional and local variants (Duchesne and Frognier 1995, 2008; Marks and Hooghe 2003; Citrin and Sides 2004; Bruter 2005). This may be a consequence not only of the psychologically non-exclusive and cross-cutting nature of identifications, but also of an 'echo effect' of the batteries of indicators used when administering the interviews – given that the items relative to 'attachment' are usually put to the respondents one after the other.[16] Keeping this in mind, one way to bring out the European component of identification is to calculate the difference between the sense of belonging to Europe and the sense of belonging to the other political–territorial communities (the nation, the region and the city/town/village). Technically, this simply involves subtracting the average of the scores relative to the other three items from the score attributed on the Likert scale for 'attachment to Europe'. The index obtained varies between +3 (the extreme case in which the interviewee said that s/he was 'very' attached to Europe and 'not at all' attached to the other political–territorial units) and −3 (in the opposite extreme case). This measure – which I call the 'identity spread' – helps one grasp the relative intensity of the feeling of proximity to Europe compared with more traditional collective identifications.

In all the samples examined, in 2004 and 2010–2011, the 'identity spread' was on average negative (Figure 6.2). This means that EU citizens – both stayers and movers – had a stronger sense of belonging to national and subnational political–territorial units than to Europe. This is a finding which reinforces the view of Europe as conveying predominantly an ancillary identity. However, there are exceptions. And these are much more frequent among mobile Europeans that in the rest of the population. Those interviewees for whom the identity spread assumed positive values represented 34.6 per cent of the European movers surveyed in 2004 (13.4 per cent among stayers) and 30.5 per cent of the interviewees in 2010–2011 (7.4 per cent among stayers). The average levels by nationality, illustrated in Figure 6.2, exhibit the smallest distance between European and other identifications in the two samples of intra-EU migrants. Whilst the maximum spread within the population was recorded in the UK (in both 2004 and 2010–2011), in the Moveact sample the widest gap was among Romanian citizens living abroad, perhaps in part because of the shorter duration of their migratory experiences. Located at the opposite extreme are German movers, who were the only national category recording a positive, though marginal, spread, thereby revealing a stronger attachment to Europe than to the other political–territorial units.

Of course, this preliminary analysis yields only inconclusive findings, given that the difference between movers and stayers may also be due to the differing composition of the samples. To neutralize this possibility,

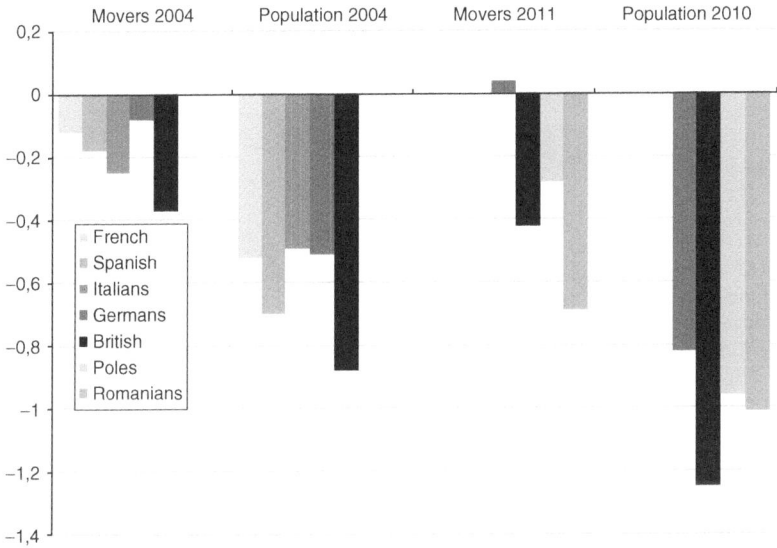

Figure 6.2 Identity spread: difference between level of attachment to Europe and average level of attachment to nation/region/city (or town or village) among EU movers and stayers (2004 and 2010–2011)
Sources: 2004: Eurobarometer 62 and EIMSS (N = 10,507); 2011: Eurobarometer 73 and Moveact (N = 6,138).

I conducted multi-variate analyses which control for the simultaneous effect of the main sociological factors that can influence the level of European identification. Table 6.1 presents the results of two logistic regression models of such factors on the dichotomous dependent variable described in Figure 6.1: that is, self-definition as being 'very attached to Europe'.[17] The first model refers to the 2004 sample (consisting of the Eurobarometer 62 and EIMSS data), the second to the 2010–2011 sample (consisting of Eurobarometer 73 and Moveact data). In both cases, experiencing intra-EU mobility is one of the strongest predictors of attachment to Europe. In 2011, in fact, assuming the overall combination of the reference modalities of the control variables introduced into the model, mobility is associated with four times higher odds of feeling 'very attached' to Europe, standing out as the single most powerful independent variable of the model. As can be expected, education – in particular, up to tertiary level (that is, after the age of 19) – tends to engender a greater sense of Europeanness as well. By contrast, upper-class membership is significant in the first but not the second model. Likewise, whilst in the first model

Table 6.1 Determinants of attachment to Europe in 2004 and 2010–2011: logit regressions ('very attached' vs 'fairly, not very or not at all attached')

	2004	2010–2011
Intra-EU mobility	1.734**	3.857**
Age (ref: >60 years old)		
15–30	0.781*	0.942
31–40	0.804*	0.961
41–50	0.905	0.803
51–60	1.112	0.905
Gender (=woman)	0.732**	0.827*
Education (ref: Low, up to 15)		
Middle (up to 16–19)	1.304*	1.105
High (after 19)	2.032**	1.751**
Social class (ref: EGP VII)		
EGP I–II	1.383**	1.209
EGP III	1.167	0.852
EGP IV	1.189	1.127
EGP V–VI	1.042	0.827
Nationality (ref: German)		
French	0.918	
British	0.472**	0.368**
Spanish	1.214*	
Italian	1.060	
Polish		0.698**
Romanian		0.423**
Local identification	1.041	1.259*
Regional identification	3.324**	
National identification	2.182**	2.691**

Sources: 2004: Eurobarometer 62 and EIMSS: $N = 9{,}254$; df = 19; chi-square = 3,852.56; Nagelkerke $R^2 = 0.18$. 2010–2011: Eurobarometer 73 and Moveact: $N = 6{,}344$; df = 17; chi-square = 1,916.80; Nagelkerke $R^2 = 0.17$.
Notes: *$p < 0.05$, **$p < 0.01$. Coefficients are odds ratios.

attachment to Europe was significantly lower among interviewees in the younger age groups, this is not the case in the 2010–2011 surveys. Gender differences are in line with most of the literature: men are more inclined to describe themselves as European (Nelson and Guth 2000; Citrin and Sides 2004; Risse 2010).

Unfortunately, the two data sets do not contain data relative to values and political attitudes that might be important (for instance, self-placement on the right–left scale). But information regarding the other competing political–territorial identities is indeed available. Analysis reveals that strong regional and national identities – to which local ones were also added in 2011 – are associated with attachment to

Europe. This may be the substantive expression of a sensibility underlying the collective dimension of social life in its territorial variants. More prosaically, however, not to be excluded is the already-mentioned presence of a 'response set' which reduces the discriminatory capacity of these indicators.

Finally, British origin is associated negatively – and considerably so – with European identification in both surveys. It is especially negative in comparison with the reference category – German nationality – which is significantly associated with an attachment to Europe greater than that of the other nationalities in 2010–2011, but not in 2004, when a more marked effect was exerted by Spanish and Italian origin (the latter with a non-significant statistical difference).

In a similar manner, it is worth evaluating whether the association between intra-European mobility and identity spread, as defined above, persists when controlling for the influence of other possible intervening factors (Table 6.2). The answer is 'yes'. Moreover, this analysis also shows that the effect of mobility on European identification (understood here in relative terms) was stronger in the 2010–2011 sample. The huge influence of mobility was offset by the modest effect of all the other variables, apart from nationality. In the relative terms that characterize this index, the greater European identification of German citizens clearly emerges in both surveys. The weak nationalism exhibited by the German population since the post-war period widens the identity spread in all comparative analyses (Smith and Kim 2006). By contrast, the Europeanness of the Spanish diminishes when it is parameterized to the sense of belonging to other levels of political–territorial organization. It should also be pointed out that, if measured with this index, the Europeanness of more elderly interviewees is less robust than that of the other cohorts, contrary to what was shown in the previous analysis. Closer inspection shows the over-60s express stronger attachment to all the political–territorial levels – which may also be due to their greater conformism in the interview situation (that is, response set).

The analyses presented in this section showed that mobile Europeans have a sense of belonging to Europe decidedly and significantly stronger than that of the rest of the population. Other studies conducted at local (Verwiebe 2004; Block 2007; Gaspar 2008), national (SVR 2013, 28 ff.) and international–comparative (Roeder 2011) levels have obtained similar results. Nonetheless, the causal relationship between mobility and identity cannot be definitively proved in the absence of longitudinal data: is it mobility that produces a stronger European identification or European identification that induces people to move to other EU countries? The

Table 6.2 Determinants of identity spread in 2004 and 2010–2011: OLS regressions of the difference between attachment to Europe and attachments to nation/region/city (or town or village)

	2004	2010–2011
Intra-EU mobility	0.182**	0.287**
Age (ref: >60 years old)		
15–30	0.064**	−0.001
31–40	0.052**	−0.030*
41–50	0.050**	−0.024
51–60	0.034**	−0.002
Gender (=woman)	−0.063**	−0.044**
Education (ref: Low, up to 15)		
Middle (up to 16–19)	0.100**	0.003
High (after 19)	0.194**	0.064**
Social class (ref: EGP VII)		
EGP I–II	0.082**	0.013
EGP III	0.033*	−0.019
EGP IV	0.034*	−0.004
EGP V–VI	−0.002	−0.002
Nationality (ref: German)		
French	−0.002	
British	−0.131**	−0.176**
Spanish	−0.033**	
Italian	−0.012	
Polish		−0.060**
Romanian		−0.128**

Sources: 2004: Eurobarometer 62 and EIMSS: $N = 10,506$; df = 16; $R^2 = 0.11$. 2010–2011: Eurobarometer 73 and Moveact: $N = 6,137$; df = 15; $R^2 = 0.12$.
Notes: *$p < 0.05$, **$p < 0.01$. Coefficients are betas.

theoretical reasonings outlined earlier in this chapter favour the former hypothesis – social practices construct identity more than the other way round. But there is more. Among the mobile Europeans interviewed in both 2004 and 2011, European identification was significantly more frequent the longer the period spent living abroad (Table 6.3). Time creates the conditions for a reconfiguration of collective identities within a broader framework. More precisely, the relationship between the duration of mobility and European identification is not linear; rather, it tends to be exponential. People who have been migrants for fewer than five years are significantly less likely to declare a strong attachment to Europe. Conversely, European identification is particularly strong among people who have lived in another EU member state for more than 20 years. The fact that 'feeling European' arises among interviewees who have lived

Table 6.3 Determinants of attachment to Europe among EU movers in 2004 and 2010–2011: logit regressions ('very attached' vs 'fairly, not very or not at all attached')

	2004	2011
Duration of mobility (ref: ≥20 years)		
1–5 years	0.763*	0.560**
6–10 years	0.951	0.779
11–19 years	0.852	0.684*
Age	1.010**	1.001
Gender (=woman)	0.748**	0.787*
Education (ref: Low, up to 15)		
Middle (up to 16–19)	1.537**	0.970
High (after 19)	2.509**	1.682**
Social class (ref: EGP VII)		
EGP I–II	1.150	1.323
EGP III	1.041	0.613*
EGP IV	0.990	1.221
EGP V–VI	0.951	0.852
Nationality (ref: German)		
French	1.073	
British	0.577**	0.275**
Spanish	1.284*	
Italian	0.094	
Polish		0.677*
Romanian		0.343**

Sources: 2004: EIMSS: $N = 4{,}270$; df = 15; chi-square = 3,239.99; Nagelkerke $R^2 = 0.05$.
2011: Moveact: $N = 1{,}972$; df = 14; chi-square = 1,683.51; Nagelkerke $R^2 = 0.13$.
Notes: *$p < 0.05$, **$p < 0.01$. Coefficients are odds ratios.

abroad longer is strongly indicative of the direction taken by the causal relationship between mobility and identity.[18]

5. Beyond mobility: transnational practices and European identity

European citizens who move from one EU member state to another feel more European than their peers who spend their lives within the boundaries of their country of birth. But freedom of movement does not exhaust the opportunities for interaction across national borders created by European integration and, simultaneously, globalization. From the structuralist perspective outlined earlier, inspired by Karl Deutsch, mobility is only one of a broad set of transnational behaviours that spill over into a stronger European identity.

138 Mobile Europe

Recent studies have sought to give a more precise definition to what is meant by 'transnationalism', exploring the entire range of 'border-crossing work relations, communication networks, social interactions, everyday practices' (Mau et al. 2008, 2). An *ad hoc* survey conducted in Germany in 2006 found that around half of the sample had at least one regular cross-border contact, while 60 per cent had visited a foreign country during the previous year (Mau 2010). A subsequent comparative inquiry revealed marked variations in the scale and patterns of transnationalism across six EU countries: people who have visited another EU member state over the last 24 months, for instance, range from 35.5 per cent of Romanians to 74.3 per cent of Danes (Salamońska et al. 2013).[19] Mau (2010, 118) also found a significant relation between transnationalism and European identification, though not as strong as the one with education.[20] In a more recent study, Mau has also sought to specify the macro- and micro-determinants of individual transnationalism on a supranational scale (Mau and Mewes 2012). However, the impact of transnationalism on European identification remains to be assessed systematically in cases other than Germany.

Eurobarometer 73 provides an opportunity in this regard as it contains a series of dichotomous items which concern important aspects of transnational experiences and practices. I therefore constructed an additive index of 'individual transnationalism' as a summary of these items. Indicators were divided into three categories – *strong*, *moderate* and *weak*[21] transnational behaviours – assigning them different weights in the index (15 per cent, 10 per cent and 5 per cent):

- Had worked abroad for more than three months (15 per cent)
- Had studied abroad for more than three months (15 per cent)
- Had lived abroad for more than three months (for reasons other than work or study) (15 per cent)
- Had or had had a partner who was or had been a citizen of another country (15 per cent)
- Normally spent holidays abroad (10 per cent)
- Owned property abroad (10 per cent)
- Had family members living abroad (5 per cent)
- Had friends living abroad (5 per cent)
- Regularly followed news about another country (5 per cent)
- Regularly cooked typical dishes of another country (5 per cent)

The index of individual transnationalism thus constructed varied from 0 (no transnational experience) to 20 (involvement in all transnational practices). Its distribution in the sample was, in fact, markedly

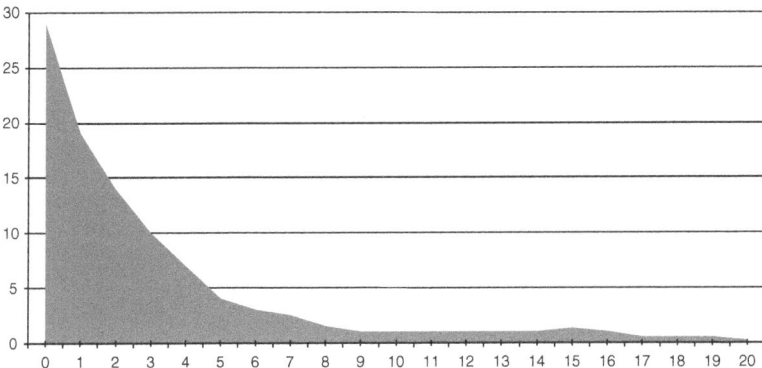

Figure 6.3 Distribution of the index of individual transnationalism (in %)
Source: Eurobarometer 73 (2010). Weighted sample of EU27 countries.

unbalanced (Figure 6.3). Only 6.6 per cent of the interviewees recorded scores over 10, while fully 48.1 per cent recorded 2 (the median) or less. The average score was 3.04. Multi-variate analysis (not presented here: see Baglioni and Recchi 2013) confirmed that people in the upper class, with higher educational qualifications, younger, male and resident in large cities were likely to have higher scores. Moreover, not surprisingly, transnationalism was found to be more widespread among people living in the richest and most globalized countries (Recchi 2012b).

Table 6.4 sets out the results of three multi-level logistic regression models used to test the hypothesis that international mobility and transnationalism influence the sense of belonging to the EU.[22] The first model did *not* include the independent variables of interest – that is, the experience of international mobility (having lived abroad for more than three months) and the individual transnationalism index – so as to highlight their separate explanatory power.

In general, multi-level models are used if it is believed that the parameters relative to the individual factors do not vary independently but according to patterns typical of the higher-order units – in the present case, countries (Snijders and Bosker 1999). The analysis was thus able to account for a more complex variability compared with the non-hierarchical models employed previously, given the larger number of countries considered (the then 27 member states of the EU).[23] It was also possible to control for a number of potentially significant context variables, in particular, the membership of the residence country in the EU15, postulating that European identification is stronger the longer a country

Table 6.4 Mobility experiences, individual transnationalism and attachment to the EU in the EU population: multi-level logit regressions ('very attached' vs 'fairly, not very or not at all attached')

	Model 1	Model 2	Model 3
	Only control variables	Past mobility abroad (≥3 months)	Individual transnationalism index
Individual-level variables			
International mobility (≥3 months)		1.654***	
Individual transnationalism index			1.103***
Gender (=woman)	0.885**	0.902*	0.896*
Age	0.986*	0.983*	0.978**
Age (squared)	1.000	1.000	1.000
Education (ref: Low, up to 15)			
Middle (up to 16–19)	1.078	1.082	1.059
High (over 19)	1.496***	1.461***	1.339***
Social class (ref: Inactive)			
Bourgeoisie (I)	1.408**	0.757*	0.820
Salariat (II)	0.856	0.899	0.960
Routine white collar (III)	1.038	1.073	1.112
Petty bourgeoisie (IV)	0.855	0.895	0.932
Working class (V–VI–VII)	1.063	1.106	1.155
Internet use (7-points scale)	1.068***	1.064***	1.048***
Local identification	1.347***	1.350***	1.340***
Region/county identification	1.808***	1.844***	1.916***
National identification	4.005***	4.084***	4.380***
National-level variables			
EU15 member state	0.736	0.748	0.824
Population (millions)	1.120*	1.126*	1.133**
GDP per capita (thousands, $)	1.055*	1.035	1.032
Unemployment rate	1.013	0.998	0.996
Globalization index (KOF)	1.004	1.004	1.005
Intercept	0.017	0.014	0.013
Variance of random intercept	0.506	0.513	0.507
Log likelihood	−7708.84	−7664.49	−7561.52
Wald chi-square	1184.82	1259.70	1414.60

Source: Eurobarometer 73 (2010). $n = 26{,}582$, $N = 27$.
Notes: *$p < 0.05$, **$p < 0.01$, ***$p < 0.001$. Coefficients are odds ratios.

has been a member state of the EU (Nissen 2005); national demographic size, presuming that smaller states have a higher interest in European integration (Steinmetz and Wivel 2010); per capita income and the unemployment rate, given the greater utility deriving to economically weaker countries from EU membership (Eichenberg and Dalton 1993; Gabel and Palmer 1995) and the country's level of globalization (measured with the KOF index already used in the Introduction), on the assumption that societal openness to the global dimension creates a climate conducive to supranational identities (Jung 2008; Haller and Roudometof 2010).

Contrary to expectations, a firmer European identification was more likely to be found in demographically larger and richer countries. Unemployment and globalization levels, though, had no effect, and GDP per capita lost its significance once the models took into account respondents' mobility experiences and transnationalism. To single out better the conditions under which a more solid European identification develops requires shifting the focus to factors operating at the individual level. The results obtained previously in this chapter were confirmed, with the sole exception of age, which here turned out to be inversely correlated with European identification. This difference is evidently due to the effects registered in the group of the countries not included in the analyses of Tables 6.1 and 6.2. and particularly many new member states, where the younger generation is more attached to Europe (Segatti 2013). The model also included an additional variable measuring the frequency of Internet use among the interviewees. Although not a direct expression of transnationalism (the web can be used to search for local information), the fact that this variable was significantly associated with a stronger attachment to the EU seemed to bear out the central hypothesis that activities spanning over national borders foster a sense of supranational identification.

This hypothesis was decidedly corroborated when the experience of (past or current) mobility abroad (model 2) and the individual transnationalism index (model 3) were introduced. The effect of each of these variables was markedly positive and significant. But that of transnationalism, including a range of practices wider than only sojourns in another country, was even stronger – when comparing the coefficients, consider that 'mobility' is a dichotomy, while the transnationalism index varies on a 20-point scale. It is also noteworthy that the model including the social transnationalism index had a better overall fit, but the significance of GDP per capita and upper-class membership disappeared. This finding resonates with a qualitative study on managers in Paris, Madrid and Milan showing quite differentiated levels and modalities of transnationalism within urban bourgeoisies (Andreotti et al. 2013). Moreover, once the social transnationalism index was introduced, the effect of education diminished. It is likely that in the first model, the large part of class and education effects 'incorporated' transnationalism, which thus emerges as a more direct cause of supranational identification. Again the globalization index, which captures transnationalism at an aggregate and contextual level and that thus turns out not to have a straightforward impact on individual practices, was non-significant.

Other recent studies shed further light on Deutsch's transactionalist thesis – revised and corrected in line with the theoretical considerations developed in the first part of this chapter – showing that individual transnationalism translates into more convinced support for European integration (Kuhn 2011a; Recchi and Kuhn 2013). Moreover, Kuhn (2012) has evidenced that transnationalist practices play a stronger role in reinforcing European identification among less-educated people. In a certain sense, highly educated individuals do not need transnational networks and mobilities to feel European: intellectual activities and relationships formed throughout their educational career have already brought them to a supranational outlook. This explains the surprising finding of analyses of longitudinal data on Erasmus students that the Erasmus experience by itself does not increase their attachment to Europe (Sigalas 2010; Wilson 2011).[24] The point is that all the participants in the Erasmus Programme are university students, that is, individuals whose self-perception as European is already substantially greater than that of the rest of the population. If anything, transnational practices can be a substitute for education in producing a sense of proximity to the EU. This has profound implications for the 'identity technology' used by the European institutions (Kaina and Karolewski 2009) – in particular, to design future intra-European mobility programmes or to promote other forms of transnational exchange. For Deutsch's theory to be translated into a stronger common European identity, thus, the population involved in free movement should be widened beyond the 'usual suspects'.

6. Mobility, belonging, participation: a concluding note

In this chapter I have argued for the existence of two distinct theoretical models underlying research on European identification. The first model considers identification to be the direct outcome of exposure to symbols and narratives with specifically identitarian content. The second views identification as a property which emerges from spatially connoted social interactions. This latter model is somewhat less popular in the literature, but its application to explain the differences in levels of European identification seems particularly fruitful. The analyses reported in this chapter showed that cross-national mobility is a practice accompanied by the presence – and perhaps the maturation – of a sense of Europeanness unknown to the majority of the population. In short, cross-national mobility makes Europe 'blossom' within Europeans. Moreover, as shown in the last part of the chapter, mobility is only one component of a broader set of social practices which extend the boundaries of life-worlds – and also, consequently, of social identities – beyond the borders of nation states.

This empirical evidence may appear to contradict the conclusion that I drew from the analysis of EU movers' political participation in Chapter 5: those Europeans who decide to profit from their citizenship by going to live in another EU member state are not particularly inclined to activate such citizenship in the public sphere. But it is not necessarily the case that identity and mobilization correlate. The reality is that intra-European mobility combines more with belonging than with active citizenship. A plausible reason is that the latter has higher costs. The sense of belonging sediments, grows and strengthens with practice, even in the absence of the particularly intense emotions and values instead required for political commitment – participating in street protests, joining a political party, attending meetings and rallies or even turning out regularly to vote. Being an active citizen demands an awareness and an identity salience which may not have taken root among mobile Europeans. But at least mobility helps sow the seeds.

To conclude, the travails of European integration in the second decade of the twenty-first century have brought the importance of popular legitimacy to the front. 'Making Europe' in the absence of widespread solidarity has proved to be a fanciful utopia – or perhaps, more sinisterly, an elitist stratagem (Haller 2008). But there can be no solidarity without a sense of common identity (Kaina 2013). Identity matters. A shared space and experience of belonging to that space are necessary incubators of identification. Hence mobility, not just as a legal principle but as a social practice, is of crucial importance for the future of a united Europe.

Conclusion
Free Movement in Europe: Epitomizing the Age of Mobility?

1. The EU as a 'human mobility system'

After delving into the genealogy, the institutional framework, the demographic picture and the individual-level outcomes of free movement in Europe, in these final pages I will try to climb a step in the ladder of abstraction and argue that the topic speaks to a broader sociological theme – namely, the changing relationship between human beings and space. Rather than summarize previous chapters, I prefer to launch a bridge to future research that may be inspired by the knowledge of the workings and implications of intra-EU migration.

As must be clear at the end of this book, European integration has paved the way to a supranational area in which the traditional power of nation states to control individuals' choices of travel and settlement has been curbed, creating a sort of 'natural experiment' of a borderless world region. The EU has established the market-embedded political infrastructure of a unique 'human mobility system' – the European free movement regime. Nothing alike exists elsewhere, in spite of the proliferation of international agreements and alliances in different regions of the globe. The freedom of movement of persons across states is 'the very hallmark of why the EU is not like NAFTA or other purely top-down "neo-liberal" regional integration projects' (Favell 2014, 282) – indeed, a historically most unusual and forward-looking legal achievement.

As such, the free movement regime is also the single piece of EU legislation that most explicitly alludes to a federalization of the Union – that is, its possible future as a United States of Europe. This is the reason why an EU–US comparison of cross-state population movements sometimes proves tempting (for example, Janiak and Wasmer 2008, 21 ff.). The socioeconomic integration of American society is predicated on the proverbial mobility of US residents: is anything similar emerging in Europe? Data are usually interpreted as responding that it is not. In brief, intra-EU migrants amount to approximately 1,600,000 persons a year, while cross-state internal US migrants hover around 5,500,000, that is, 0.32 per cent of the population in the EU against 1.79 per cent in the USA.[1] Intra-EU migration flows are proportionally almost six times lower than cross-state movements in America. However, this is perhaps not the correct comparison to make. The USA is a federal state, the EU is not; the USA is a nation, the EU is not; in the USA, there is one predominant language, in the EU there are more than 20; the USA has a relatively more integrated domestic market and a more extensive network of firms with subsidiaries in the various states.[2] If the interest lies on internal population migration as an index of structural socioeconomic integration, it is more correct to make not a *spatial* but a *temporal* comparison. This second type of comparison reveals that the relative share of EU citizens who choose to live in a member state of the Union different from their state of origin has gradually increased, whereas in the USA it has constantly declined since the 1990s.[3] In particular, the EU accession of economically less-developed Central-Eastern new member states has fuelled migratory flows without precedence in Europe – at least since the 1970s (see Chapter 3). What is surprising, however, is that the number of West Europeans who have moved to live in another EU member state has *also* continued its slow growth, up by 37.3 per cent between 1990 and 2010 (the vast majority still residing in the 'old' Europe). The neo-classical economic theory of migration would have forecast a drop, on the grounds that people cross borders only if there is a significant difference between national incomes (Sjaastad 1962; Harris and Todaro 1970; Borjas 2001, 3–4). In fact, Figure 7.1 clearly shows that since the mid-1980s, the volume of intra-EU movers (dotted line) has progressively increased even though income differentials (solid line) in the EU15 countries have diminished.[4]

Applied to the EU case, the neo-classical economic theory of migration needs to be refined to take into account two additional effects. The first is public policies geared to support intra-European mobility. The large spectrum of EU pro-mobility legislation (see Chapter 2) has contributed to offset the disincentive to spatial mobility which is due to economic convergence among the member states – slowed but not halted by the economic crisis of the late 2000s (Stanisić 2012). Migration policies matter. Usually they are designed to inhibit and limit population movements. Instead, the pro-mobility activism of the EU has encouraged migration by lowering its costs.[5]

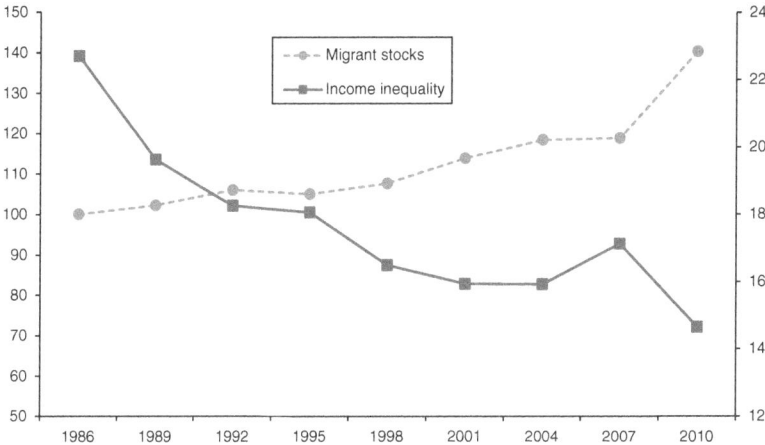

Figure 7.1 Income inequality between countries and intra-EU movers' stocks in EU15 (1986–2010)

Sources: Groningen Growth and Development Centre, Total Economy Database, www.ggdc.net; World Bank (for 2010 data), www.worldbank.org on GNPs per capita (in 1990 GK$); Eurostat database online, http://epp.eurostat.ec.europa.eu/portal/page/portal/statistics/search_database for data on movers' stocks.

Note: The left-hand axis shows changes in stocks of intra-EU migrants from 1986 (1986 = 100); the right-hand axis shows income inequality between countries measured as the coefficient of variation of their GNPs per capita. Luxembourg data are excluded.

The second shortcoming of the theory is that it underestimates non-economic factors in social choices. The increasing diversification of migration evidences the importance of the affective and self-fulfilment dimensions of mobility projects (Smith and King 2012). The concept of 'migration' itself appears reductive. In fact, it is not so much migration but human mobility writ large that has been growing tremendously, shaping a major social trend of our age boosted by technological and cultural developments. I will discuss this in the next section.

2. Beyond the EU: the age of migration or the age of mobility?

Migration is usually mentioned as a prime sociological feature of globalization. As a widely read and cited handbook put it, 'international population movements constitute a key dynamic within globalization – a complex process which intensified from the mid-1970s onward' (Castles and Miller 2003, 1). The timing also coincides, as historical accounts of globalization agree that its contemporary wave began between the late 1960s and the 1980s (Robertson 1992, 58–9).

Indeed, the number of human beings that change their CoR has increased considerably since the 1960s. According to the UN (2013), 232 million persons reside in a state other than the one where they were born, which corresponds to 3.2 per cent of the world population. In particular, about one in every ten persons living in the more-developed regions of the world is a migrant. Yet the expansion of the migrant population has been somewhat overstated, presenting ours as 'the age of migration' (Castles and Miller 2003). True, there were fewer than 70 million international migrants at the end of the 1960s. They have tripled in 40 years. A spectacular rise *per se*, but less so if viewed jointly with demographic trends. The world population and the migrant population soared in parallel for about two decades, in the 1970s and 1980s. Only since the early 1990s, in part due to the break-up of the USSR (which moved borders, not people), has the increase of migrant stocks surpassed the global population increase. Both, however, pale in comparison with the growth rate of international journeys – from 69 million in 1960 to 983 million in 2011 (Figure 7.2).[6] In proportional terms, this constitutes a 1,400 per cent increase rate. Ours is the age of mobility more than the age of migration.

While it is conceptually true that 'mobility is central to what it is to be modern' (Cresswell 2006, 20), only in the final decades of the twentieth century has the travel revolution gained momentum in scale and scope. At the outset, moon-landing epitomized the hyperbolic promise of mankind reaching out beyond its apparently insuperable frontiers. In the end, the ubiquitous spread of the Internet popularized another extreme – virtual travelling. In between, there have been technological advances, cultural shifts, economic progress and political changes – symbolized in Europe by the fall of the Berlin Wall in 1989 – that have combined to make it enormously more accessible and widespread to move out of nation-state containers.

Before this multi-dimensional revolution, international travelling was still a matter of social extremes. It was practiced by the privileged or the poorer classes, so that it was either 'tourism' or 'migration'.[7] Most people moved relatively seldom and usually between two points – an origin and a destination. This is less and less the case. Of the total trips reported by the United Nations World Tourism Organization (UNWTO) in 2006, only 51 per cent had the purpose of 'leisure, recreation and holidays', while 27 per cent were justified by 'visiting friends and relatives, religious reasons/pilgrimages, and health treatment; 16 per cent [by] business; and

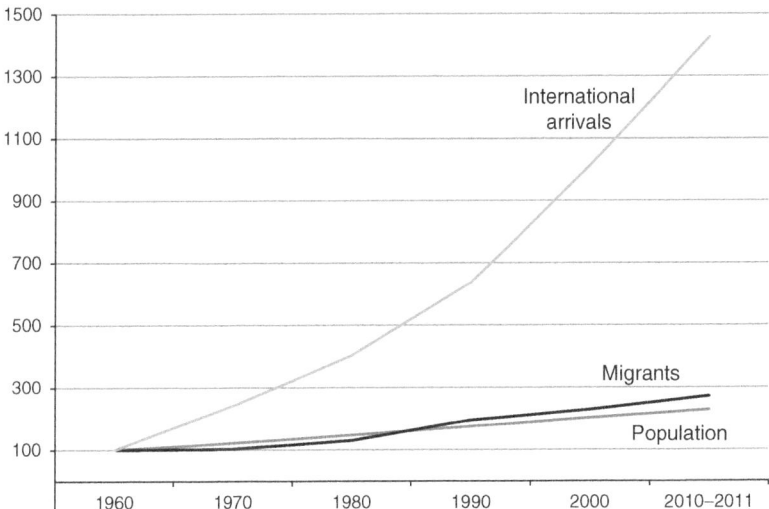

Figure 7.2 Mobility more than migration: Growth of world population, migrant stocks and international arrivals, 1960–2011 (1960 = 100)
Sources: http://www.un.org/en/development/desa/population/publications/policy/international-migration-policies-2013.shtml (consulted on 9 June 2013), UNWTO (2006, Annex 3). Most recent world population and migrant stocks refer to 2010, international arrivals to 2011, http://www.unwto.org/facts/eng/barometer.htm (consulted on 9 June 2013).

the purpose of the remaining 6 per cent was not specified' (Koslowski 2011, 54). Add to this that the declared reasons of travelling are scarcely reliable – it is well known, for instance, that the bulk of irregular migration originates with tourism visas – and you get a picture of the multifaceted nature and composition of movements across borders in the contemporary world.

International migration – conventionally defined as a form of human mobility that fulfils a space-based (that is, crossing state borders) and a time-based (usually, one year of residency) condition – does not tell the full story. *Migration* is only one specific, politically shaped subset of all the possible manifestations of human *mobility*. In the past, a variety of significant population movements predated the emergence of nation-state border controls (Moch 1992; Bade 2003; Lucassen and Lucassen 2009), possibly constituting a decisive ingredient in the emergence of capitalist societies in the Northwest of Europe (Tilly 1978). In our days, 'other movers, who are not staying and whose presence is indifferent to the receiving society, cross borders – such as tourists, business people, international lorry drivers – but they remain wholly indifferent and largely invisible forms of movement from the migration/immigration perspective' (Favell 2007, 270). The free movement regime of the EU makes such diverse mobility projects and practices easier and more secure than anywhere else on the globe. Transnationalism, which has entered the migration literature from US-based research, is in fact relatively more viable in Europe because of its supranational political framework. As Favell (2007, 271) concludes, 'Physical movement across space is the natural, normal given of human social life; what is abnormal, changeable, and historically constructed is the idea that human societies need to build political borders and institutions that define and constrain spatial mobility in particular, regularized ways, such that immobility becomes the norm.' For its part, the EU free movement regime is thus revealing of the state-centred reification of all human mobility into 'migration'. Not by chance, perhaps, as I will show in the next and final section, it is in Europe that the social sciences are opening up new perspectives on the relations between individuals and space.

3. Advancing the sociological study of human mobility

Traditionally, more than sociology, which for a long time conflated societies into nation states, it has been human geography that has dealt with the mobility of individuals and populations in physical space. Since the 1950s, this discipline has pivoted on the study of the 'role of distances and remoteness in the functioning of the social fabric' (Claval 1991). Especially inspired by Torsten Hägerstrand's seminal ideas on time geography (Shaw 2012), today's 'geographers are not coming to mobilities anew but are revisiting an old friend' (Cresswell and Merriman 2011, 4; see also Adey 2010). And it is human geographers (Janelle 1969; Harvey 1989; Leyshon 1995) who have proposed the crucial notion of 'time–space compression' as the distinctive feature of the contemporary age, engendered by the combined effect of technical progress in transport and telecommunications and the international expansion of the capitalist organization of the economy. In its turn, this compression constitutes the essential premise for the process of globalization.[8]

Among sociologists interested in globalization, John Urry stands out for his emphasis on movements of persons, objects and images as the essential and defining components of this process. In his book manifesto *Sociology beyond Societies* (Urry 2000), as well as in subsequent revisions (Urry 2007) and applications of his approach (Elliott and Urry 2010), adoption of a new paradigm is urged for the study of social phenomena in late modernity, given that the current age has experience of, and sets

Conclusion 151

value on, a 'circulation' unprecedented in history. The 'new mobilities paradigm' solicits the study of the not-only-human 'flows' rather than the 'structures' which underpin relations among social actors (Büscher et al. 2010; Sheller 2014).

Urry draws on the notions set out in his celebrated book co-authored with Scott Lash on the end of 'organized capitalism' (Lash and Urry 1987) to relate the post-industrial and post-Fordist transformations of the economy to, on the one hand, the dispersion and internationalization of production and consumption strategies, and on the other, the loss of sovereignty by nation states (but see also Sassen 2006). Such a change in the organization of the economy, and to a lesser extent, in the political sphere, brings about unstable and fluctuating social relationships. This conclusion has been nuanced but substantially shared by prominent end-of-century social theorists (Giddens 1990, 1999; Beck 1997; Bauman 1998). In particular, it resonates with Castells' (2000) interpretation of social change, according to which the specificity of globalization consists in the transformation of late-modern society into a 'network society'. Multiple, dynamic and potentially infinite connections, which find in the Internet both a metaphor and the technological basis for their development, increasingly inform the organization of social life. In this scenario, it is not the structure that defines the relations, but rather the relations that define the structure: networks are formed, deformed and constantly reformed according to the interactions among their nodes – that is, the actors (see also Latour 2007).

Given these premises, Urry's 'mobility turn' suggests a classification of the 'forms of mobility' that substantiate social life in late modernity: 'corporeal journeys', 'physical movements of objects', 'imaginary journeys' (through the *passive* perceptions of the media), 'virtual journeys' (through *active* interactions with distant places) and 'communicative journeys' (through personal exchanges of letters, telephone and Internet calls, texts, emails, conversations in chat rooms) (Urry 2007, 47). These mobilities, Urry emphasizes, are interconnected: they trigger and generate each other. Hence, virtual interactions in particular fuel the desire for face-to-face contact rather than substituting it. The result is an exponential growth of the different types of movement, and therefore also of individuals' movements in space, with very different forms and purposes. At the micro level, the changes just described affect 'human extensibility' (Janelle 1973) and reshape the scope of individuals' experience of physical space.

To grasp this phenomenon concisely, I introduce here the concept of 'space-set'.[9] A 'space-set' can be defined as the complex of geographical sites where individuals spend their social existence. This concept is patterned after Robert Merton's notions of 'status-set' and 'role-set' to refer to the array of statuses and roles that a person holds (Merton 1968, 422).[10] The only difference is that while status-sets change as people shift social positions (for instance, by changing jobs), space-sets are formed by spatial contexts that are not occupied at the moment and are not constantly accessible in everyday life because of travel constraints. A space-set is the outcome of an individual's spatial career, stemming from *present* and *past* practices, unified by remembering one's presence in a geographical place. In this sense, inasmuch as it includes a career-like personal history of significant places, a space-set differs from Doreen Massey's 'activity space' defined as 'the spatial network of links and activities, of spatial connections and locations, within which a particular agent operates' (Massey 1995, 54). Space-sets do not depend on current actions only; rather, they can be conceived as personal maps of the physically experienced world.[11] They can also be depicted as ego-centred networks, in which the points are not other people but significant places people have been to.

As in social network analysis, the *size, range* and *salience* of space-sets vary dramatically across time, space and social strata. All three properties need be considered. *Size* is an objective measure: it measures the number of places where individuals have physically been in their lives (the scale of measurement may be more or less fine-tuned: by neighbourhood, city, county, state, etc.). *Range* captures the geographical width of space-sets – typically, the distance between the furthest places that form it. Extreme cases are people who are familiar with many highly spatially concentrated places (for example, within a single county) and people who only mention two very distant localities (like traditional transatlantic migrants). *Salience*, finally, is subjectively defined. Different parts of a space-set are ordered by the intensity of the individual's ties with each of them: the place where one lives or was raised is usually prominent, while sites where one has travelled occasionally are kept in the periphery of personal maps. More precisely, the salience of space-sets can be analytically distinguished into two subdimensions: the average *strength* of the subjective attachment to places and their degree of *centralization*, which depends on the difference in the level of attachment to such places.

These dimensions of an individual's space-set lend themselves well to empirical research – via both survey data and content-analytical tools (interviews, diaries, life histories). They should help social scientists make sense of the sweeping fact that mobility is on the rise: in particular, by examining the social stratification of movements and the differential control of space across social classes. Geographical mobility can be an outcome but also a relevant source of social differentiation. Space-sets constitute a form of capital, partly cultural (entailing 'spatial competence', which in turn engenders 'motility': Kaufmann et al. 2004; Kellerman 2012) and partly social (as a means to gain access to other capitals). As such, they need to be factored in when accounting for status attainment processes. Existing research on social stratification, in fact, is almost entirely silent on how they affect individual life chances (for exceptions, see Berger and Weiss 2008; Ohnmacht et al. 2009).

The cultural effects of mobility experiences are equally worth exploring. Is mobility polarizing societies along some revised version of the classic 'local/cosmopolitan' divide (Gouldner 1957, 1958; Merton 1968, 368 ff.)? Does this divide overlap with the 'integration/demarcation' cleavage that, according to Kriesi et al. (2008, 2012), separates the 'winners' and 'losers' of globalization? Are different mobility patterns across social groups reflected in an emerging 'cosmopolitanism/sovereigntism' ideological struggle that, around the theme of the permeability of nation-state borders, is supplanting the traditionalism/libertarianism dialectic in advanced societies (Azmanova 2011)?

None of these questions can be properly answered for the time being. Since this conceptual framework is novel, consistent data on space-sets have not yet been generated. But while we lack a map of the space-sets of individuals that articulates the social impact of enhanced geographical movements, the concept can guide the logical next research step in the sociological study of human mobility in the contemporary age. For not everybody wants to move, and not everybody can move, even when they want to. If some frontiers have disappeared, as has exceptionally occurred in Europe, others have been strengthened and adapted – consider only the persisting capacity of authoritarian regimes to shield physical travel, telecommunications and Internet access within and across their borders in the face of a too hastily presumed 'flat' world.

In this light, the possibility of cross-national free movement with citizenship rights granted by the EU stands out as a real and undisputed achievement – one of the few – of European integration. But it would be a mistake to take it as an established status quo that cannot be attacked, curtailed or reversed for good – especially in times of mounting uncertainties. Seldom does history unfold linearly. And like all freedoms, freedom of movement is not exempt from the risk of 'escape' (Fromm 1968) when the future grows bleak and anxieties loom large.

Methodological Appendix

1. The Pioneur research data

The Pioneur research project (full title: Pioneers of European Integration 'From Below': Mobility and the Emergence of European Identity Among National and Foreign Citizens in the EU) was conducted between 2003 and 2006 as part of the Fifth Framework Programme of the European Commission, which financed it (contract: HPSE-CT-2002-00128). Five national research units participated in the project: CIUSPO (University of Florence, lead unit, coordinator: Ettore Recchi), OBETS (University of Alicante, coordinator: Antonio Alaminos), ZUMA (Mannheim, coordinator: Michael Braun), CEVIPOF (Sciences Po, Paris, coordinator: Anne Muxel) and CSLS (University of Oxford, coordinator: Damian Tambini). The project explored the dynamics of European integration in light of the experiences of mobile European citizens. At the empirical level, both qualitative and quantitative data were collected. The qualitative data were gathered by semi-structured interviews with 40 West-European citizens resident in the countries covered by the survey (Italy, Spain, Germany, France and the UK: the five largest countries of the EU15) and 40 Poles and Romanians already present in those countries in the autumn of 2004. An analysis of this latter set of interviews is in Favell and Nebe (2009). The quantitative data were collected in 2004 (specifically between May 2004 and January 2005), through the European Internal Movers Social Survey (EIMSS). This survey consists of 5,000 interviews carried out via a structured questionnaire administered by telephone in the respondent's mother tongue using Computer Assisted Telephone Interviews (CATI). One thousand interviews were conducted in each country. They were equally divided among the following nationalities of Europeans movers: Italian, Spanish, French, German and English (obviously excluding the nationality of the country in which the interview was being conducted).[1]

The questionnaire was constructed by drawing on principal international social surveys (such as the International Social Survey Programme, the Eurobarometer and the European Social Survey) and the replies collected by the qualitative survey, endeavouring to ensure the maximum possible comparability with those surveys. The English text of the questionnaire can be consulted in Recchi and Favell (2009, 255 ff.).

The sampling procedure was particularly complex. An innovative procedure called the 'onomastic method' was used, which preserved the random nature of the sampling while at the same time minimizing the costs of retrieving a small segment of the population (Santacreu et al. 2006). The starting point was each country's telephone directory. Surnames and names were ordered according to their frequency in the directory, each being assigned a decreasing probability value. In Italy, for example, Rossi, Bianchi and Verdi, on the one hand, and Giovanni, Giuseppe and Maria, on the other, were classified as having a 'high probability of Italianness'. This information was then used to select the names of persons to be randomly extracted from the telephone directories of the other countries as potential subjects of interviews with Italians living abroad. This method did not entirely eliminate the risk of false positives (consider the many descendants of Italian emigrants to France), and it was necessary to discard the intra-EU migrants with more unusual ethnic backgrounds (for example, Italian citizens who have the surnames of foreign forebears) or ones belonging to linguistic minorities (such as migrants from Alto Adige). But this seemed an acceptable cost compared with those of alternative strategies like snowball sampling, or the use of lists compiled by consulates and associations, which are notoriously incomplete and biased. To be borne in mind is that mobile Europeans, precisely because of the rights granted to them by European citizenship, are not enrolled on consular registers or present in other institutional records. They constitute a population particularly difficult to reach; indeed, they are sometimes entirely invisible.

Finally to be specified is that the interviewees had to fulfil the following criteria: majority age at the time of migration, migration between 1974 and 2003 and residence in the country of the interview for at least one year. Further methodological details are available in Braun and Santacreu (2009).

2. The Moveact research data

The Moveact research project (full title: 'All Citizens Now': Intra-EU Mobility and Political Participation of British, Germans, Poles and Romanians in Western and Southern Europe) was conducted between 2011 and 2013 as part of the Fundamental Rights and Citizenship Programme of the Directorate-General for Justice, Fundamental Rights and Citizenship of the European Commission, which financed it (contract: JUST/2010/FRAC/AG/1186-30-CE-0377115/00-16). The research was coordinated by the 'G. d'Annunzio' University of Chieti-Pescara (coordinator: Ettore Recchi), and the partners were the Hellenic Foundation for European and Foreign Policy (ELIAMEP, Athens, coordinator: Anna Triandafyllidou), the University of Alicante (coordinator: Antonio Alaminos), the François Rabelais University of Tours (coordinator: Sylvie Strudel) and the Centro Europeo di Ricerche e Studi Sociali of Florence (CEURISS, coordinator: Valentina Bettin).

The objective of the Moveact project was to analyse the knowledge, awareness and effective use of citizenship rights by mobile European citizens. The project focused on British, German, Polish and Romanian citizens resident in Greece, France, Italy and Spain. The choice of countries was determined with the intention to select destinations equally attractive to intra-EU migrants from the 'old' and 'new' Europe (Triandafyllidou 2006; Recchi and Triandafyllidou 2010). The nationalities selected were the two most numerous among Western Europeans (German and British) and among Central-Eastern Europeans (Polish and Romanian).

The study used both qualitative and quantitative data-collection techniques. Fieldwork included:

1 The Moveact telephone survey (2,000 interviews);
2 A mapping of mobile European citizen associations, integrated with interviews conducted by telèphone and/or email in order to collect systematic

information on each association (for a total of 194 associations in the four countries);
3 Forty-eight in-depth interviews (12 per country) with politically and socially active EU movers.

This book has mainly used data from the telephone survey, which covered a sample of 500 mobile citizens in each country, 125 per nationality. The survey was conducted in the four countries between November 2011 and March 2012 with the same sampling and case-selection criteria successfully used by the EIMSS. To be noted is that other sampling options were tested in a preliminary phase, especially in view of the difficulty of extracting a random sample from landline telephone directories, as well as the spread in recent years of cell phones and alternatives to landlines for high-speed internet connection. Bias risks were probably even greater in the case of the population covered by the survey precisely because of its mobility. Initially, use was made of the Skype VoIP phone service as a possible option to construct the sample and administer the questionnaire. A search was carried out to collect the most common names and surnames of movers of the four nationalities – according to the Skype search mask – resident in the four countries subject to the research. The persons thus identified were sent an invitation to take part in the survey. The invitation included a link to an online questionnaire, together with the project's webpage address if further information was required. As a variant, the message asked the recipient if s/he was willing to be interviewed via Skype, and if so, to arrange an appointment with the interviewer. A total of 400 invitation messages were sent. However, with both strategies, the percentage of replies was very low (less than 5 per cent).Therefore, the option of online panels – lists of individuals, already profiled on the basis of a series of characteristics, who have given their permission to be contacted for the purpose of answering questionnaires and surveys – was considered. These are widely used in marketing research, and they are beginning to be employed in social research as well. However, it turned out that the main national companies and multinationals active in the field did not subdivide their panels by nationality.

After these alternatives had been explored, the onomastic method applied to telephone directories once again – like in the EIMSS of 2004 – proved to be the most effective. Probably, in 2011, given the above-mentioned innovations in communication technologies, use of this method reduced the presence in the sample of more recently settled movers, but this was in any case consistent with the aim of the study, which was not targeted at people with temporary or volatile mobility like seasonal workers or Erasmus students.

The interviews were conducted on the basis of a standardized questionnaire which combined questions from the Eurobarometer, the European Social Survey and the European Internal Movers' Social Survey, the purpose being to maximize opportunities for comparison. The interviews were administered by bilingual interviewers, so that the interviewees could answer in their mother tongue (the option most frequently chosen) or in the language of the country of residence. In all the countries, the overrepresentation of women and elderly persons – due to the greater ease of finding these two social categories at home – required the sample to be rebalanced by means of snowball sampling, which generated ten per cent of the cases included in the final dataset.

Notes

Preface and Acknowledgements

1 This proportion refers to *currently* non-national EU citizens residing in EU member states, with some minor oscillations over time (see Chapter 3). In fact, the share of EU citizens who have ever lived in another European country is definitely higher. On the basis of a question in Eurobarometer 73.3, it can be estimated that 16.8 per cent of EU citizens have spent 'three or more *consecutive* months' of their life in another country. Most likely, the great majority of them did so in another EU member state.

2 In this book I shall use the terms 'EU movers' and 'EU stayers' consistently with the terminology of studies on *internal* migration which distinguish between 'movers' and 'stayers' in analogy with the 'immigrants' versus 'natives' distinction used in studies on *international* migrations (see Borjas 2001, 34).

3 On the Pioneer and Moveact projects, see the Methodological Appendix. The Eucross project (The Europeanisation of Everyday Life: Cross-Border Practices and Transnational Identifications Among EU and Third-Country Citizens) has been funded by the European Commission as part of the Seventh Framework Programme (contract 266767). The aim of the project is to map the individual transnational practices fostered by European integration and globalization – that is, the experiences of foreign countries which Europeans gain from physical or virtual mobility (see www.eucross.eu).

Introduction – Between Individualization and Globalization: The Long-Term Premises to Free Movement

1 The text of the question asked by the Eurobarometer at varying time intervals is: 'Which of the following statements best describe(s) what the European Union means to you personally?' Between 2003 and 2012 the question was put 15 times, and 'freedom to travel' was invariably the preferred item (with percentages ranging from 41 to 53).

2 It is also true that the early-modern meaning of freedom applies primarily to 'freedom of movement' out of feudal obligations to land labour. As has been noted, 'the very process of individualization in the modern sense begins when traditional social ties become weakened and the individual is "released" from those ties through the possibility of "going anywhere": individuality, this typically Western modern concept, was born *as* a form of mobility' (Mubi Brighenti 2012, 403).

3 The final generation of rights for which there is growing demand for recognition comprises the rights of animal species other than *homo sapiens*. Mobilization and claim-making for these rights are growing substantially throughout the world in recent decades (Pocar 2005).

4 Logically, enjoyment of 'frontierless' rights presupposes the right 'to cross borders' – that is, a universal right to *im*migration specular to the right to *out*migration enshrined in the Universal Declaration of Human Rights at article 13.2. What is the ethical status of this right (Barry and Goodin 1992; Bader 2005)? Some political philosophers have argued that it is a 'primary right', restrictions on which are not morally justifiable (Carens 1987, 1992; Shachar and Hirschl 2007). By contrast, others have defended the legitimacy of border controls as serving to protect a common good (Walzer 1983, ch. 2; see also Engelen 2003). For a discussion of the unintended effects of a world completely without frontiers, see Bauböck (2009), who proposes a 'stakeholder criterion' to immigration claims of non-citizens. Albeit from a position favourable to a universal right to mobility, Pécoud and De Guchteneire (2007a) and Wihtol de Wenden (2014) furnish good overviews of the debate and try to assess the economic, political and social consequences of an open-borders world. Incidentally, the philosophical–political literature on free global movement has burgeoned simultaneously with the introduction of European citizenship, perceived as a pioneering advance towards a possible cosmopolitan order.

5 However, subsequently Joppke (2007) admitted that there is increasing convergence among national policies concerning the integration of immigrants in Europe.

6 Exemplary in this regard is Germany, where immigrant communities and their defenders campaigned for decades to obtain the de-ethnicization of the law on naturalization, which was eventually achieved in 2000.

7 These figures result from a search conducted using www.scholar.google.com on 6 July 2012. It may be that the amounts for the earliest years are underestimated, owing to the smaller coverage of publications from those years by the Google database.

8 One of the most controversial issues in defining globalization concerns the part played by the subjective dimension – the 'awareness of globality' emphasized by some of the first sociologists to deal with the topic (Robertson 1992). Without denying the importance of the social representation of globalization, I nevertheless believe that it should be kept analytically distinct from the structural component.

9 To be precise, the globalization indices have been calculated using only the core subset of KOF indicators. For the economic component, therefore, the index uses the indicators relative to 'economic flows': foreign trade, the stock of direct foreign investments (FDIs), foreign financial investments and payments to resident foreign nationals (all these variables expressed as proportions of the GDP), while the indicators relative to 'restrictive foreign trade policies' are omitted. For the social component, the index employed includes indicators relative to 'personal transnational contacts': international telephone traffic (minutes per person), international correspondence (per capita), the number of foreign tourists (in proportion to residents), the resident foreign population (as a proportion of residents) and remittances by foreign residents (as a proportion of GDP), while the indicators relative to 'information flows' (for example, Internet traffic) and 'cultural proximity' (which in fact measures 'Westernization' with indicators such as the presence of McDonald's and IKEA) are omitted.

10 What is the relationship between Europeanization and globalization? According to Wallace (2000), the European single market is a 'regional variant' of globalization. Likewise, but citing more extensive transformation dynamics, Delanty and Rumford (2005, 5) maintain that the EU, 'despite its power of regulation', participates in a process of global change which transcends it. In a similar vein, Castells (2000, 348) argues that European integration is simultaneously a form of globalization and a reaction to its indiscriminate extension. Fligstein and Mérand (2002; see also Fligstein 2011), by contrast, contend that the institutionally regulated nature of Europeanization radically differentiates it from globalization in that the latter is not politically controlled. As Beckfield (2006, 966) puts it, they are 'alternative *forms* of international embeddedness'. For a discussion attentive to the sociological dimension of Europeanization, see Favell et al. (2011, 8–13).

1 A Frontierless Continent: History of an Idea and Its Realization

1 Although on a much smaller scale, perhaps the only precedent is the creation of the Swiss Confederation. On the political history of Switzerland and its nationalism, see Zimmer (2003). For an original comparison with the process of European integration, see Blondel (1998).
2 To be precise, the right to free movement is not entirely unconditional. After three months of stay, EU movers are required not to be an 'unreasonable burden on the social assistance system of the host Member State during their period of residence and have comprehensive sickness insurance cover in the host Member State' (Directive 2004/38, article 7.b). Moreover, 'Member States may restrict the freedom of movement and residence of Union citizens and their family members, irrespective of nationality, on grounds of public policy, public security or public health' (article 27), if justified by 'the personal conduct of the individual concerned' and taking into account the 'principle of proportionality' and the level of integration of the individual in the host country (article 28).
3 The legal literature on the right to free movement in the EU is abundant and detailed, especially in regard to the impact of the Court of Justice's case-law on its evolution. Among others, see Martin and Guild (1996), O'Leary (1996), O'Keeffe (1998), Wiener (1998), Weiss and Wooldridge (2002), van der Mei (2003), Guild (2004), Rogers and Scannell (2005), Carlier and Guild (2006), Giubboni and Orlandini (2007), Barnard (2007, part three) and Blome et al. (2012). Updates and comments on upcoming cases can be found at www. europeanlawblog.eu (especially in the sections on citizenship and freedom of movement of persons).
4 This applies only to persons who hold European citizenship; differences deteriorate into social inequalities in the case of migrants from third countries (Geddes 2003; Recchi and Baldoni 2005). Among the latter, however, the citizens of countries that have signed a treaty of association with the EU (such as Turkey, Morocco, Algeria and Tunisia), thanks to extensive interpretations by the European Court of Justice, enjoy a status which closely resembles that of European citizens (see Joppke 2010b, 27).

5 The complete text of this essay is available at www.altierospinelli.org (accessed on 19 August 2011).
6 On a smaller scale, in those same years, the right to free movement was introduced in the Benelux with the 1953 Hague Protocol on coordination of the economic and social policies of Belgium, Netherlands and Luxembourg; in Scandinavia with creation of the Common Nordic Labour Market among Denmark, Sweden, Norway and Finland; in the Western European Union (France, Netherlands, Belgium, Luxembourg and the United Kingdom) with a series of conventions which between 1949 and 1954 introduced a free movement regime. The right to travel without a passport among Great Britain, Ireland and the Channel Islands (the Common Travel Area) was introduced in 1922.
7 According to Romero (2001, 403–4), in the immediate post-war period among Italian political leaders, and especially for De Gasperi, 'the search for migratory outlets was the central paradigm of a vision of European interdependence and integration'.
8 As in the case, for example, of the agreements reached between Germany and Portugal in 1964 and between Germany and Yugoslavia in 1968.
9 In this specific case, by 'material dimension' of citizenship is meant the capacity for individual action in the social context which, through the combined use of personal qualities and capital on the one hand, and the resources made available by political institutions on the other, can generate social inclusion in the absence of its 'formal dimension' (that is, the status of citizen) (Baglioni 2009, 44–5).
10 Nevertheless, the controversial position of posted workers (that is, workers temporarily sent abroad by their employers) was clarified only twenty years later with Directive 96/71, according to 'a rule which had the merit of simplicity: the laws of the host country were applied, but the worker maintained the superior protection afforded by those of the state of origin' (Giubboni and Orlandini 2007, 114; see also Cremers 2013).
11 This last category included all persons without access to freedom of intra-European movement by other means.
12 From June 2007 onwards, the new text was drafted by the Intergovernmental Conference and received official approval at the Lisbon Council of December 2007. It was a scaled-down version of the Constitution which, even though it made no reference to its nature as a founding act, incorporated large part of the measures and innovations proposed by the Convention. Thus relinquished was the ideal objective of the original constitutional text but not the substantial one. Given the experience of the previous failures, the document drafted to replace the European Constitution was submitted for approval by member state parliaments so that it would not be necessary to resort to perilous consultative referenda. Ratification of the new text was initially obstructed when it was rejected by the June 2008 referendum held in Ireland – the only country to conduct a confirmatory referendum – but the process resumed after the favourable vote cast in the repeated Irish referendum of October 2009. Ratified in November, on 1 December 2009, the treaty for reforming the EU, which was agreed upon in Lisbon two years earlier, finally came into effect.

13 The directive clarified that the rights conferred extend to the citizen's co-resident family members even if they are third-country nationals (except for possession of a short-term visa in the case of residence for less than three months, when the host state requires it). The directive also specifies those family members who have an automatic right of entry and residence and those whose entry must instead only be 'facilitated' (on this see Barnard 2007, 416 ff.).

14 In 2008, the European Commission presented a report to the Parliament and Council on the transposition of the Directive into national legislations (COM/2008/0840). The conclusions leave little doubt as to the reluctance of the member states to comply with EU law: 'Communication by Member States of national implementing measures was incomplete and late in a large number of cases. Between June 2006 and February 2007 the Commission initiated infringement proceedings under Article 226 of the EC Treaty against 19 Member States for their failure to communicate the text of the provisions of national law adopted to transpose the Directive. Since then, as all Member States have gradually adopted the transposition measures, the infringement proceedings for non-communication have been closed [. . .] The overall transposition of Directive 2004/38/EC is rather disappointing. Not one Member State has transposed the Directive effectively and correctly in its entirety. Not one Article of the Directive has been transposed effectively and correctly by all Member States.' On the particularly problematic implementation of the directive in the UK, see Shaw and Miller (2012).

15 The extent and nature of access by mobile Europeans to the welfare systems of the EU member states is a delicate and constantly changing issue which concerns not harmonization but, more limitedly, the coordination of national measures (whose basis is Regulation EC 883/2004). As Giubboni and Orlandini point out (2007, 140), 'The coordination of national social security regimes constitutes [. . .] one of the most extensive and complex bodies of EC law, a matter of sophisticated specialist knowledge and the result of periodic stratifications and recodifications.'

16 A less spectacular but not insignificant enlargement involves Switzerland, since Swiss nationals and their family members can benefit from the free movement regime in accordance with the Agreement of 21 June 1999 between the Swiss Confederation and the EU (curbed in 2013, see below). The EEA agreement (article 28) grants free movement rights to employees and self-employed persons from and to Norway, Iceland and Liechtenstein as well.

17 Less vocally, passport and ID checks are occasionally reinstated, in breach of Schengen rules, at particular internal borders, as EU citizens themselves can and do denounce at an *ad hoc* website: https://freemovement.net

2 Why Free Movement? Assessing Policies and Rationales

1 The figure refers to the 2011–2012 academic year (European Commission 2013).
2 European Commission decision 93/569/EEC of 22 October 1993.

3   Curiously, and somewhat clumsily, the EURES website does not have its own web address but instead a secondary address at the EU portal (http://ec.europa.eu/EURES). The domains www.EURES.org, www.EURES.net and www.EURES.com have been adroitly registered by third parties and put on sale (the last website also states the asking price: $112,180, consulted on 30 August 2014).

4   The portal includes a database on 'Living and Working' which provides information on everyday issues in another EU member state (finding accommodation or a school, taxes, cost of living, health, social legislation or comparability of qualifications). The 'Labour Market Information' section contains information by country, region and sector of activity on trends in the European labour market. Other information is available from the 'Events Calendar'. The 'Learning' section draws on the PLOTEUS portal (Portal on Learning Opportunities Throughout Europe). Created by the Directorate General for Education and Culture of the European Commission and updated by the Euroguidance network, PLOTEUS highlights the opportunities for study available, and also provides information on learning opportunities, exchange programmes and grants, national education systems and transfer to another EU member state.

5   For instance, on 21 April 2013 there were 1,413,787 job vacancies, 1,103,283 CVs and 30,537 employers registered.

6   The cross-border partnerships currently in effect are EURES Channel (which involves Belgium, France and the UK), Scheldemond (Belgium and the Netherlands), EURES Triregio (Czech Republic, Germany and Poland), EURES Maas-Rhin (Belgium, Germany and the Netherlands), PED (Belgium, France and Luxembourg), Saar-Lor-Lux-Rheinland Pfalz (Germany, France and Luxembourg), Bayern-Tschechien (Germany and Czech Republic), EURES Cross Border Denmark–Germany (Germany and Denmark), Euregio Rhein-Waal (Germany and the Netherlands), Danubius (Slovakia and Hungary), Pannonia (Hungary and Austria), Northern Ireland–Ireland (Ireland and the UK), Trans Tirolia (Italy, Austria and Switzerland), Øresund (Denmark and Sweden), Galicia-Região Norte (Spain and Portugal), Oberrhein (France, Germany and Switzerland), Euradria (Italy and Slovenia) and EURES-T Beskydy (Czech Republic, Poland and Slovakia).

7   The Schengen Information System (SIS) consists of a computerized database which stores and shares information on foreign citizens, asylum seekers, criminals and individuals under surveillance. Its purpose is to furnish information to consular and police authorities on suspect persons, and on lost or stolen goods. It is a tool for information and investigation made necessary by the opening of internal borders, aiming at closer international cooperation among the law enforcement agencies of the member states. Implementation of the SIS has gone through various stages, constituting a sort of Hobbesian counterpoint to the increase in freedom of movement. It contains identity photographs, fingerprints and sensitive data of various kinds (car number plates, DNA), geared to combating illegal immigration, terrorism and international crime. Its accessibility to European police forces has been gradually extended (Broeders 2009). 'Basically, if a person is registered, (s)he will be denied entry at one of the 1792 official border-crossing points. In 2006, the number of people registered in the data bank was 751,954. [In that year,] about 4 people in 1000 were denied entry' (Mau et al. 2012, 137).

8 Although they belong to the SIS, the UK and Ireland are not included in the Schengen area and keep their own area of free transit. Cyprus, Romania, Bulgaria and Croatia are committed to joining the Schengen area at some point, but only after the green light of the European Parliament and the European Council.
9 A major controversy was raised in 2009 when Slovakia apparently resorted to this clause to ban the entry of the Hungarian president, who was supposed to inaugurate a statue of Saint Stephen of Hungary on Slovakian territory. The event was unfortunately planned on the anniversary of the invasion of Czechoslovakia of 1968, in which Hungarian troops took part, possibly leading to public protests and demonstrations. Hungary brought the case to the ECJ, but the plea was dismissed on the ground that international law imposes EU member states to protect foreign heads of state when visiting their country. In this sense, international law may create a limitation to the free movement rights of top political office-holders unknown to ordinary citizens (for a legal discussion, see www.europeanlawblog.eu/?p=1084, consulted on 12 June 2014).
10 Persons wishing to visit a member state of the Schengen area must apply for a visa at the embassy or consulate of that state. However, this obligation applies only to the third-country citizens mentioned in European Council Regulation 539 of 15 March 2001.
11 In exceptional cases, visitors who do not fulfil the common entry conditions are issued with a visa valid solely for the member state concerned. These exceptions are made for humanitarian reasons, in compliance with international obligations, or for national interest.
12 Although mobility is the central pillar of Erasmus, the programme devotes one-fifth of its funds to further initiatives to support the European space of higher education. It fosters the creation of study programmes which are followed in different countries and which lead to joint or at least equivalent qualifications. It contributes to the creation of virtual campuses based on new communication technologies. And it promotes joint initiatives by universities of different countries for organizing courses on topics of common interest.
13 The Socrates Programme is divided into eight chapters. The first three correspond to the various stages of the education process: Comenius (school education); Erasmus (university education); Grundtvig (adult education). The remaining five chapters are more diverse in content: Language (the teaching and learning of European languages); Minerva (open and distance learning, and information and communication technologies); Joint Actions (coordination of activities between Socrates and other European programmes); Observation and Innovation (education policies and systems); Accompanying Measures (awareness raising, information, dissemination and training).
14 The *Lifelong Learning Programme* gathered all European cooperation initiatives in education and training for the period from 2007 to 2013, integrating previous programmes into a single framework. From 2014 to 2020, in turn, it has been replaced by the Erasmus + Programme.
15 Long before contemporary social theorists, such as Habermas (2003), Bauman (2006) and Beck and Grande (2004, 2007), or intellectuals like Vaclav Havel

(1998), this argument had a passionate and tragic herald in Stefan Zweig between the two World Wars (Zweig 2014).

16 On the basis of Eurobarometer data collected from a sample of young adults, Fertig and Schmidt (2002) report that interviewees with unemployed parents were significantly less willing to work in another European country than were their peers. Apparently, the costs of migration were still regarded as too onerous by a population that instead, in theory, should be prone to mobility.

17 A parallel question is whether intra-EU migration helps reduce the effects of unemployment and favours economic convergence among European regions. In other words, does migration from the poorer areas of the EU enable them to catch up with the economically wealthier regions? The empirical results are contradictory (for a survey see Janiak and Wasmer 2008, 12 ff.). Faini (2003) found a significant association between mobility and convergence among European regions (at the Nuts2 level) in the 1980s, but not in the 1990s. He reached the conclusion that 'mobility is not an unmitigated blessing': its virtuous effects are conditional on the removal of country-based labour market distortions like the creation of 'public sector jobs to compensate for the employment depressing impact of unionized wages' (ibid., 7).

18 For a more detailed treatment of the economic virtues of human capital density see Glaeser (2000) and Carlino et al. (2005), who maintain that this variable can explain why high-technology industries benefit from proximity to universities and other research centres. The most striking examples in the USA are Silicon Valley and the Boston area. In Europe, however, although there are close links between certain Nuts3 areas with high innovation rates and the presence of universities, significant exceptions exist: in Germany and in Italy, for example, the coincidence between scientific institutions and local areas of marked technological development is very low (Zitt et al. 2003).

3 EU Movers: How Many Are There, Where Are They, What Do They Do?

1 The flows from Italy to Central-Northern Europe peaked in 1961, when almost 350,000 people departed (Recchi 2005, 8). Thereafter, however, the numbers progressively decreased as internal migration to the industrial areas of Northern Italy replaced international migration.

2 In the UK, for instance, in 1978, 51,000 new residence permits were granted to foreigners, among whom only 8,000 were citizens of other EEC member states, while immigrants from former Commonwealth countries amounted to 32,000 (Lebon and Falchi 1980, 579).

3 Posted workers are registered via A1 (formerly E101) forms, which guarantee them health and social security coverage in the host country. On the basis of these forms, it is calculated that in 2011 European enterprises sent around 1,200,000 people to work in another EU member state. Compared to 2009, this represents about a 20 per cent increase. Germany is the country hosting by far the largest number (311,000), with France coming second with about half that number (162,000). The majority of these posted workers (228,000) are of Polish nationality (European Commission 2011a, 257; Maslauskaite 2014).

4   Although I am aware that EU15 does not coincide with Western Europe, nor the countries which joined the Union in the 2000s with Eastern Europe, for the sake of brevity I shall sometimes refer to citizens of the former group of countries as 'Western Europeans' and to citizens of the latter group of countries as 'Eastern Europeans'.
5   All the statistics presented here define immigrants in terms of citizenship, that is, as 'foreigners'. It should be specified that in the literature, due to a tradition predominant in the English-speaking countries, it is equally common to come across figures which instead adopt the criterion of the country of birth, so that immigrants are persons born in a country different from the one in which they reside.
6   Well-known is the glaring error in a report compiled for the UK Home Office in 2003, which, on the basis of econometric estimates, predicted that 'net immigration from the AC-10 to the UK after the current enlargement of the EU will be relatively small, at between 5,000 and 13,000 immigrants per year up to 2010' (Dustmann et al. 2003, 59). It is fair to say, though, that such estimates assumed that the same entry conditions were adopted by all EU15 member states, which eventually was not the case.
7   To be noted among Western Europeans, however, is the case of the Portuguese, who have a long migratory tradition. Even in 2011 there were 993,000 Portuguese living in another country of the EU, corresponding to 9.7 per cent of the Portuguese population. Also numerically conspicuous is the Italian diaspora in Europe, which comprises 1,278,000 people (2.2 per cent of the Italian population).
8   For example, in 2001 the Romanians and Poles legally resident in Italy following the regularization amnesties of the previous years already amounted to almost one-third of the intra-EU migrants in the country.
9   Bonifazi (2009) has estimated that the incidence of immigrants in Italy's resident population between 1992 and 2009 was larger than that recorded even in the 'golden' period of post-war migration to Germany (between 1955 and 1972). Obviously, in both cases the figures include European and non-European migrants in unequal but probably similar proportions (especially in the second halves of the periods considered).
10 In the international classification of occupations proposed by the ILO (ISCO-88), 'elementary occupations' (major group 9 of the classification) comprise the lowest-level manual occupations performed by workers with minimal skills, such as cleaners, doorkeepers, transport workers or builders (see http://www.ilo.org/public/english/bureau/stat/isco/isco88/publ4.htm).
11 Existing studies also show that intra-EU migrants tend to perform better than third-country nationals in the Western European labour markets. Compared with native workers, however, they are penalized, especially in Southern Europe (Bernardi et al. 2011; Reyneri and Fullin 2011a, 2011b).
12 This result holds at the aggregate level, distinguishing between countries of the 2004 and 2007 enlargements. The employment rate of EU15 movers is equal to that of the stayers.
13 Data on flows confirm this picture for the whole of the EU. Recchi and Salamońska (2015) show that outflows of nationals from troubled countries of Western Europe have been, overall, on par with those from more prosperous economies. Most strikingly, the number of Germans who decided to leave

their homeland increased by 9.3 per cent between 2006 and 2011 – twice as large as the increase of Spaniards (4.8 per cent) and Italians (4.5 per cent).

4 'Old' and 'New' EU Movers: Integration Pathways Compared

1. The characteristics of the survey and the sampling procedures are described in detail in the methodological appendix.
2. A notable exception is Braun and Glöckner-Rist (2011), which, however, adopts a different analytical strategy to assess the degree of denationalization of integration patterns of EU movers in distinct countries of residence. In this regard, Britain is found to provide the most fertile ground for mixed friendship networks and partner choices.
3. A previous version of this section, but limited to the analysis of EIMSS data, is in Braun and Recchi (2009).
4. Notoriously, there are two ways of interpreting factors in multiple correspondence analysis: 'factorial', which focuses on the absolute most important contributions, and 'geometric-structural', which mainly analyses relative distances (Le Roux and Rouanet 2010).
5. Used here is a simplified version of Erikson and Goldthorpe's (1992) schema. It includes (a) service class (entrepreneurs, senior executives, free professionals); (b) white-collar middle class; (c) self-employed middle class (shopkeepers, artisans, self-employed manual workers); (d) skilled and semi-skilled manual workers; (e) unskilled manual workers.
6. In theory, labour-market integration could also comprise the variables used to measure status. Nevertheless, in our case, for the large majority of respondents, education level and class were still those that they possessed on arrival in the CoR.
7. On transnationalization and inequalities see Weiss (2005) and Berger and Weiss (2008).
8. Originally, there were five modalities for the language variable, ranging from 'no knowledge' to 'near mother-tongue competence'. Subsequently, however, the first two and the last two modalities were unified ('no/scant = low', 'good/excellent = high'), while the middle one remained the same.
9. Braun and Recchi (2009) also report an analysis of this set of variables in light of the various periods of migration considered (1974–1983, 1984–1993 and 1994–2003). Put briefly, marked changes emerge in the degree and type of integration of certain nationalities. In the first period, Germans in Spain were very poorly integrated – they did not speak the language, they had no contacts with locals and they did not use the Spanish media. In the second period, but even more so in the third, they were joined by Britons, whose status also diminished over time: retirement migration thus seems to have become more massified. Again, in the first period Italians and Spaniards had very low levels of status and integration in Germany. Only in the third period did Italians, whilst their status remained low, exhibit somewhat stronger integration – so that their position moved towards the centre. The Spaniards fared decidedly better, and in the third period advanced in terms of both status and integration to a level similar to that of the other nationalities.

10   As in the EIMSS survey, moreover, the 'CoO/CoR' variable (or better, the modalities of which it is composed) reproduces the relatively largest amount of total variance.

5   A Sterile Citizenship? Intra-European Mobility and Political Participation

1   These figures are taken from http://www.results-elections2014.eu/en/turnout.html (consulted on 11 August 2014).
2   However, in the same period (spring 2007–spring 2013), the decrease in trust in EU institutions was not matched by growing trust in national parliaments and governments, testifying that the tendency is part of a broader scenario of crisis of democracy in Europe (see http://europa.eu/rapid/press-release_IP-14-543_en.htm, consulted on 11 August 2014).
3   Another view that is sometimes aired in policy-making circles points to 'insufficient marketing': European institutions are little known and their role is misunderstood and thus overlooked. But it seems that this interpretation serves a self-consolatory purpose more than a descriptive one accredited by EU scholars.
4   At the institutional level, the White Paper on European Governance (European Commission 2001) set up a strategy to increase participation by civil society in the formation of EU public policies. In reality, however, the opening up of decision-making processes has mainly involved a European elite of transnational activists. The various projects implemented after the White Paper seemed intended more to build consensus on the European Commission's policies than to foster the development of a European public sphere, and therefore an active citizenship (Raffini 2010, 99 ff.). At the same time, the growth of new opinion movements and the emergence of transnational mobilizations are indicative of the advent of a proactive opposition to the European project. Some authors have perceived this as the basis for Europe's self-constitution from below by citizens who for the first time talk about 'Europe', thus contributing to the formation of a European public sphere (Trenz and Eder 2007; for different aspects, see della Porta and Caiani 2009). Paradoxically, anti-EU neo-nationalist parties may also be part of this trend.
5   The figures for Poland are taken from the ESS of 2010, while those on Romania are from the ESS of 2008.
6   To be noted is that interest in politics in the CoO does not conflict with interest in politics in the CoR. On the contrary, the EU movers interested in politics combine the two interests, and also prove very interested in European politics (for details, see Recchi et al. 2012).
7   The index covers a broad but not exhaustive array of conventional political actions on the basis of the indicators available. Voting in European elections has not been included for methodological reasons (see note 10 of this chapter) and to avoid overrepresentation of voting as a form of participation. The index is calculated by attributing one point to each of the items of which it is composed; it therefore ranges from 0 to 7.
8   Note that in both countries it is possible to vote at consulates. Obviously, this involves logistical problems, considering that it is more difficult to

reach a consulate, which may be hundreds of kilometres from the place of residence, than a neighbourhood polling station. By contrast British and German citizens resident in foreign countries are allowed to vote by post, which to some extent – impossible to estimate – may explain their greater electoral participation (see Ellis et al. 2007).

9 Although on paper European citizens are eligible anywhere regardless of nationality, in 2009 only 81 candidates for the European Parliament were not citizens of the member state in which they stood for election (European Commission 2010, 7).

10 To be precise, the EIMSS survey began in May 2004 and therefore spanned the European Parliament election of that year. This required adjustment of the question on this issue (intention to vote for interviewees before 13 June 2004, actual turnout to vote thereafter). In Spain, the survey was carried out in its entirety before the elections, in Germany almost wholly after them (only 53 interviewees referred to their intention to vote). Altogether, 3,018 cases referred to intention to vote and 1,695 to turnout to vote. Although in general the proportion of respondents who said that they intended to vote was greater than the proportion of those who reported that they had actually done so, the relative distances among nationalities remained constant in the two subsamples.

6 Intra-EU Mobility and European Identity: Towards a Sense of Shared Belonging

1 Studies on European identity by now fill numerous shelves in university libraries. But closer inspection shows that they form a nebulous melange of notions drawn from different disciplines, with the most disparate treatments of their subject. It should therefore be clarified that here European identity is defined as 'a psycho-sociological or socio-political process of citizens' attachment to the European space or to the political community designed by integration' (Duchesne 2010, 7).

2 This linkage between cultural heritage and identity recurs also in the workings of the Council of Europe. A significant example is provided by the 2000 European Landscape Convention, which emphasizes shared European-scale protection of the natural environment (Sassatelli 2009).

3 An earlier version of this section is in Recchi (2014).

4 See Pettigrew (1998) for an overview of this strand of experimental social psychology.

5 For example, in a pioneering work on European identity, Kohli (2000, 117) notes that the sociological study of collective identities 'continues the basic theoretical agenda set by Marx in the domain of class'.

6 Simmel demonstrates the influence of spatial organization on personality in his famous essay on *The Metropolis and Mental Life* (Simmel 1903). The blasé outlook born from the dense and impersonal social interactions typical of the urban environment, however, attests that the connection between space and identity is far from being linear.

7 Here the term 'habitus' is used in Bourdieu's (2000, 138) sense as a set of 'schemes of perception, appreciation and action [which enable social

actors] to perform acts of practical knowledge, based on the identification and recognition of conditional, conventional stimuli to which they are predisposed to react; and, without any explicit definition of ends or rational calculation of means, to generate appropriate and endlessly renewed strategies'. The expression 'concert of interests' instead refers to cooperative processes in line with the theory of rational action. The two options are not incompatible.

8 Curiously enough, existing theorizations of the sources of European identity tend to sideline the issue of the *mechanisms* of collective identification – that is, what I have discussed here. They instead concentrate on sets of sociopolitical antecedents or attitudinal correlates of identity, such as *cognitive mobilization, instrumental rationality, political mobilizations* and *affective orientations*. For a comprehensive review and testing of such perspectives see Bellucci et al. (2012).

9 An exception is the book edited by Checkel (2005), which thoroughly examines the theory of socialization. A more recent study (Risse 2010, 31), which to some extent covers the same ground, treats the concept of socialization in a less well-informed manner. Indeed, it distorts the sociological concept of socialization by confusing it with the frequency of interpersonal contacts.

10 See, for example, Morin (1987), Delanty (1995), Lützeler (1997), Mikkeli (1998), Stråth (2002), Brague (1992) and Eder (2009). Cotesta (2011) provides a classification of the paradigms guiding these studies, which deal with European 'civilization' rather than 'identity'. It should also be pointed out that, although they do not adopt an overtly normative perspective, many of these studies criss-cross the subtle dividing line between description and prescription.

11 This might be taken to suggest that Deutsch was a functionalist, given that, in his view, actions for strategic purposes also have cultural 'spillovers'. His thesis thus relates to Haas's (1958) neo-functionalist theory of European integration. But Deutsch's works also consider the sociopsychological dynamics of learning and adjustment to the norms of the Other, thus linking with Allport's (1954) theory of prejudice. Put briefly, this theory postulates that the intensity of positive interactions among different groups weakens the cognitive distinction between the 'in-group' and the 'out-group' (see also Tajfel 1974). As a consequence, individuals become aware of their commonalities and eventually develop a shared identity (for an application to the European case, see Recchi and Nebe 2003).

12 In the concluding paragraphs of his doctoral thesis, Deutsch already envisaged the possibility of creating higher-order communities in the form of regional blocks (Deutsch 1953, 193).

13 Deutsch (1969, 97) accordingly noted that the 'boundaries are not just lines on a map [. . .] what really makes a *boundary* is a sharp drop in the frequency of some relevant transaction flow'.

14 Another spatial aspect of identity anchorage, in line with Simmel's insights discussed above, has been treated differently by Berezin and Díez Medrano (2008), who show a positive association between proximity to the geographic centre of the EU and support in public opinion for European integration.

15 None of the 2011 Eurobarometers contain the dependent variable common to all the other surveys: the question on 'attachment to Europe'. I therefore had to rely on the survey closest in time able to ensure full comparability:

the Eurobarometer 73.3 of March–April 2010. Moreover, to be precise, in the latter survey the response item was not phrased as 'Europe' but rather as the 'European Union'. This is an unfortunate change which must be factored in, but – also in consideration of the question structure, which is for the rest unaltered – I assume it to be an analogously trustworthy measurement of the European component of identification.

16 This is the well-known 'response set' phenomenon, which, as Marradi observes (2007, 117), 'is a drawback endemic in questionnaires which include batteries'.

17 As Mood (2010) has shown, caution is needed when interpreting parameters of logistic regressions conducted on different samples. As long as it cannot be assumed that unobserved heterogeneity is the same across such samples, effects cannot be compared properly. In this light, the two models examined here (and in following analyses of this chapter) must be read as two parallel takes on the issue rather than a way to gauge changes in the influence of only apparently comparable factors.

18 The only other possible, but not plausible, explanation is that it is due to generation effects determined by the greater sense of belonging to Europe of people who migrated in the distant past.

19 This is one of the many findings of the Eucross Project (www.eucross.eu), a large study on transnationalism whose results are unfortunately still preliminary when the present book goes to press.

20 Moreover, transnationalism proves to be empirically associated with cosmopolitanism (Mau et al. 2008), although the indicators used to operationalize the latter concept are not entirely convincing (Favell et al. 2011).

21 This classification of transnational behaviours according to their intensity seems to be the best one possible given the indicators available in Eurobarometer 73. In theoretical terms, I have elsewhere proposed a more composite classification which rests on a fundamental distinction between transnationalism practices which depend on *physical* mobility (long/brief residence abroad) and *virtual* mobility (personal/impersonal) (Recchi 2012a, 2014). Another classification distinguishes three dimensions of transnationalism relative to background, practices and human capital (Kuhn 2011b, 814–15). The human capital component is not strictly speaking a transnational behaviour, and thus remains outside the present analysis. At the same time, it is evident that knowledge of foreign languages is a *sine qua non* of individual transnationalism whose identitarian consequences deserve closer scrutiny (see Gerhards 2012).

22 Differently from previous models, in this analysis the 'international mobility' variable is not restricted to *current* mobility but also includes past experiences, and it is not limited to movements within the EU but to any possible foreign country. Moreover, the sample is the EU-wide Eurobarometer, and not a case-control combination of two different surveys as before. All this provides an even stronger test of the mobility–supranational identity link.

23 In the logistic regression models estimated previously, by contrast, the number of countries was too small to use hierarchical models (Steenbergen and Jones 2002, 219; see also Steenbergen 2011). Moreover, EU movers and stayers share nationality but not residence: therefore, a common dependence on the context would have been an unrealistic assumption.

24 Previous research, but mostly qualitative and based on small samples, had instead shown that Erasmus students, when interviewed on their return home, declared a particularly deep-rooted European identity which they attributed to the mobility experience (see De Federico de la Rúa 2002; Fernández 2005; Taglioli 2008).

Conclusion – Free Movement in Europe: Epitomizing the Age of Mobility?

1 The EU data are taken from the Eurostat online database. They relate to 2010 (http://appsso.eurostat.ec.europa.eu/nui/submitViewTableAction.do). The American data (again relative to 2010) originate from the Tax Foundation website, which compares the states in which taxpayers have paid federal taxes from one year to the next (http://interactive.taxfoundation.org/migration/). To this absolute figure, I have added an estimate of cross-state migrants among people who do not file income tax returns, assuming an analogous propensity to mobility.
2 A more systematic comparison of US–EU differences is in Martinelli (2007); a particularly concise but sharp parallel is in Hix (2008, 10–12).
3 Interstate mobility in the USA has progressively shrunk since the beginning of the 1990s; indeed, it has been halved in 20 years (see Schachter 2001; Kaplan and Schulhofer-Wohl 2012). Theodos (2009) shows that the same trend is also to be found at the substate level, albeit to a less marked extent. Kaplan and Schulhofer-Wohl (2012) argue that the trend is independent from the ageing of the population and from the economic cycle. They hypothesize that it instead depends on the decline in the geographical specificity of employment opportunities in the USA, and on the greater ability of workers to obtain information about possible destinations for their migratory projects thanks to the Internet. According to these authors, this has a dissuasive effect on spatial mobility.
4 For more detailed analysis of this convergence in Western Europe see Beckfield (2006, 2009), who shows that, as an effect of political integration, income inequalities have decreased *between* countries but have increased *within* countries.
5 A prime pro-mobility factor is foreign language proficiency, which is rising in Europe over time due to educational expansion and cohort replacement. Of course, establishing a single common lingua franca would make the real difference. But 'while the EU in many policy areas strives for a unity and convergence of the member states – a single market, a single currency, a single jurisprudence – this is not the case when it comes to language policy. [The point is that] the question of regulating the languages [. . .] belongs to the areas which must be decided concurrently between all the governments. A change in the present regulations is practically impossible, because each of the [. . .] member countries has the right of veto' (Gerhards 2012, 98). Having said this, there remains a non-negligible, but still unexplored, room to manoeuvre for a common policy designed to – at least – standardize foreign language teaching at all levels of national education systems.
6 Taking into account potential return trips in home countries and other movements not included in tourism statistics, Koslowski (2011, 55) estimates a worldwide total of over two billion border crossings in 2010.

174 *Notes*

7 This does not imply that mobility has been 'democratized' – in fact, as I discuss in the next section, the social stratification of mobility is an underdeveloped area of research. As has been observed, 'different social groups have distinct relationships to this anyway differentiated mobility: some people are more in charge of it than others; some initiate flows and movement, others don't; some are more on the receiving-end of it than others; some are effectively imprisoned by it' (Massey 1994, 149; see also Shamir 2005). This argument has been popularized by Bauman (1998, 92 ff.) using the icons of the 'tourist' and the 'vagabond', which resonates with the medieval split in the disciplining of mobility for aristocrats on one side and marginals on the other (Cresswell 2006, 10–12). In fact, in contemporary society not only the population involved but also spatial trajectories, temporal patternings and subjective rationales of mobility are becoming more diversified and stratified.

8 Extreme versions of this view foresee the 'end of distance' in social relationships, by analogy with the organization of the global financial system, in which investment and speculation decisions flow electronically and in which geographical origin is of little importance. This conclusion has been endorsed by numerous globalization scholars who have more or less explicitly resumed and adapted into quasi-sociological terms the vision of a deterritorialized world put forward by Deleuze and Guattari (1980). Despite the intellectual success of this radical scenario, however, its empirical bases are weak and unconvincing (for a discussion see Kennedy 2010, 27 ff.).

9 For an earlier discussion and application of this concept, see Recchi and Kuhn (2013).

10 Merton defines the status-set as 'the complex of distinct positions assigned to individuals both within and among social systems' (1968, 434), while the role-set is 'that complement of role relationships which persons have by virtue of occupying a particular social status' (ibid., 423). Elsewhere in his work, Merton paid special attention to the spatial orientation of influential people, classifying them into 'locals' and 'cosmopolitans' (ibid., 447 ff.). This classification is based on different 'orientations' but echoes a difference in 'the structure of social relations in which each type is implicated' (ibid.), thus encapsulating the intuition of different spatial references – or, as I propose to call them, 'space-sets'.

11 While here the focus is on 'physical' mobility, I do not underscore the effect of 'virtual' forms of mobility on 'personal communities' (Wellman 2001; Castells 2001). Some research has found, in fact, that surfing the web does not take most people very far from home (Hampton and Wellman 2003). Nevertheless, the features and scope of virtual space-sets definitely deserve more systematic scrutiny.

Methodological Appendix

1 The dataset is deposited, and can be accessed on request, at the GESIS Archive of Cologne: Alaminos, Antonio; Recchi, Ettore; Braun, Michael; Muxel, Anne; Tambini, Damian; Santacreu, Oskar (2007): *European Internal Movers Social Survey (Pioneer project)*. Gesis Data Archive, Cologne. ZA4512 Data file Version 1.0.0, doi:10.4232/1.4512.

References

Ackers, D. (2012) *The Experience of EURES*, High level conference 'Improving Access to Labour Market Information for Migrants and Employers', European Commission, DG Employment Social Affairs and Inclusion, Brussels, 6 November.

Ackers, L. (1998) *Shifting Spaces: Women, Citizenship and Migration within the European Union*, Bristol: Policy Press.

Ackers, L. (2005) 'Moving People and Knowledge: Scientific Mobility in the European Union', *International Migration*, 43, 99–131.

Ackers, L. and Stalford, H. (2004) *A Community for Children? Children, Citizenship and Internal Migration in the EU*, Aldershot: Ashgate.

Adey, P. (2010) *Mobility*, New York: Routledge.

Alaminos, A. and Santacreu, O. (2009) 'Living across Cultures in a Transnational Europe', in E. Recchi and A. Favell (eds), *Pioneers of European Integration: Citizenship and Mobility in the EU*, Cheltenham: Elgar.

Aledo Tur, A. (2005) 'Los otros immigrantes: residents europeos en el sudeste español', in J. Fernández-Rufete and M. Jiménez (eds), *Movimientos migratorios contemporáneos*, Murcia: Fundación Universitaria San Antonio.

Alfieri, A. and Havinga, I. (2005) 'Definition of Universe for the Framework of the Movement of Natural Persons', Issue Paper # 2, United Nations Statistics Division, at http://unstats.un.org/unsd/tradeserv/tsgdocuments/issuepaper2.pdf (accessed June 16, 2013).

Allport, G. W. (1954) *The Nature of Prejudice*, New York: Doubleday.

Ambrosini, M. (2008) *Un'altra globalizzazione. La sfida delle migrazioni transnazionali*, Bologna: Il Mulino.

Anderson, B., Ruhs, M., Rogaly, B. and Spencer, S. (2006) *Fair Enough? Central and East European Migrants in Low-Wage Employment in the UK*, Oxford: Joseph Rowntree Foundation.

Andreotti, A., Le Galès, P. and Moreno Fuentes, F. J. (2013) 'Transnational Mobility and Rootedness: The Upper Middle Classes in European Cities', *Global Networks*, 13, 41–59.

Anghel, R. G. (2008a) 'Changing Statuses: Freedom of Movement, Locality and Transnationality of Irregular Romanian Migrants in Milan', *Journal of Ethnic and Migration Studies*, 34, 787–802.

Anghel, R. G. (2008b) 'Come hanno fatto i rumeni ad arrivare in Italia', in A. Colombo and G. Sciortino (eds), *Stranieri in Italia: Trent'anni dopo*, Bologna: Il Mulino.

Archibugi, D. (1995) 'Immanuel Kant, Cosmopolitan Law and Peace', *European Journal of International Relations*, 1, 429–56.

Aron, R. (1974) 'Is Multinational Citizenship Possible?', *Social Research*, 41, 638–56.

Auer, P., Berg, J. and Coulibaly, I. (2004) *Is a Stable Workforce Good for the Economy? Insights into the Tenure–Productivity–Employment Relationship*, working paper

2004/15, Employment Analysis and Research Unit – Employment Strategy Department, Geneva: ILO.
Azmanova, A. (2011) 'After the Left–Right (Dis)continuum: Globalization and the Remaking of Europe's Ideological Geography', *International Political Sociology*, 5, 384–407.
Bachan, R. and Sheehan, M. (2011) 'On the Labour Market Progress of Polish Accession Workers in South-East England', *International Migration*, 49, 104–34.
Baczynska, G. (2009) 'Few Poles Returning Home Despite Crisis – Survey', *Reuters*, 29, www.reuters.com (accessed May 29, 2009).
Bade, K. (2003) *Migration in European History*, Oxford: Blackwell.
Bader, V. M. (2005) 'The Ethics of Immigration', *Constellations*, 12, 331–61.
Baglioni, L. G. (2009) *Sociologia della cittadinanza*, Soveria Mannelli: Rubbettino.
Baglioni, L. G. and Recchi, E. (2013) 'La classe media va in Europa? Transnazionalismo e stratificazione sociale nell'Unione Europea', *SocietàMutamentoPolitica*, 4, 47–69.
Bailly, F., Mohoud, E. M. and Oudinet, J. (2004) 'Les pays de l'Union Européenne face aux nouvelles dynamiques des migrations internationales', *Revue française des affaires sociales*, 58, 33–60.
Baldoni, E. (2003) *The Free Movement of Persons in the EU: A Legal-Historical Overview*, Pioneur working paper # 2, Firenze: Ciuspo.
Baldwin-Edwards, M. and Arango, J. (eds) (1999) *Immigrants and the Informal Economy in Southern Europe*, London: Frank Cass.
Balibar, E. (2004) *We, The People of Europe?* Princeton (NJ): Princeton University Press.
Barberis, E. (2008) *Imprenditori immigrati. Tra inserimento sociale e partecipazione allo sviluppo*, Roma: Ediesse.
Barnard, C. (2007) *The Substantive Law of the EU: The Four Freedoms*, Oxford: Oxford University Press.
Barou, J. and Prado, P. (1995) *Les Anglais dans nos campagnes*, Paris: L'Harmattan.
Barrett, A. and Duffy, D. (2008) 'Are Ireland's Immigrants Integrating into Its Labour Market?', *International Migration Review*, 3, 597–619.
Barry, B. and Goodin, R. E. (eds) (1992) *Free Movement. Ethical Issues in the Transnational Migration of People and of Money*, Philadelphia: Pennsylvania University Press.
Bauböck, R. (2003) 'Towards a Political Theory of Migrant Transnationalism', *International Migration Review*, 37, 700–23.
Bauböck, R. (2009) 'Global Justice, Freedom of Movement and Democratic Citizenship', *Archives Européens de Sociologie*, 50, 1–31.
Bauböck, R. (2010) 'Cold Constellations and Hot Identities: Political Theory Questions about Transnationalism and Diaspora', in R. Bauböck and T. Faist (eds), *Diaspora and Transnationalism: Concepts, Theories and Methods*, Amsterdam: Amsterdam University Press.
Bauböck, R. (2011) 'Citizenship and Free Movement', in R. Smith (ed.), *Citizenship, Borders, and Human Needs*, Philadelphia: University of Pennsylvania Press.
Bauböck, R., Ersbøll, E., Groenendijk, K. and Waldrauch, H. (eds) (2006) *Acquisition and Loss of Nationality. Policies and Trends in 15 European States. Volume 2: Country Analyses*, Amsterdam: Amsterdam University Press.
Bauman, Z. (1998) *Globalization. The Human Consequences*, Cambridge and Oxford: Polity Press.

Bauman, Z. (2006) *L'Europa è un'avventura*, Roma-Bari: Laterza.
Beck, U. (1997) *Was ist Globalisierung?* Frankfurt am Main: Suhrkamp.
Beck, U. and Grande, E. (2004) *Das kosmopolitische Europa. Gesellschaft und Politik in der Zweiten Moderne*, Frankfurt am Main: Suhrkamp.
Beck, U. and Grande, E. (2007) 'Cosmopolitanism: Europe's Way Out of Crisis', *European Journal of Social Theory*, 10, 67–85.
Beckfield, J. (2006) 'European Integration and Income Inequality', *American Sociological Review*, 71, 964–85.
Beckfield, J. (2009) 'Remapping Inequality in Europe: The Net Effect of Regional Integration on Total Income Inequality in the European Union' *International Journal of Comparative Sociology*, 50: 486–509.
Bellamy, R., Castiglione, D. and Shaw, J. (eds) (2006) *Making European Citizens: Civic Inclusion in a Transnational Context*, London: Palgrave Macmillan.
Bellucci, P., Sanders, D. and Serricchio, F. (2012) 'Explaining European Identity', in D. Sanders, P. Bellucci, G. Tóka and M. Torcal (eds), *The Europeanization of National Polities? Citizenship and Support in a Post-Enlargement Union*, Oxford: Oxford University Press.
Bendix, R. (1977) *Nation-Building and Citizenship: Studies of Our Changing Social Order*, Berkeley: University of California Press.
Benson, M. and O'Reilly, K. (2009) 'Migration and the Search for a Better Way of Life: A Critical Exploration of Lifestyle Migration', *The Sociological Review*, 57, 608–25.
Berezin, M. (2003) 'Territory, Emotion and Identity: Spatial Recalibration in a New Europe', in M. Berezin and M. Schain (eds), *Europe Without Borders: Remapping Territory, Citizenship, and Identity in a Transnational Age*, Baltimore: Johns Hopkins University Press.
Berezin, M. and Díez Medrano, J. (2008) 'Distance Matters: Place, Political Legitimacy and Popular Support for European Integration', *Comparative European Politics*, 6, 1–32.
Berger, P. A. and Weiss, A. (eds) (2008) *Transnationalisierung sozialer Ungleichheit*, Wiesbaden: VS Verlag für Sozialwissenschaften.
Bernardi, F., Garrido, L. and Miyar, M. (2011) 'The Recent Fast Upsurge of Immigrants in Spain and Their Employment Patterns and Occupational Attainment', *International Migration*, 49, 149–87.
Bettin Lattes, G. (2011) 'Socializzazione politica', in G. Bettin Lattes and L. Raffini (eds), *Manuale di sociologia*, Padova: Cedam.
Bettin Lattes, G. and Bontempi, M. (eds) (2008) *Generazione Erasmus? L'identità europea tra vissuto e istituzioni*, Firenze: Firenze University Press.
Beyers, J. (2005) 'Multiple Embeddedness and Socialization in Europe: The Case of Council Officials', *International Organization*, 59, 899–936.
Billig, M. (1995) *Banal Nationalism*, London: Sage.
Blanchflower, D. G. and Lawton, H. (2010) 'The Impact of the Recent Expansion of the EU on the UK Labour Market', in M. Kahanec and K. F. Zimmermann (eds), *EU Labor Markets After Post-Enlargement Migration*, Berlin: Springer.
Blatter, J., Erdmann, S. and Schwanke, K. (2009) *Acceptance of Dual Citizenship: Empirical Data and Political Contexts*, working paper # 2, Global Governance and Democracy series, Luzern: Universität Luzern.
Block, L. (2007) *Where the Heart Is: On the European Identity of Intra-EU Migrants*, Maastricht European Studies papers # 2, Maastricht: Universiteit Maastricht.

Blome, K., Friedrich, D. and Nanz, P. (2012) 'Personenfreizügigkeit und die Herausbildung europäischer sozialer Bürgerschaft', *Österreichische Zeitschrift für Politikwissenschaft*, 4, 383–98.
Blondel, J. (1998) 'Il modello svizzero: un futuro per l'Europa?', *Rivista italiana di scienza politica*, 28, 203–27.
Bobbio, N. (1990) *L'età dei diritti*, Torino: Einaudi.
Bonifazi, C. (2009) 'Toh, una nuova sanatoria!', *Neodemos*, www.neodemos.it (accessed November 16, 2009).
Borjas, G. J. (2001) 'Economics of Migration', in N. J. Smelser and P. B. Baltes (eds), *International Encyclopedia of the Social and Behavioral Sciences*, Oxford and New York: Elsevier.
Bourdieu, P. (2000 [1997]) *Pascalian Meditations*, Stanford (CA): Stanford University Press.
Bousiou, P. (2008) *The Nomads of Mykonos: Performing Liminalities in a 'Queer' Space*, Oxford: Berghahn.
Boy, D. and Mayer, N. (eds) (1997) *L'électeur a ses raisons*, Paris: Presses de Sciences Po.
Brague, R. (1992) *Europe, la voie romaine*, Paris: Critérion.
Braun, M. and Arsene, C. (2009) 'The Demographics of Movers and Stayers in the European Union', in E. Recchi and A. Favell (eds), *Pioneers of European Integration: Citizenship and Mobility in the EU*, Cheltenham: Elgar.
Braun, M. and Glöckner-Rist, A. (2011) 'Patterns of Social Integration of Western European Migrants', *Journal of International Migration and Integration*, 13, 403–22.
Braun, M. and Recchi, E. (2009) 'Free-Moving Western Europeans: An Empirically Based Portrait', in H. Fassmann, M. Haller and D. Lane (eds), *Migration and Mobility in Europe: Trends, Patterns and Control*, Cheltenham: Elgar.
Braun, M. and Santacreu, O. (2009) 'Methodological Notes', in E. Recchi and A. Favell (eds), *Pioneers of European Integration: Citizenship and Mobility in the EU*, Cheltenham: Elgar.
Braunerhjelm, P., Faini, R., Norman, V., Ruane, F. and Seabright, P. (2000) *Integration and the Regions of Europe: How the Right Policies Can Prevent Polarization*, London: Centre for Economic Policy Research.
Broeders, D. (2009) 'Tracing, Identifying and Sorting: The Role of EU Migration Databases in the Internal Control on Irregular Migrants', in H. Fassmann, M. Haller and D. Lane (eds), *Migration and Mobility in Europe: Trends, Patterns and Control*, Cheltenham: Elgar.
Brubaker, R. (1992) *Citizenship and Nationhood in France and Germany*, Cambridge (MA): Harvard University Press.
Brubaker, R. (1995) 'Aftermaths of Empire and the Unmixing of Peoples: Historical and Comparative Perspectives', *Ethnic and Racial Studies*, 18, 189–218.
Bruter, M. (2003) 'Winning Hearts and Minds for Europe: The Impact of News and Symbols on Civic and Cultural Identity', *Comparative Political Studies*, 36, 1148–79.
Bruter, R. (2005) *Citizens of Europe? The Emergence of a Mass European Identity*, Basingstoke: Palgrave Macmillan.
Büscher, M., Urry, J. and Witchger, K. (eds) (2010) *Mobile Methods*, London: Routledge.
Campbell, D. (2011) 'Economic Crisis: The Pain in Spain', *The Observer*, 4 December.

Canovi, A. (2011) 'L'immagine degli italiani in Belgio. Appunti geostorici', *Diacronie. Studi di storia contemporanea*, 5, 1–16.
Carens, J. H. (1987) 'Aliens and Citizens: The Case for Open Borders', *The Review of Politics*, 49, 251–73.
Carens, J. H. (1992) 'Migration and Morality. A Liberal Egalitarian Perspective', in B. Barry and R. E. Goodin (eds), *Free Movement. Ethical Issues in the Transnational Migration of People and of Money*, Philadelphia: Pennsylvania University Press.
Caritas-Migrantes (2009) *Immigrazione. Dossier statistico 2009*, Roma: IDOS.
Carlier, J.-Y. and Guild, E. (eds) (2006) *L'avenir de la libre circulation des personnes dans l'U. E.*, Brussels: Bruylant.
Carlino, G., Chatterjee, S. and Hunt, R. (2005) *Matching and Learning in Cities: Urban Density and the Rate of Invention*, working paper 04/16, Philadelphia: Federal Reserve Bank of Philadelphia.
Carmel, E. (2013) 'Mobility, Migration and Rights in the European Union: Critical Reflections on Policy and Practice', *Policy Studies*, 34, 238–53.
Carmel, E. and Paul, R. (2013) 'Editorial', *Policy Studies*, 34, 113–21.
Carrera, S. (2013) *Shifting Responsibilities for EU Roma Citizens: The 2010 French Affair on Roma Evictions and Expulsions Continued*, CEPS Papers in Liberty and Security in Europe # 55, Brussels: CEPS.
Casado Díaz, M. (2006) 'Retiring to Spain: An Analysis of Difference among North European Nationals', *Journal of Ethnic and Migration Studies*, 32, 1321–39.
Casey, J. P. (2009) 'Open Borders: Absurd Chimera or Inevitable Future Policy?', *International Migration*, 48, 14–62.
Castells, M. (2000) *The Rise of the Network Society*, Oxford: Blackwell.
Castells, M. (2001) *Diffusion and Uses of Internet in Catalonia and in Spain*, IN3 Working Paper Series 1, Barcelona: Internet Interdisciplinary Institute.
Castles, S. (2006) 'Guestworkers in Europe: A Resurrection?', *International Migration Review*, 40, 741–66.
Castles, S. and Miller, M. J. (2003) *The Age of Migration*, New York: Guilford Press.
Catanzaro, R. and Colombo, A. (eds) (2009) *Badanti & co. Il lavoro domestico straniero in Italia*, Bologna: Il Mulino.
Chan, K. M. (2008) 'Internal Migration in China: Trends, Geographical Distributions, and Policies', in Department of Social and Economic Affairs, *United Nations Expert Group Meeting on Population Distribution, Urbanization, Internal Migration and Development*, New York: United Nations.
Chase-Dunn, C., Kawann, Y. and Brewer, B. D. (2000) 'Trade Globalization since 1795: Waves of Integration in the World-System', *American Sociological Review*, 65, 77–95.
Checkel, J. (ed.) (2005) *International Institutions and Socialization in Europe*, special issue of *International Organization*, 59.
Cicchelli, V. (2012) *L'esprit cosmopolite. Voyages de formation des jeunes en Europe*, Paris: Presses de Sciences Po.
Cingolani, P. (2009) *Romeni d'Italia. Migrazioni, vita quotidiana e legami transnazionali*, Bologna: Il Mulino.
Citrin, J. and Sides, J. (2004) 'More than Nationals: How Identity Choice Matters in the New Europe', in R. K. Herrmann, T. Risse, and M. B. Brewer (eds), *Transnational Identities: Becoming European in the EU*, Lanham, MD: Rowman & Littlefield.

Clark, K. and Drinkwater, S. (2008) 'The Labour-Market Performance of Recent Migrants', *Oxford Review of Economic Policy*, 3, 495–516.
Claval, P. (1991) *Geografia umana*, in *Enciclopedia delle scienze sociali*, Rome: Istituto della Enciclopedia Italiana (accessed May 5, 2011).
Cook, J., Dwyer, P. and Waite, L. (2011) 'The Experiences of Accession 8 Migrants in England: Motivations, Work and Agency', *International Migration*, 49, 54–79.
Cotesta, V. (2011) 'Paradigmi per lo studio dell'identità europea', *Quaderni di sociologia*, 55, 11–22.
Cram, L., Patrikios, S. and Mitchell, J. (2011) *What Does the European Union Mean to Its Citizens? Implicit Triggers, Identity(ies) and Attitudes to the European Union*, http://ssrn.com/abstract=1900063, APSA 2011 Annual Meeting Paper.
Cremers, J. (2013) 'Free Provision of Services and Cross-Border Labour Recruitment', *Policy Studies*, 34, 201–20.
Cresswell, T. (2006) *On the Move: Mobility in the Modern Western World*, New York: Routledge.
Cresswell, T. and Merriman, P. (2011) 'Introduction: Geographies of Mobilities – Practices, Spaces, Subjects', in T. Cresswell (ed.), *Geographies of Mobilities: Practices, Spaces, Subjects*, Farnham: Ashgate.
Critchley, J. (1996) 'The Great Betrayal. Tory Policy towards Europe from 1945 to 1955', in M. Bond, J. Smith and W. Wallace (eds), *Eminent Europeans: Personalities Who Shaped Contemporary Europe*, London: Greycoat Press.
Csedő, K. (2008) 'Negotiating Skills in the Global City: Hungarian and Romanian Professionals and Graduates in London', *Journal of Ethnic and Migration Studies* 35, 803–23.
Cyrus, N. (2006) 'Recent Polish Immigrants in the UK', in A. Triandafyllidou (ed.), *Contemporary Polish Migration in Europe: Complex Patterns of Movement and Settlement*, Washington (DC): Edward Mellen.
Cyrus, N. and Vogel, D. (2006) 'Managing Access to the German Labour Market: Opportunities and Restrictions', in F. Düvell (ed.), *Illegal Immigration in Europe beyond Control?* Basingstoke: Palgrave Macmillan.
Dawson, R. E. and Prewitt, K. (1969) *Political Socialization*, Boston: Little Brown and Company.
De Bruycker, P. (2006) *La libre circulation des citoyens européens entre codification et reforme*, in J.-Y. Carlier and E. Guild (eds), *L'avenir de la libre circulation des personnes dans l'U. E.*, Brussels: Bruylant.
De Federico de la Rúa, A. (2002) 'Amistad e identificación: las micro fundaciones de las pertenencias macro. Amigos europeos e identitad europea', *Redes – Revistahispana para el análisis de redes sociales*, 3, http://redalyc.uaemex.mx/src/inicio/HomRevRed.jsp?iCveEntRev=931, accessed June 23, 2009).
Delanty, G. (1995) *Inventing Europe. Idea, Identity, Reality*, Basingstoke: Palgrave Macmillan.
Delanty, G. (2006) 'Borders in a Changing Union: An Analysis of Recent Trends', *Comparative European Politics*, 4, 183–202.
Delanty, G. and Rumford, C. (2005) *Rethinking Europe: Social Theory and the Implications of Europeanization*, New York: Routledge.
Deleuze, G. and Guattari, F. (1980) *Mille plateaux*, Paris: Editions de Minuit.
Delhey, J. (2004) *European Social Integration. From Convergence of Countries to Transnational Relations between Peoples*, WZB Discussion Paper SP I 2004-201, Berlin: WZB.

Delhey, J., Deutschmann, E., Graf, T. and Richter, K. (2014) 'Measuring the Europeanization of Everyday Life: Three New Indices and an Empirical Application', *European Societies*, 16, 355–77.
Della Porta, D. and Caiani, M. (2009) *Social Movements and Europeanization*, Oxford: Oxford University Press.
Déloye, Y. (2005) *Dictionnaire des élections européennes*, Paris: Economica.
Der Spiegel (2013) *Die neuen Gastarbeiter. Europas junge Elite fuer Deutschlands Wirtschaft*, March, issue 9.
Deutsch, K. W. (1953) *Nationalism and Social Communication: An Inquiry into the Foundations of Nationality*, Cambridge (MA): MIT Press.
Deutsch, K. W. (1969) *Nationalism and Its Alternatives*, New York: Knopf.
Deutsch, K. W., Burrell, S., Kann, R., Lee, M., Lichterman, M., Lindgren, R., Loewenheim, F. and van Wagenen, R. (1957) *Political Community and the North Atlantic Area: International Organization in the Light of Historical Experience*, Princeton (NJ): Princeton University Press.
De Vries, C. E. and Edwards, E. E. (2009) 'Taking Europe to Its Extremes: Extremist Parties and Public Euroscepticism', *Party Politics*, 15, 5–28.
Díez Medrano, J. and Gutiérrez, P. (2001) 'Nested Identities: National and European Identity in Spain', *Ethnic and Racial Studies*, 24, 753–78.
Drake, H. and Collard, S. (2008) 'A Case Study of Intra-EU Migration. 20 Years of "Brits" in the Pays d'Auge, Normandy, France', *French Politics*, 6, 214–33.
Dreher, A., Gaston, N. and Martens, P. (2008) *Measuring Globalisation: Gauging Its Consequences*, New York: Springer.
Duchêne, F. (1996) 'Jean Monnet. Pragmatic Visionary', in M. Bond, J. Smith and W. Wallace (eds), *Eminent Europeans: Personalities Who Shaped Contemporary Europe*, London: Greycoat Press.
Duchesne, S. (2010) 'L'identité européenne, entre science politique et science fiction. Introduction', *Politique européenne*, 30, 7–16.
Duchesne, S. and Frognier, A. P. (1995) 'Is There a European Identity?', in O. Niedermayer and R. Sinnott (eds), *Public Opinion and Internationalized Governance*, Oxford: Oxford University Press.
Duchesne, S. and A.-P. Frognier (2008) 'National and European Identifications: A Dual Relationship', *Comparative European Politics*, 6, 143–68.
Dustmann, C., Casanova, M., Fertig, M., Preston, I. and Schmidt, C. M. (2003) *The Impact of EU Enlargement on Migration Flows*, London: Home Office Online Report 25/03, http://eprints.ucl.ac.uk/14332/1/14332.pdf (accessed September 21, 2012).
Düvell, F. (2006) 'Polish Immigrants in the United Kingdom', in A. Triandafyllidou (ed.), *Contemporary Polish Migration in Europe: Complex Patterns of Movement and Settlement*, Lewiston (NY): Edwin Mellen Press.
Eade, J. (2007) *Class and Ethnicity: Polish Migrant Workers in London. Full Research Report*, ESRC End of Award Report, RES-000-22-1294, Swindon: ESRC.
Eade, J., Drinkwater, S. and Garapich, M. (2006) *Class and Ethnicity. Polish Migrants in London*, Final Project Report, www.surrey.ac.uk/Arts/CRONEM/polish/Polish_final_research-report_web.pdf (accessed February 18, 2010).
Easton, D. and Hess, R. D. (1962) 'The Child's Political World', *Midwest Journal of Political Science*, 6, 229–46.
Eder, K. (2006) 'Europe's Borders. The Narrative Construction of Boundaries of Europe', *European Journal of Social Theory*, 9, 255–71.

Eder, K. (2009) 'A Theory of Collective Identity. Making Sense of the Debate on a "European Identity"', *European Journal of Social Theory*, 12, 427–47.

Ederveen, S. and Bardsley, N. (2003) *The Influence of Wage and Unemployment Differentials on Labour Mobility in the EU: A Meta-Analysis*, The Hague: CPB.

Eichenberg, R. C. and Dalton, R. J. (1993) 'Europeans and the European Union: The Dynamics of Public Support for European Integration', *International Organization*, 47, 507–34.

Elliott, A. and Urry, J. (2010) *Mobile Lives*, London: Routledge.

Ellis, A., Navarro, C., Morales, I., Gratschew, M. and Braun, N. (2007) *Voting from Abroad: The International IDEA Handbook*, Stockholm: International Institute for Democracy and Electoral Assistance.

Elster, J. (1986) *An Introduction to Karl Marx*, Cambridge: Cambridge University Press.

Emirbayer, M. and Goodwin, J. (1994) 'Network Analysis, Culture and the Problem of Agency', *American Journal of Sociology*, 99, 1411–54.

Engbersen, G., Snel, E. and de Boom, J. (2010) '"A Van Full of Poles": Liquid Migration from Central and Eastern Europe', in R. Black, G. Engbersen, M. Okolski and C. Pantiru (eds), *A Continent Moving West? EU Enlargement and Labour Migration from Central and Eastern Europe*, Amsterdam: Amsterdam University Press.

Engelen, E. (2003) 'How to Combine Openness and Protection? Citizenship, Migration, and Welfare Regimes', *Politics & Society*, 31, 503–36.

Eriksen, E. O. (2005) 'An Emerging European Public Sphere', *European Journal of Social Theory*, 8, 341–63.

Erikson, R. and Goldthorpe, J. H. (1992) *The Constant Flux*, Oxford: Clarendon Press.

Eurobarometer (2010) *European Union Citizenship. Analytical Report*, Flash EB 294, Luxembourg: Office for Official Publications of the European Communities.

Euronews (2014) *Belgium Sends 'Burden' EU Citizens Letters Asking Them to Leave the Country*, 30 January, http://www.euronews.com/2014/01/30/belgium-sends-burden-eu-citizens-letters-asking-them-to-leave-the-country (accessed May 5, 2014).

European Commission (2001) *European Governance: A White Paper*, COM(2001)428 final, Brussels: European Commission.

European Commission (2002) *Action Plan for Skills and Mobility*, COM(2002)72, Brussels: European Commission.

European Commission (2007a) *Labour Mobility in the Euro Area*, Directorate General Economic and Financial Affairs, ECFIN/E3(2007)REP/52147, Brussels: European Commission.

European Commission (2007b) *Labour Market Reforms and Adjustment Mechanisms in the Euro Area*, Directorate General Economic and Financial Affairs, ECFIN/E3(2007)REP/54240, Brussels: European Commission.

European Commission (2008) *Employment in Europe 2008*, Luxembourg: Office for Official Publications of the European Communities.

European Commission (2010) *EU Citizenship Report 2010. Dismantling the Obstacles to EU Citizens' Rights*, COM(2010)602-605 final, Brussels: European Commission.

European Commission (2011a) *Employment in Europe 2011*, Luxembourg: Office for Official Publications of the European Communities.

European Commission (2011b) *European Territorial Cooperation: Building Bridges between People*, Directorate General Regional Policies, Luxembourg: Office for Official Publications of the European Communities.
European Commission (2013) *On the Way to ERASMUS +. A Statistical Overview of the ERASMUS Programme in 2011–12*, Luxembourg: Office for Official Publications of the European Communities.
European Travel Commission (2012) *European Travel Commission Factsheet*, http://www.etc-corporate.org/etc-factsheet (accessed 3 December 2014).
Eurostat (2009) *Key Figures on Europe. 2009 Edition*, Luxembourg: Office for Official Publications of the European Communities.
Eurostat (2014) *International Trade in Goods: Statistics Explained*, http://epp.eurostat.ec.europa.eu/statistics_explained (accessed 3 December 2014).
Faas, D. (2010) *Negotiating Political Identities: Multiethnic Schools and Youth in Europe*, Farnham: Ashgate.
Faini, R. (2003) *Migration and Convergence in the Regions of Europe: A Bit of Theory and Some Evidence*, Flowenla Discussion Paper # 9, Hamburg: Hamburgisches Welt-Wirtschaft-Archiv.
Faist, T. (ed.) (2007) *Dual Citizenship in Europe. From Nationhood to Societal Integration*, Farnham: Ashgate.
Faist, T. (2014) 'On the Transnational Social Question: How Social Inequalities Are Reproduced in Europe', *Journal of European Social Policy*, 24, DOI: 10.1177/0958928714525814.
Favell, A. (2003) 'Games Without Frontiers? Questioning the Transnational Social Power of Migrants in Europe', *Archives Européennes de Sociologie*, 46, 397–427.
Favell, A. (2004) 'London as Eurocity: French Free Movers in the Economic Capital of London', *Global and World Cities Research Bulletin*, 150, 1–16.
Favell, A. (2007) 'Rebooting Migration Theory: Interdisciplinarity, Globality, and Postdisciplinarity in Migration Studies', in C. Brettell and J. Hollifield (eds), *Migration Theory: Talking across Disciplines* (2nd edition), London: Routledge.
Favell, A. (2008a) *Eurostars and Eurocities: Free Movement and Mobility in an Integrating Europe*, Oxford: Blackwell.
Favell, A. (2008b) 'The New Face of East-West Migration in Europe', *Journal of Ethnic Migration Studies*, 34, 701–16.
Favell, A. (2014) 'The Fourth Freedom: Theories of Migration and Mobilities in "Neo-Liberal" Europe', *European Journal of Social Theory*, 17, 275–89.
Favell, A. and Guiraudon, V. (eds) (2011) *Sociology of the European Union*, Basingstoke: Palgrave Macmillan.
Favell, A. and Nebe, T. (2009) 'Internal and External Movers: East-West Migration and the Impact of EU Enlargement', in E. Recchi and A. Favell (eds), *Pioneers of European Integration: Citizenship and Mobility in the EU*, Cheltenham: Elgar.
Favell, A. and Recchi, E. (2011) 'Social Mobility and Spatial Mobility', in A. Favell and V. Guiraudon (eds), *Sociology of the European Union*, Basingstoke: Palgrave Macmillan.
Favell, A., Recchi, E., Kuhn, T., Solgaard Jensen, J. and Klein, J. (2011) *The Europeanisation of Everyday Life: Cross-Border Practices and Transnational Identifications among EU and Third-Country Citizens. State of the Art Report*, Eucross working paper # 1, Chieti: Università di Chieti-Pescara.
Fernández, O. (2005) 'Towards European Citizenship through Higher Education?', *European Journal of Education*, 40, 60–8.

Ferrera, M. (2005) *The Boundaries of Welfare: European Integration and the New Spatial Politics of Social Protection*, Oxford: Oxford University Press.
Fertig, M. and Schmidt, C. M. (2002) *Mobility within Europe: What Do We (Still Not) Know?* IZA DP # 447, Bonn: ForschungsinstitutzurZukunft der Arbeit.
Fibbi, R. and D'Amato, G. (2008) 'Transnationalisme des migrants en Europe: Une preuve par les faits', *Revue européenne des migrants internationales*, 24, 7–22.
Fidrmuc, J. and Doyle, O. (2006) *Does Where You Live Affect How You Vote? An Analysis of Migrant Voting Behavior*, manuscript, http://www.fidrmuc.net/research/emigrants.pdf (accessed June 10, 2012).
Fischer, C. (2005) 'Bowling Alone: What's the Score?', *Social Networks*, 27, 155–67.
Fligstein, N. (2008) *Euroclash: The EU, European Identity, and the Future of Europe*, Oxford: Oxford University Press.
Fligstein, N. (2011) 'Markets and Firms', in A. Favell and V. Guiraudon (eds), *Sociology of the European Union*, Basingstoke: Palgrave Macmillan.
Fligstein, N. and Mérand, F. (2002) 'Globalization or Europeanization? Evidence on the European Economy since 1980', *Acta Sociologica*, 45, 7–22.
Flipo, A. (2013) 'Mobilité et passage à l'âge adulte', *Agora débats/jeunesses*, 65, 23–35.
Florida, R. (2002) *The Rise of the Creative Class*, New York: Basic Books.
Føllesdal, A. and Hix, S. (2006) 'Why There Is a Democratic Deficit in the EU: A Response to Majone and Moravcsik', *Journal of Common Market Studies*, 44, 533–62.
Foster, N. (2011) *Foster on EU Law*, Oxford and New York: Oxford University Press.
Fouarge, D. and Ester, P. (2009) 'Understanding Migration Decisions in Eastern and Western Europe: Perceived Costs and Benefits of Mobility', in H. Fassmann, M. Haller and D. Lane (eds), *Migration and Mobility in Europe: Trends, Patterns and Control*, Cheltenham: Elgar.
Fox, J. (2005) 'Unpacking Transnational Citizenship', *Annual Review of Political Science*, 8, 171–201.
Fromm, E. (1968 [1941]) *Escape from Freedom*, New York: Avon Books.
Gabel, M. and Palmer, H. (1995) 'Understanding Variation in Public Support for European Integration', *European Journal of Political Research*, 27, 3–19.
Garapich, M. (2008) 'The Migration Industry and Civil Society: Polish Immigrants in the United Kingdom Before and After EU Enlargement', *Journal of Ethnic and Migration Studies*, 34, 735–52.
Garth, B. G. (1986) 'Migrant Workers and Rights of Mobility in the European Community and the United States: A Study of Law, Community and Citizenship in the Welfare State', in M. Cappelletti, M. Seccombe and J. Weiler (eds), *Integration through Law*, vol. 1, *Methods, Tools and Institutions*, book III, *Forces and Potential for a European Identity*, Berlin and New York: De Gruyter.
Gaspar, S. (2008) *Towards a Definition of European Intra-Marriage as a New Social Phenomenon*, CIES e-working paper # 46, Lisbon: CIES-ISCTE.
Geddes, A. (2003) *The Politics of Migration and Immigration in Europe*, London and Thousand Oaks (CA): Sage.
Gellner, E. (1983) *Nations and Nationalism*, Oxford: Blackwell.
Gerhards, J. (2012) *From Babel to Brussels. European Integration and the Importance of Transnational Linguistic Capital*, Berlin Studies on the Sociology of Europe (BSSE) # 28, Berlin: Freie Universität Berlin.

Giddens, A. (1973) *The Class Structure of Advanced Societies*, London: Hutchinson.
Giddens, A. (1990) *The Consequences of Modernity*, Cambridge: Polity Press.
Giddens, A. (1999) *Runaway World: How Globalisation Is Reshaping Our Lives*, London: Profile.
Giubboni, S. (2007) 'Free Movement of Persons and European Solidarity', *European Law Journal*, 13, 360–79.
Giubboni, S. (2010) 'Coordinamento europeo della sicurezza sociale e regimi di previdenza complementare', *Rivista del diritto della sicurezza sociale*, 2, 193–210.
Giubboni, S. and Orlandini, G. (2007) *La libera circolazione dei lavoratori nell'Unione Europea*, Bologna: Il Mulino.
Glaeser, E. L. (2000) 'Demand for Density? The Functions of the City in the 21st Century', *The Brookings Review*, 18, 10–13.
Glick Schiller, N., Basch, L. and Blanc-Szanton, C. (1992) *Transnationalism: A New Analytical Framework for Understanding Migration*, New York: New York Academy of Sciences.
Gouldner, A. W. (1957) 'Cosmopolitans and Locals: Toward an Analysis of Latent Social Roles – I', *Administrative Science Quarterly*, 2, 281–306.
Gouldner, A. W. (1958) 'Cosmopolitans and Locals: Toward an Analysis of Latent Social Roles – II', *Administrative Science Quarterly*, 2, 444–80.
Grabowska, I. (2003) *Irish Labour Migration of Polish Nationals: Economic, Social and Political Aspects in the Light of the EU Enlargement*, working paper 51 (migration series), Warsaw: Institute for Social Studies, University of Warsaw.
Greenacre, M. J. and Blasius, J. (ed.) (1994) *Correspondence Analysis in the Social Sciences: Recent Developments and Applications*, London: Academic Press.
Greenstein, F. (1965) *Children and Politics*, New Haven: Yale University Press.
Guild, E. (2004) *The Legal Elements of European Identity: EU Citizenship and Migration Law*, The Hague: Kluwer.
Guild, E. (2006) 'Preface', in J.-Y. Carlier and E. Guild (eds), *The Future of Free Movement of Persons in the EU*, Brussels: Bruylant.
Guiraudon, V. (2003) 'The Constitution of a European Immigration Policy Domain: A Political Sociology Approach', *Journal of European Public Policy*, 10, 263–83.
Guiraudon, V. and Joppke, C. (ed.) (2001) *Controlling a New Migration World*, London: Routledge.
Grundy, S. and Jamieson, L. (2007) 'European Identities: From Absent-Minded Citizens to Passionate Europeans', *Sociology*, 41, 663–80.
Haas, E. B. (1958) *The Uniting of Europe*, Stanford (CA): Stanford University Press.
Habermas, J. (1997) 'Kant's Idea of Perpetual Peace, with the Benefit of Two Hundred Years' Hindsight', in J. Bohman and M. Lutz-Bachmann (eds), *Perpetual Peace: Essays on Kant's Cosmopolitan Ideal*, Cambridge (MA): MIT Press.
Habermas, J. (2003) 'Toward a Cosmopolitan Europe', *Journal of Democracy*, 14, 86–100.
Hadler, M. (2006) 'Intentions to Migrate within the European Union: A Challenge for Simple Economic Macro-level Explanations', *European Societies*, 8, 111–40.
Hajer, M. (2000) 'Transnational Networks as Transnational Policy Discourse: Some Observations on the Politics of Spatial Development in Europe', in W. Salete and A. Faludi (eds), *The Revival of Strategic Spatial Planning*, Amsterdam: Koninklijke Nederlandse Akademie van Wetenschappen.

Hakhverdian, A., van Elsas, E., van der Brug, W. and Kuhn, T. (2013) 'Euroscepticism and Education: A Longitudinal Study of 12 EU Member States, 1973–2010', *European Union Politics*, DOI: 10.1177/1465116513489779.

Haller, M. (2008) *European Integration as an Elite Process: The Failure of a Dream?* London: Routledge.

Haller, W. and Roudometof, V. (2010) 'The Cosmopolitan-Local Continuum in a Cross-National Perspective', *Journal of Sociology*, 46, 277–97.

Hampton, K. and Wellman, B. (2003) 'Neighboring in Netville: How the Internet Supports Community and Social Capital in a Wired Suburb', *City & Community*, 2, 277–311.

Hansen, P. (2009) 'European Integration, European Identity and the Colonial Connection', *European Journal of Social Theory*, 5, 483–98.

Harris, J. R. and Todaro, M. P. (1970) 'Migration, Unemployment and Development: A Two-Sector Analysis', *American Economic Review*, 60, 126–42.

Harvey, D. (1982) *Limits to Capital*, Oxford: Blackwell.

Harvey, D. (1989) *The Condition of Postmodernity*, Oxford: Blackwell.

Havel, V. (1998) 'Europe as Task', in H. M. Enzensberger (ed.), *The European Challenge*, The Hague: Vuga.

Herm, A. (2008) 'Recent Migration Trends: Citizens of EU-27 Member States Become Ever More Mobile while EU Remains Attractive to Non-EU Citizens', *Eurostat – Statistics in Focus*, 98, http://epp.eurostat.ec.europa.eu/cache/ITY_OFFPUB/KS-SF-08-098/EN/KS-SF-08-098-en.pdf (accessed October 10, 2009).

Herrmann, R. K., Risse, T. and Brewer, M. B. (eds) (2004) *Transnational Identities: Becoming European in the EU*, Lanham (MD): Rowman & Littlefield.

Hinderliter Ortloff, D. (2005) 'Becoming European: A Framing Analysis of Three Countries' Civics Education Curricula', *European Education*, 37, 35–49.

Hix, S. (2008) *What's Wrong with the European Union and How to Fix It*, Cambridge: Polity Press.

Hix, S. and Høyland, B. (2011) *The Political System of the European Union*. Basingstoke: Palgrave Macmillan.

Hoggart, K. and Buller, H. (1994) 'The Social Integration of British Home Owners into French Rural Communities', *Journal of Rural Studies*, 10, 197–210.

Hooghe, L. (2005) 'Several Roads Lead to International Norms, but Few via International Socialization: A Case Study of the European Commission', *International Organization*, 59, 861–98.

Hooghe, L. (2007) 'What Drives Euroskepticism? Party-Public Cueing, Ideology and Strategic Opportunity', *European Union Politics*, 8, 5–12.

Hooghe, L. and Marks, G. (2009) 'A Postfunctionalist Theory of European Integration: From Permissive Consensus to Constraining Dissensus', *British Journal of Political Science*, 39, 1–23.

Huber, A. (2004) 'Geographical and Ethnographic Perspectives on the Rainbow: Settlements of the Spanish Coast', in A. M. Warnes (ed.), *Older Migrants in Europe*, Sheffield: Sheffield Institute for Studies on Ageing.

Hüller, T. (2007) 'Assessing EU Strategies for Publicity', *Journal of European Public Policy*, 14, 563–81.

Immerfall, S. Boehnke, K. and Baier, D. (2010) 'Identity', in S. Immerfall and G. Therborn (eds), *Handbook of European Societies. Social Transformations in the 21st Century*, New York: Springer.

Inglehart, R. (1970) 'Cognitive Mobilization and European Identity', *Comparative Politics*, 3, 45–70.

Ireland, P. (1994) *The Policy Challenge of Ethnic Diversity: Immigrant Politics in France and Switzerland*, Cambridge (MA): Harvard University Press.
Janelle, D. G. (1969) 'Spatial Reorganization: A Model and Concept', *Annals of the Association of American Geographers*, 59, 348–64.
Janelle, D. G. (1973) 'Measuring Human Extensibility in a Shrinking World', *The Journal of Geography*, 72, 8–15.
Janiak, A. and Wasmer, E. (2008) *Mobility in Europe. Why It Is Low, the Bottlenecks and the Policy Solutions*, Economic Paper # 340, Directorate-General for Economic and Financial Affairs, Brussels: European Commission.
Jensen, O. B. and Richardson, T. (2004) *Making European Space: Mobility, Power and Territorial Identity*, London: Routledge.
Jensen, O. B. and Richardson, T. (2007) 'New Region, New Story: Imagining Mobile Subjects in Transnational Space', *Space and Polity*, 11, 137–50.
Joppke, C. (1999) *Immigration and the Nation-State: The United States, Germany and Great Britain*, Oxford: Oxford University Press.
Joppke, C. (2007) 'Beyond National Models: Civic Integration Policies for Immigrants in Western Europe, *West European Politics*, 30, 1–22.
Joppke, C. (2010a) *Citizenship and Immigration*, Cambridge: Polity Press.
Joppke, C. (2010b) 'The Inevitable Lightening of Citizenship', *Archives Européens de Sociologie*, 51, 9–32.
Jordan, B. and Düvell, F. (2002) *Irregular Migration: Dilemmas of Transnational Mobility*, Cheltenham: Elgar.
Judt, T. (2005) *Postwar: A History of Europe since 1945*, London: Heinemann.
Jung, J. K. (2008) 'Growing Supranational Identities in a Globalising World? A Multilevel Analysis of the World Values Surveys', *European Journal of Political Research*, 47, 578–609.
Kaczmarczyk, P. (2010) 'Brains on the Move? Recent Migration of the Highly Skilled from Poland and Its Consequences', in R. Black, G. Engbersen, M. Okolski and C. Pantiru (eds), *A Continent Moving West? EU Enlargement and Labour Migration from Central and Eastern Europe*, Amsterdam: Amsterdam University Press.
Kaczmarczyk, P. and Okolski, M. (2008) *Economic Impacts of Migration on Poland and the Baltic States*, FAFO Paper # 1, Oslo, http://www.fafo.no/pub/rapp/10045/10045.pdf (accessed October 11, 2009).
Kaina, V. (2013) 'How to Reduce Disorder in European Identity Research', *European Political Science*, 12, 184–96.
Kaina, V. and Karolewski, I. P. (2009) 'EU Governance and European Identity', *Living Reviews in European Governance*, 4, http://europeangovernance.livingreviews.org/Articles/lreg-2009-2 (accessed February 10, 2012).
Kaplan, G. and Schulhofer-Wohl, S. (2012) *Understanding the Long-Run Decline in Interstate Migration*, working paper # 697, Minneapolis: Federal Reserve Bank of Minneapolis.
Kaufmann, V., Bergmann, M. M. and Joyé, D. (2004) 'Motility: Mobility as Capital', *International Journal of Urban and Regional Research*, 28, 745–56.
Kellerman, A. (2012) 'Potential Mobilities', *Mobilities*, 7, 171–83.
Kennedy, P. (2010) 'Mobility, Flexible Lifestyles and Cosmopolitanism: EU Postgraduates in Manchester', *Journal of Ethnic and Migration Studies*, 36, 465–82.
Kępińska, E. (2007) *Recent Trends in International Migration. The 2006 SOPEMI Report for Poland*, Center of Migration Research working paper 15/73, Warsaw: CMR.

Kesselring, S. (2006) 'Pioneering Mobilities: New Patterns of Movement and Motility in a Mobile World', *Environment and Planning A*, 38, 269–79.

King, R. (2002) 'Towards a New Map of European Migration', *International Journal of Population Geography*, 8, 89–106.

King, R. and Ruiz-Gelices, E. (2003) 'International Student Migration and the European "Year Abroad": Effects on European Identity and Subsequent Migration Behavior', *International Journal of Population Geography*, 9, 229–52.

King, R. and Skeldon, R. (2010) '"Mind the Gap!" Integrating Approaches to International and Internal Migration', *Journal of Ethnic and Migration Studies*, 36, 1619–46.

King, R., Warnes, A. M. and Williams, A. M. (1998) 'International Retirement Migration in Europe', *International Journal of Population Geography*, 4, 157–82.

King, R., Warnes, A. M. and Williams, A. M. (2000) *Sunset Lives: British Retirement Migration to the Mediterranean*, Oxford: Berg.

Kleingeld, P. (1998) 'Kant's Cosmopolitan Law: World Citizenship for a Global Order', *Kantian Review*, 2, 72–90.

Klingemann, H. D. (1979) 'Ideological Conceptualization and Political Action', in S. H. Barnes and M. Kaase (eds), *Political Action: Mass Participation in Five Western Democracies*, Beverly Hills and London: Sage.

Kohli, M. (2000) 'The Battlegrounds of European Identity', *European Societies*, 2, 113–37.

Koikkalainen, S. (2013) *Making It Abroad: Experiences of Highly Skilled Finns in the European Union Labour Markets*, Rovaniemi: University of Lapland.

Koopmans, R. (2007) 'Who Inhabits the European Public Sphere? Winners and Losers, Supporters and Opponents in Europeanised Political Debates', *European Journal of Political Research*, 46, 183–210.

Koopmans, R. and Erbe, J. (2004) 'Towards a European Public Sphere? Vertical and Horizontal Dimensions of a Europeanized Political Communication', *Innovation*, 17, 97–118.

Koryś, I. (2003) *Migration Trends in Selected EU Applicant Countries: Poland*, CEFMR working paper # 5, Warsaw: Central European Forum for Migration and Population Research.

Koslowski, R. (2011) 'The International Travel Regime', in R. Koslowski (ed.), *Global Mobility Regimes*, Basingstoke: Palgrave Macmillan.

Kostoris Padoa Schioppa, F. (1999) *Regional Aspects of Unemployment in Europe and in Italy*, CEPR Discussion Paper # 2108, London: Centre for Economic Policy Research.

Kriesi, H., Grande, E., Dolezal, M., Helbling, M., Hoeglinger, D. and Hutter, S. (2012) *Political Conflict in Western Europe*, Cambridge: Cambridge University Press.

Kriesi, H., Grande, E., Lachat, R., Dolezal, M., Bornschier, S. and Frey, T. (2008) *West European Politics in the Age of Globalization*, Cambridge: Cambridge University Press.

Krings, T., Bobek, A., Moriarty, E., Salamońska, J. and Wickham, J. (2009) 'Migration and Recession: Polish Migrants in Post-Celtic Tiger Ireland', *Sociological Research Online*, 14, http://www.socresonline.org.uk/14/2/9.html

Krings, T., Bobek, A., Moriarty, E., Salamońska, J. and Wickham, J. (2011) 'From Boom to Bust: Migrant Labour and Employers in the Irish Construction Sector', *Economic and Industrial Democracy*, 3, 459–76.

Krings, T., Bobek, A., Moriarty, E., Salamońska, J. and Wickham, J. (2013) 'Polish Migration to Ireland: "Free Movers" in the New European Mobility Space', *Journal of Ethnic and Migration Studies*, 39, 87–103.

Kuhn, T. (2011a) *Individual Transnationalism and EU Support. An Empirical Test of Deutsch's Transactionalist Theory*, PhD thesis, Fiesole, European University Institute.

Kuhn, T. (2011b) 'Individual Transnationalism, Globalisation and Euroscepticism: An Empirical Test of Deutsch's Transactionalist Theory', *European Journal of Political Research*, 50, 811–37.

Kuhn, T. (2012) 'Why Educational Exchange Programmes Miss Their Mark: Cross-Border Mobility, Education and European Identity', *Journal of Common Market Studies*, 50, 994–1010.

Landuyt, A. (2004) 'L'Italia e l'unificazione europea tra dibattito ideale e fasi di attuazione', in A. Landuyt (ed.), *Idee d'Europa e integrazione europea*, Bologna: Il Mulino.

Lash, S. and Urry, J. (1987) *The End of Organized Capitalism*, Cambridge: Polity.

Latour, B. (2007) *Reassembling the Social: An Introduction to Actor-Network-Theory*, Oxford: Oxford University Press.

Lebon, A. and Falchi, G. (1980) 'New Developments in Intra-European Migration since 1974', *International Migration Review*, 14, 539–79.

Le Roux, B. and Rouanet, H. (2010) *Multiple Correspondence Analysis*, Thousand Oaks (CA): Sage.

Lewis, J. (2005) 'The Janus Face of Brussels: Socialization and Everyday Decision Making in the European Union', *International Organization*, 59, 937–71.

Leyshon, A. (1995) 'Annihilating Space? The Speed-Up of Communications', in J. Allen and C. Hamnett (eds) *A Shrinking World? Global Unevenness and Inequality*, Oxford: Oxford University Press/The Open University.

Lieberson, S. (1969) 'Measuring Population Diversity', *American Sociological Review*, 34, 850–62.

Limmer, R. and Schneider, N. F. (2008) 'Studying Job-Related Mobility in Europe', in N. F. Schneider and G. Meil (eds), *Mobile Living across Europe 1: Relevance and Diversity of Job-Related Spatial Mobility in Six European Countries*, Opladen: Barbara Budrich.

Lindberg, L. and Scheingold, S. (1970) *Europe's Would Be Polity: Patterns of Change in the European Community*, Englewood Cliffs (NJ): Prentice Hall.

Livi Bacci, M. (1972) 'The Countries of Emigration', in M. Livi Bacci (ed.), *The Demographic and Social Pattern of Emigration from the Southern European Countries*, Florence: Dipartimento statistico-matematico dell'università di Firenze.

Livi Bacci, M. (2012) *A Short History of Migration*, Oxford: Polity.

Lowi, T. J. (1972) 'Four Systems of Policy, Politics, and Choice', *Public Administration Review*, 32, 298–310.

Lucassen, J. and Lucassen, L. (2009) 'The Mobility Transition Revisited, 1500–1900: What the Case of Europe Can Offer to Global History', *Journal of Global History*, 4, 347–77.

Lűtzeler, P. M. (1997) *Europäischer Identität und Multikultur*, Tübingen: Stauffenburg.

Maas, W. (2007) *Creating European Citizens*, Lanham (MD): Rowman & Littlefield.

Marcu, S. (2013) 'Entre migración y movilidad: prácticas de movilidad transfronteriza de los europeos del este hacia España', *Revista de Estudios Europeos*, 62, 33–54.

Marks, G. and Hooghe, L. (2003) *National Identity and Support for European Integration*, Veröffentlichungsreihe der Abteilung Demokratie: Strukturen, Leistungsprofil und Herausforderungen des Schwerpunkts Zivilgesellschaft, Konflikte und Demokratie, No. SP IV 2003–202 [National Identity and Support for European Integration. Social Science Research Centre. WP 2003–202], Berlin: WZB.

Marradi, A. (2007) *Metodologia delle scienze sociali*, Bologna: Il Mulino.

Marsh, D. (1971) 'Political Socialization: The Implicit Assumptions Questioned', *British Journal of Political Science*, 1, 453–65.

Marsh, M. (1998) 'Testing the Second-Order Election Model after Four European Elections', *British Journal of Political Science*, 28, 591–607.

Marshall, T. H. (1963) 'Citizenship and Social Class', in T. H. Marshall (ed.), *Sociology at the Crossroads*, London: Heinemann.

Martin, D. and Guild, E. (1996) *Free Movement of Persons in the European Union*, London: Butterworths.

Martinelli, A. (ed.) (2007) *Transatlantic Divide: Comparing American and European Society*, Oxford: Oxford University Press.

Maslauskaite, K. (2014) *Travailleurs détachés dans l'UE: état des lieux et évolution réglementaire*, Policy Paper 107, Paris: Notre Europe – Institut Jacques Delors.

Massey, D. (1994) *Space, Place and Gender*, Cambridge: Polity Press.

Massey, D. (1995) 'The Conceptualization of Place', in D. Massey and P. Jess (eds), *A Place in the World? Places, Cultures and Globalization*, Oxford: Oxford University Press.

Massey, D. S. (1999) 'Why Does Migration Occur? A Theoretical Synthesis', in C. Hirschman, P. Kasinitz and J. DeWind (eds), *The Handbook of International Migration: The American Experience*, New York: Russell Sage Foundation.

Matei, S. (2002) 'La participation electorale dans les démocraties post-communistes (1989–2001)', in B. Cautrès and D. Reynié (eds), *L'opinion européenne*, Paris: Presses de Sciences Po.

Mau, S. (2010) *Social Transnationalism. Lifeworlds beyond the Nation-State*, London: Routledge.

Mau, S., Brabandt, H., Laube, L. and Roos, C. (2012) *Liberal States and the Freedom of Movement: Selective Borders, Unequal Mobility*, Basingstoke: Palgrave Macmillan.

Mau, S. and Mewes, J. (2012) 'Horizontal Europeanisation in Contextual Perspective', *European Societies*, 14, 7–34.

Mau, S., Mewes, J. and Zimmermann, A. (2008) 'Cosmopolitan Attitudes through Transnational Social Practices?', *Global Networks*, 8, 1–24.

Mau, S. and Verwiebe, R. (2010) *European Societies: Mapping Structure and Change*, Bristol: Policy Press.

Mayer, N. and Perrineau, P. (1992) *Les comportements politiques*, Paris: Armand Colin.

Mayne, R. (1996) 'Schuman, De Gasperi, Spaak. The European Frontiersmen', in M. Bond, J. Smith and W. Wallace (eds), *Eminent Europeans: Personalities Who Shaped Contemporary Europe*, London: Greycoat Press.

Meardi, G. (2009) 'A Suspended Status: The Puzzle of Polish Workers in the West Midlands', in H. Fassmann, M. Haller and D. Lane (eds), *Migration and Mobility in Europe: Trends, Patterns and Control*, Cheltenham: Elgar.

Meil, G. (2008) 'Summary – Job Mobility in Europe: Greater Differences among Social Groups than among Countries', in N. F. Schneider and G. Meil (eds),

Mobile Living across Europe 1: Relevance and Diversity of Job-Related Spatial Mobility in Six European Countries, Opladen: Barbara Budrich.
Merton, R. (1968) *Social Theory and Social Structure*, Glencoe: Free Press.
Metz-Göckel, S., Morokvasic, M. and Senganata Münst, A. (eds) (2008) *Migration and Mobility in an Enlarged Europe: A Gender Perspective*, Opladen: Barbara Budrich.
Meyer, J. (2010) 'World Society, Institutional Theories, and the Actor', *Annual Review of Sociology*, 36, 1–20
Meyers, E. (2002) *Multilateral Cooperation, Integration and Regimes: The Case of International Labor Mobility*, Center for Comparative Immigration Studies, working paper # 61, San Diego: University of California at San Diego.
Miera, F. (2008) 'Transnational Strategies of Polish Migrant Entrepreneurs in Trade and Small Business in Berlin', *Journal of Ethnic and Migration Studies*, 34, 753–70.
Mikkeli, H. (1998) *Europe as an Idea and an Identity*, Basingstoke: Palgrave.
Milbrath, L. W. and Goel, M. L. (1977) *Political Participation: How and Why Do People Get Involved in Politics?* Lanham (MD): University Press of America.
Mitchell, K. (2012) 'Student Mobility and European Identity: Erasmus Study as a Civic Experience?', *Journal of Contemporary European Research*, 8, 490–518.
Mitchell, K. (2014) 'Rethinking the "Erasmus Effect" on European Identity', *Journal of Common Market Studies*, 52, DOI:10.1111/jcms.12152.
Moch, L. P. (1992) *Moving Europeans: Migration in Western Europe since 1650*, Bloomington (IN): Indiana University Press.
Molle, W. and van Mourik, A. (1988) 'International Movements of Labour under Conditions of Economic Integration: The Case of Western Europe', *Journal of Common Market Studies*, 16, 317–47.
Monnet, J. (1955) *Les États-Unis d'Europe ont commencé*, Paris: Robert Laffont.
Mood, C. (2010) 'Logistic Regression: Why We Cannot Do What We Think We Can Do, and What We Can Do About It', *European Sociological Review*, 26, 67–82.
Morales, L. and Giugni, M. (eds) (2011) *Social Capital, Political Participation and Migration in Europe*, Basingstoke: Palgrave Macmillan.
Moravcsik, A. (2002) 'In Defense of the "Democratic Deficit": Reassessing the Legitimacy of the European Union', *Journal of Common Market Studies*, 40, 603–24.
Morawska, E. (2002) 'Transnational Migration in the Enlarged European Union: A Perspective from East and Central Europe', in J. Zielonka (ed.), *Europe Unbound*, Oxford: Oxford University Press.
Morawska, E. (2008) *East European Westbound Income-Seeking Migrants: Some Unwelcome Effects on the Sender- and Receiver-Societies (A Report on a Study in Progress)*, paper presented at the conference 'The impact of 1989 on Europe: structural integration but ideational divergence?', European University Institute, Fiesole.
Morelli, A. (2004) *Gli italiani del Belgio: Storia e storie di due secoli di migrazioni*, Foligno: Editoriale Umbra.
Morin, E. (1987) *Penser l'Europe*, Paris: Seuil.
Moro, G. (2009) *Cittadini in Europa. L'attivismo civico e l'esperimento democratico comunitario*, Roma: Carocci.
Morokvasic, M. (2004) '"Settled in Mobility": Engendering Post-Wall Migration in Europe', *Feminist Review*, 77, 7–25.

Moskal, M. (2011) 'Transnationalism and the Role of Family and Children in Intra-European Labour Migration', *European Societies*, 13, 29–50.
Mouhoud, E. M. and Oudinet, J. (2004) 'Les déterminants des migrations dans l'Union Européenne: une prime aux effets de réseaux', *Revue française des affaires sociales*, 58, 87–108.
Mubi Brighenti, A. (2012) 'New Media and Urban Motilities: A Territoriologic Point of View', *Urban Studies*, 49, 399–414.
Mulé, R. and Galassi, F. (2003) 'The Shape of Politics to Come? Intra-European Migration in a Rural French Community', *French Politics*, 1, 279–303.
Mundell, R. A. (1961) 'A Theory of Optimum Currency Areas', *American Economic Review*, 51, 509–17.
Muxel, A. (2009) 'EU Movers and Politics: Towards a Fully-Fledged European Citizenship?', in E. Recchi and A. Favell (eds), *Pioneers of European Integration: Citizenship and Mobility in the EU*, Cheltenham: Elgar.
Nelson, B. and Guth, J. (2000) 'Exploring the Gender Gap: Women, Men and Public Attitudes toward European Integration', *European Union Politics*, 1, 267–91.
Neundorf, A. (2010) 'Democracy in Transition: A Micro Perspective on System Change in Post-Socialist Societies', *Journal of Politics*, 72, 1096–108.
Nissen, S. (2005) 'European Identity and the Future of Europe', in M. Bach, C. Lahusen and G. Vobruba (eds), *Europe in Motion: Social Dynamics and Political Institutions in an Enlarging Europe*, Berlin: Sigma.
Ohmae, K. (1990) *The Borderless World*, London: Collins.
O'Keeffe, D. (1998) 'Freedom of Movement for Workers in Community Law', in J.-Y. Carlier and M. Verwilghen (eds), *Thirty Years of Free Movement of Workers in Europe*, Brussels: European Commission.
Okolski, M. (2001) 'Incomplete Migration: A New Form of Mobility in Central and Eastern Europe. The Case of Polish and Ukrainian Migrants', in C. Wallace and D. Stola (eds), *Patterns of Migration in Central Europe*, Basingstoke: Palgrave.
O'Leary, S. (1996) *The Evolving Concept of Community Citizenship*, The Hague: Kluwer.
Olsen, E. D. H. (2012) *Transnational Citizenship in the European Union: Past, Present, and Future*, London: Continuum.
Ohnmacht, T., Maksim, H. and Bergman, M. (eds) (2009) *Mobilities and Inequality*, Farnham: Ashgate.
O'Reilly, K. (2000) *The British on the Costa del Sol*, London: Routledge.
Padilla, A. M. (ed.) (1980) *Acculturation: Theory, Models and Some New Findings*, Boulder (CO): Westview Press.
Padoa Schioppa, F. (ed.) (1991) *Mismatch and Labour Mobility*, Cambridge: Cambridge University Press.
Pajares, M. (2007) *Inmigrantes del Este: procesos migratorios de los rumanos*, Barcelona: Icaria.
Pascouau, Y. (2013) *Strong Attack against the Freedom of Movement of EU Citizens: Turning Back the Clock*, European Policy Centre, http://www.epc.eu/pub_details.php?cat_id=4&pub_id=3491 (accessed May 2, 2013).
Paul, R. (2013) 'Strategic Contextualisation: Free Movement, Labour Migration Policies and the Governance of Foreign Workers in Europe', *Policy Studies*, 34, 122–41.
Paxton, P. (1999) 'Is Social Capital Declining in the United States? A Multiple Indicator Assessment', *American Journal of Sociology*, 105, 88–127.

Pécoud, A. and De Guchteneire, P. (eds) (2007a) *Migration Without Borders: Essays on the Free Movement of People*, New York: Berghahn.

Pécoud, A. and De Guchteneire, P. (2007b) 'Introduction: The Migration Without Borders Scenario', in A. Pécoud and P. De Guchteneire (eds), *Migration Without Borders: Essays on the Free Movement of People*, New York: Berghahn.

Perrineau, P. (ed.) (2005) *Le vote européen 2004–2005. De l'élargissement au referendum français*, Paris: Presses de Sciences Po.

Pettigrew, T. (1998) 'Intergroup Contact Theory', *Annual Review of Psychology*, 49, 65–86.

Pinder, J. (1996) 'Prewar Ideas of European Union. The British Prophets', in M. Bond, J. Smith and W. Wallace (eds), *Eminent Europeans: Personalities Who Shaped Contemporary Europe*, London: Greycoat Press.

Pocar, V. (2005) *Gli animali non umani. Per una sociologia dei diritti*, Roma-Bari, Laterza.

Poiares Maduro, M. (2002) 'Harmony and Dissonance in Free Movement', in M. Andenas and W.-H. Roth (eds), *Services and Free Movement in EU Law*, Oxford: Oxford University Press.

Portes, A., Guarnizo, L. E. and Landolt, P. (1999) 'The Study of Transnationalism: Pitfalls and Promise of an Emergent Research Field', *Ethnic and Racial Studies*, 22, 217–37.

Potot, S. (2007) *Vivre à l'Est, travailler à l'Ouest: les routes roumaines de l'Europe*, Paris: L'Harmattan.

Poulain, M., Perrin, N. and Singleton, A. (2006) *THESIM: Towards Harmonised European Statistics on International Migration*, Paris: Ined.

Pugliese, E. (2002) *L'Italia tra migrazioni internazionali e migrazioni interne*, Bologna: Il Mulino.

Puhani, P. A. (1999) *Labour Mobility. An Adjustment Mechanism in Euroland?* IZA Discussion Paper # 34, Bonn: Forschungs Institut zur Zukunft der Arbeit.

Putnam, R. D. (2000) *Bowling Alone: The Collapse and Revival of American Community*, New York: Simon and Schuster.

Rabikowska, M. and Burrell, K. (2009) 'The Material Worlds of Recent Polish Migrants: Transnationalism, Food, Shops and Home', in K. Burrell (ed.), *Polish Migration to the UK in the 'New' European Union: After 2004*, Farnham: Ashgate.

Raffini, L. (2010) *La democrazia in mutamento. Dallo Stato-nazione all'Europa*, Firenze: Firenze University Press.

Ralph, D. (2014) '"Always on the Move, but Going Nowhere Fast": Motivations for "Euro-commuting" between the Republic of Ireland and Other EU States', *Journal of Ethnic and Migration Studies*, 40, DOI: 10.1080/1369183X.2014.910447.

Ram, M. and Jones, T. (2008) 'Ethnic-Minority Businesses in the UK: A Review of Research and Policy Developments', *Environment and Planning C: Government and Policy*, 26, 352–74.

Rea, A. (2013) 'Les nouvelles figures du travailleur immigré: fragmentation des statuts d'emploi et européanisation des migrations', *Revue européenne des migrations internationales*, 29, 15–35.

Recchi, E. (2005) *Migrants and Europeans: An Outline of the Free Movement of Persons in the EU*, Amid working paper # 38, Aalborg: Academy of Migration Studies.

Recchi, E. (2006) 'From Migrants to Movers: Citizenship and Mobility in the European Union', in M. P. Smith and A. Favell (eds), *The Human Face of Global Mobility*, New Brunswick (NJ): Transaction.

Recchi, E. (2008) 'Cross-State Mobility in the EU: Trends, Puzzles and Consequences', *European Societies*, 10, 197–224.

Recchi, E. (2009) 'The Social Mobility of Mobile Europeans', in E. Recchi and A. Favell (eds), *Pioneers of European Integration: Citizenship and Mobility in the EU*, Cheltenham: Elgar.

Recchi, E. (2011) 'Mobilità', in G. Bettin Lattes and L. Raffini (eds), *Manuale di sociologia*, II volume, Padua: Cedam.

Recchi, E. (2012a) *Transnational Practices and European Identity: From Theoretical to Policy Issues*, Eucross working paper # 3, Chieti: Università 'G. d'Annunzio' di Chieti-Pescara.

Recchi, E. (2012b) *Europe as a Transnational Social Space: A Comparative Assessment*, paper presented at the 2nd ISA Forum of Sociology, Research Committee 20 'Comparative Sociology', Buenos Aires, 1–4 August.

Recchi, E. (2014) 'Pathways to European Identity Formation: A Tale of Two Models', *Innovation: The European Journal of Social Science Research*, 27, 119–33.

Recchi, E., Alaminos, A., Michalska, K., Maroufof, M., Penalva, C., Raffini, L., Santacreu, O., Strudel, S. and Triandafyllidou, A. (2012) *'All Citizens Now': Intra-EU Mobility and Political Participation of British, Germans, Poles and Romanians in Western and Southern Europe*, scientific report, Chieti: Università 'G. d'Annunzio' di Chieti-Pescara, www.moveact.eu (accessed September 20, 2012).

Recchi, E. and Baldoni, E. (2005) 'Partecipata e duale: la politica migratoria dell'Unione Europea', in L. Leonardi and A. Varsori (eds), *Lo spazio sociale europeo*, Firenze: Firenze University Press.

Recchi, E., Baldoni, E., Francavilla, F. and Mencarini, L. (2006) *Geographic and Job Mobility in the EU*, Report for the DG Employment, Brussels: European Commission.

Recchi, E. and Favell, A. (eds) (2009) *Pioneers of European Integration: Citizenship and Mobility in the EU*, Cheltenham: Elgar.

Recchi, E. and Kuhn, T. (2013) 'Europeans' Space-Sets and the Political Legitimacy of the EU', in N. Kauppi (ed.), *A Political Sociology of Transnational Europe*, Colchester: ECPR Press.

Recchi, E. and Nebe, T. (2003) *Migration and Political Identity in the European Union: Research Issues and Theoretical Premises*, Pioneur working paper # 1, Firenze: Ciuspo.

Recchi, E. and Salamońska, J. (2015) 'Bad Times at Home, Good Times to Move? The (Not So) Changing Landscape of Intra-EU Migration', in H.-J. Trenz, C. Ruzza and V. Guiraudon (eds), *Europe in Crisis: The Unmaking of the Political Union*, Basingstoke: Palgrave Macmillan.

Recchi, E., Tambini, D., Baldoni, E., Williams, D., Surak, K. and Favell, A. (2003) *Intra-EU Migration: A Socio-demographic Overview*, Pioneur working paper # 3, Firenze: Ciuspo.

Recchi, E. and Triandafyllidou, A. (2010) 'Crossing Over, Heading West and South: Mobility, Citizenship and Employment in the Enlarged Europe', in G. Menz and A. Caviedes (eds), *Labour Migration in Europe*, London: Palgrave Macmillan.

Reding V., Rehn, O. and Andor, L. (2013) *Labour Mobility: Europe's Chance to Battle the Crisis*, http://ec.europa.eu/commission_2010-2014/andor/headlines/articles/2013/05/20130508_en.htm, 8 May (accessed May 21, 2013).

Reichel, D. (2011) *Do Legal Regulations Hinder Naturalisation? Citizenship Policies and Naturalisation Rates in Europe*, Robert Schuman Centre for Advanced Studies,

working paper # 51, Eudo Citizenship Observatory, Fiesole: European University Institute.
Reif, K. and Schmitt, H. (1980) 'Nine Second-Order Elections. A Conceptual Framework for the Analysis of European Elections Results', *European Journal of Political Research*, 8, 3–44.
Reyneri, E. (1998) 'Immigrazione ed. economia sommersa', *Stato e mercato*, 2, 287–318.
Reyneri, E. (2004) 'Immigrazione ed economia sommersa nell'Europa meridionale', *Studi emigrazione*, 153, 91–114.
Reyneri, E. and Fullin, G. (2011a) 'Labour Market Penalties of New Immigrants in New and Old Receiving West European Countries', *International Migration*, 49, 31–57.
Reyneri, E. and Fullin, G. (2011b) 'Low Unemployment and Bad Jobs for New Immigrants in Italy', *International Migration*, 49, 118–47.
Reyneri, E., Minardi, E. and Scidà, G. (eds) (1997) *Immigrati e lavoro*, Milano: Franco Angeli.
Ribas-Mateos, N. (2004) 'How Can We Understand Immigration in Southern Europe?', *Journal of Ethnic and Migration Studies*, 30, 1045–63.
Risse, T. (2002) 'The Euro between National and European Identity', *Journal of European Public Policy*, 10, 487–505.
Risse, T. (2004) 'European Institutions and Identity Change: What Have We Learned?', in R. K. Hermann, T. Risse and M. B. Brewer (eds), *Transnational Identities: Becoming European in the EU*, Lanham (MD): Rowman & Littlefield.
Risse, T. (2010) *A Community of Europeans? Transnational Identities and Public Spheres*, Ithaca: Cornell University Press.
Robertson, R. (1992) *Social Theory and Global Culture*, London: Sage.
Ródenas Calatayud, C. (1994) *Emigración y economía en España*, Alicante: Editorial Civitas.
Roeder, A. (2011) 'Does Mobility Matter for Attitudes to Europe? A Multi-level Analysis of Immigrants' Attitudes to European Unification', *Political Studies*, 59, 458–71.
Rogers, N. and Scannell, R. (2005) *Free Movement of Persons in the Enlarged European Union*, London: Sweet and Maxwell.
Rogers, R. (1985) 'Post-World War II European Labor Migration: An Introduction to the Issues', in R. Rogers (ed.), *Guests Come to Stay*, Boulder (CO): Westview Press.
Romero, F. (2001) 'L'emigrazione operaia in Europa (1948–1973)', in P. Bevilacqua, A. De Clementi and E. Franzina (eds), *Storia dell'emigrazione italiana. Partenze*, Roma: Donzelli.
Rossini, D. (2006) *L'altra Marcinelle: dalle grandi tragedie sul lavoro alla lunga catena di vittime della silicosi*, Brussels: Acli Belgio-Patronato Acli.
Rother, N. and Nebe, T. (2009) 'More Mobile, More European? Free Movement and EU Identity', in E. Recchi and A. Favell (eds), *Pioneers of European Integration: Citizenship and Mobility in the EU*, Cheltenham: Elgar.
Rumford, C. (2006) 'Theorizing Borders', *European Journal of Social Theory*, 2, 155–69.
Salamońska, J., Baglioni, L. G. and Recchi, E. (2013) *Navigating the European Space: Physical and Virtual Forms of Cross-Border Mobility among EU Citizens*, EUCROSS working paper # 5, Chieti: Università di Chieti-Pescara.

Sandu, D. (2006) *Living Abroad on a Temporary Basis. The Romanians and the Economic Migration: 1990–2006*, Bucuresti: Open Society Foundation.
Santacreu, O., Baldoni, E. and Albert, M. C. (2009) 'Deciding to Move: Migration Projects in an Integrating Europe', in E. Recchi and A. Favell (eds), *Pioneers of European Integration: Citizenship and Mobility in the EU*, Cheltenham: Elgar.
Santacreu, O., Rother, N. and Braun, M. (2006) 'Stichprobenziehung für Migrantepopulationen in fünf Ländern. Eine Darstellung des metodischen Vorgehems im PIONEUR-Project', *ZUMA-Nachrichten*, 59, 72–88.
Sapir, A., Aghion, P., Bertola, G., Hellwig, M., Pisani-Ferry, J., Rosati, D. K., Viñals, J. and Wallace, H. (2004) *An Agenda for a Growing Europe*, Oxford: Oxford University Press.
Sassatelli, M. (2002) 'Imagined Europe: The Shaping of a European Cultural Identity through EU Cultural Policy', *European Journal of Social Theory*, 5, 435–51.
Sassatelli, M. (2009) *Becoming Europeans. Cultural Identity and Cultural Policies*, Basingstoke: Palgrave Macmillan.
Sassen, S. (2006) *Territory, Authority, Rights: From Medieval to Global Assemblages*, Princeton (NJ): Princeton University Press.
Schachter, J. (2001) *Geographical Mobility. Current Population Report*, Washington (DC): US Bureau of Census.
Scharpf, F. W. (1999) *Governing in Europe. Effective and Democratic?* Oxford: Oxford University Press.
Schissler, H. and Soysal, Y. (2005) *The Nation, Europe, and the World: Textbooks and Curricula in Transition*, New York: Berghahn.
Schmidt, V. (2006) *Democracy in Europe*, Oxford: Oxford University Press.
Schmidt, V. (2013) 'Democracy and Legitimacy in the European Union Revisited: Input, Output *and* "Throughput"', *Political Studies*, 61, 2–22.
Schmitt, H. (2005) 'The European Elections of June 2004: Still Second Order?', *West European Politics*, 28, 650–79.
Schmitter, P. C. (2003) 'Democracy in Europe and Europe's Democratization', *Journal of Democracy*, 14, 71–85.
Schneider, C. and Holman, D. (2009) *Longitudinal Study of Migrant Workers in the East of England. Interim Report*, Cambridge and Chelmsford: Anglia Ruskin University.
Schneider, M. (2007) 'Structuralism', in G. Ritzer (ed.), *The Blackwell Encyclopedia of Sociology*, Malden (MA): Blackwell.
Schneider, N. F. and Meil, G. (2008) *Mobile Living across Europe 1: Relevance and Diversity of Job-Related Spatial Mobility in Six European Countries*, Opladen: Barbara Budrich.
Scott, D. S. (2006) 'The Social Morphology of Skilled Migration: The Case of the British Middle Class in Paris', *Journal of Ethnic and Migration Studies*, 32, 1105–29.
Searing, D., Wright, G. and Rabinowitz, G. (1976) 'The Primacy Principle: Attitude Change and Political Socialization', *British Journal of Political Science*, 6, 83–113.
Segatti, P. (2013) 'Identità europea e generazioni politiche', in E. Recchi, M. Bontempi and C. Colloca (eds), *Metamorfosi sociali. Attori e luoghi del mutamento nella società contemporanea*, Rubbettino: Soveria Mannelli.
Sennett, R. (1998) *The Corrosion of Character: The Personal Consequences of Work in the New Capitalism*, New York: Norton.

References 197

Shachar, A. and Hirschl, R. (2007) 'Citizenship as Inherited Property', *Political Theory*, 35, 253–87.
Shamir, R. (2005) 'Without Borders? Notes on Globalization as a Mobility Regime', *Sociological Theory*, 23, 197–217.
Shaw, J. and Miller, N. (2012) *When Legal Worlds Collide: An Exploration of What Happens When EU Free Movement Law Meets UK Immigration Law*, School of Law Research Paper Series # 31, Edinburgh: University of Edinburgh.
Shaw, S.-L. (ed.) (2012) 'Special Issue on Time Geography', *Journal of Transport Geography*, 23, 1–91.
Sheller, M. (2014) 'Sociology after the Mobilities Turn', in P. Adey, D. Bissell, K. Hannam, P. Merriman and M. Sheller (eds), *The Routledge Handbook of Mobilities*, London: Routledge.
Shore, C. (2000) *Building Europe: The Cultural Politics of European Integration*, London: Routledge.
Siedentop, L. (2001) *Democracy in Europe*, Oxford: Oxford University Press.
Sigalas, E. (2010) 'Cross-Border Mobility and European Identity: The Effectiveness of Intergroup Contact during the Erasmus Year Abroad', *European Union Politics*, 11, 241–65.
Simmel, G. (1903) *Die Großstädte und das Geistesleben*, Dresden: Petermann.
Simmel, G. (1908) *Sociology*, Leiden and Boston: Brill.
Sjaastad, L. A. (1962) 'The Costs and Returns of Human Migration', *Journal of Political Economy*, 70, supplement, 80–93.
Smith, D. P. and King, R. (2012) 'Editorial Introduction: Re-making Migration Theory', *Population, Space and Place*, 18, 127–33.
Smith, M. P. and Favell, A. (eds) (2006) *The Human Face of Global Mobility*, New Brunswick (NJ): Transaction.
Smith, T. and Kim, S. (2006) 'National Pride in Comparative Perspective: 1995/96 and 2003/04', *International Journal of Public Opinion Research*, 18, 127–36.
Snijders, T. A. B. and Boskers, R. J. (1999) *Multilevel Analysis: An Introduction to Basic and Advanced Multilevel Modeling*, London and Thousand Oaks (CA): Sage.
Soysal, Y. N. (1994) *Limits of Citizenship. Migrants and Postnational Membership in Europe*, Chicago: University of Chicago Press.
Soysal, Y. N. (2012) 'Citizenship, Immigration, and the European Social Project: Rights and Obligations of Individuality', *British Journal of Sociology*, 63, 1–21.
Stanišić, N. (2012) 'The Effects of the Economic Crisis on Income Convergence in the European Union', *Acta Oeconomica*, 62, 161–82.
Statistische Bundesamt (2013) *Bevölkerung und Erwerbstätigkeit*, Wiesbaden.
Steinmetz, R. and Wivel, A. (eds) (2010) *Small States in Europe: Challenges and Opportunities*, Farnham: Ashgate.
Stoeckel, F. (2008) *The European Public Sphere, the Media and Support for European Integration*, in Berliner Studien zur Soziologie Europas # 20, Berlin: Freie Universität Berlin.
Stråth, B. (2002) 'A European Identity: To the Historical Limits of a Concept', *European Journal of Social Theory*, 5, 387–401.
Strudel, S. (2003) 'Polyrythmie européenne: le droit de suffrage municipal des étrangers au sein de l'Union, une règle électorale entre détournements et retardements', *Revue française de science politique*, 53, 3–34.
Strudel, S. (2005) 'Citoyen, citoyenneté européenne', in Y. Déloye (ed.), *Dictionnaire des élections européennes*, Paris: Economica.

Strudel, S. (2009) 'L'Europe, un nouvel espace de citoyenneté? Le vote des nonnationaux', *Revue internationale de politique comparée. Élections Européennes*, 16, 559–68.
SVR [Sachsverständigenrat deutscher Stiftungen für Migration und Integration] (2013) *Erfolgsfall Europa? Folgen und Herausforderungen der EU-Freizügigkeit für Deutschland. Jahresgutachten 2013 mit Migrationsbarometer*, Berlin: SVR GmbH.
Taglioli, A. (2008) 'L'Erasmus: un'espressione vitale del processo di europeizzazione', in G. Bettin Lattes and M. Bontempi (eds), *Generazione Erasmus? L'identità europea tra vissuto e istituzioni*, Firenze: Firenze University Press.
Tajfel, H. (1974) 'Social Identity and Intergroup Behaviour', *Social Science Information*, 13, 65–93.
Tambini, D. and Rother, N. (2009) 'A Common Information Space? The Media Use of EU Movers', in E. Recchi and A. Favell (eds), *Pioneers of European Integration: Citizenship and Mobility in the EU*, Cheltenham: Elgar.
Tarrius, A. (1992) *Les fourmis d'Europe. Migrants riches, migrants pauvres et nouvelles villes internationales*, Paris: L'Harmattan.
Teichler, U. (ed.) (2002) *Erasmus in the Socrates Programme: Findings of an Evaluation Study*, Bonn: Lemmens.
Theiler, T. (2005) *Political Symbolism and European Integration*, Manchester: Manchester University Press.
Theodos, B. (2009) *Geographic Mobility in the U.S. and Implications for Low-Income Families and Communities*, paper presented at the workshop "Labor Mobility in a Transatlantic Perspective: American Movers versus European Stayers?", German Marshall Fund of the United States, Washington, 6 April.
Thorogood, D. and Winqvist, K. (2003) 'Women and Men Migrating to and from the European Union', *Statistics in Focus-Eurostat*, 2, 1–8.
Tilly, C. (1978) 'Migration in Modern European History', in W. H. McNeill and B. Adams (eds), *Human Migration. Patterns and Policies*, Bloomington (IN): University of Indiana Press.
Torpey, J. (2000) *The Invention of the Passport: Surveillance, Citizenship, and the State*, Cambridge: Cambridge University Press.
Trenz, H.-J. (2011) 'Social Theory and European Integration', in A. Favell and V. Guiraudon (eds), *Sociology of the European Union*, Basingstoke, Palgrave Macmillan.
Trenz, H.-J. and Eder, K. (2007) 'The Democratizing Dynamics of a European Public Sphere. Towards a Theory of Democratic Functionalism', *European Journal of Social Theory*, 7, 5–25.
Triandafyllidou, A. (ed.) (2006) *Contemporary Polish Migration in Europe: Complex Patterns of Movement and Settlement*, Washington (DC): Edwin Mellen.
Triandafyllidou, A. and Kosic, A. (2006) 'Polish and Albanian Workers in Italy: Between Legality and Undocumented Status', in F. Düvell (ed.), *Illegal Migration in Europe: Beyond Control?* Basingstoke: Palgrave Macmillan.
Tsaliki, L. (2007) 'The Construction of European Identity and Citizenship through Cultural Policy', *European Studies: A Journal of European Culture, History and Politics*, 24, 157–82.
United Nations (2013) *International Migration 2013 Wall Chart*, New York: Department of Economic and Social Affairs, Population Division, http://esa.un.org/unmigration/wallchart2013.htm (accessed September 6, 2014).
Urry, J. (2000) *Sociology beyond Societies*, London: Routledge.

Urry, J. (2007) *Mobilities*, Cambridge: Polity.
van der Eijk, C. and Franklin, M. (1996) *Choosing Europe? The European Electorate and National Politics in the Face of the Union*, Ann Arbor (MI): University of Michigan Press.
van der Mei, A. P. (2003) *Free Movement of Persons within the European Community: Cross-Border Access to Public Benefits*, Oxford: Hart.
van Mol, C. (2013) 'Intra-European Student Mobility and European Identity: A Successful Marriage?' *Population, Space and Place*, 19, 209–22.
van Mol, C. and Timmerman, C. (2014) 'Should I Stay or Should I Go? An Analysis of the Determinants of Intra-European Student Mobility', *Population, Space and Place*, 20, 465–79.
Van Steenbergen, M. (2011) *Multilevel Analysis of Cross-National Surveys: The Role of Measurement and Estimation*, Universitat Pompeu Fabra, RECSM Seminar, Barcelona, http://www.upf.edu/survey/_pdf/Steenbergen_seminar_2.pdf (accessed September 5, 2012).
Van Steenbergen, M. and Jones, B. S. (2002) 'Modeling Multilevel Data Structures', *American Journal of Political Science*, 46, 218–37.
Vertovec, S. (1999) 'Conceiving and Researching Transnationalism', *Ethnic and Racial Studies*, 22, 217–37.
Verwiebe, R. (2004) *Transnationale Mobilität innerhalb Europas: Eine Studie zu den sozialstrukturellen Effekten der Europäisierung*, Berlin: Sigma.
Verwiebe, R. (2011) 'Why Do Europeans Migrate to Berlin? Social-Structural Differences for Italian, British, French and Polish Nationals in the Period between 1980 and 2002', *International Migration*, DOI: 10.1111/j.1468-2435.2010.00663.x.
Verwiebe, R. and Eder, K. (2006) 'The Positioning of Transnationally Mobile Europeans in the German Labour Market', *European Societies*, 8, 141–67.
Vigneswaran, D. (2013) *Territory, Migration and the Evolution of the International System*, Basingstoke: Palgrave Macmillan.
Viruela Martinez, R. (2009) 'Europeos del Este en el mercado de trabajo español: un enfoque geografico', *Revista CIDOB d'Afers Internacionals*, 84, 81–103.
Waldren, J. (1996) *Insiders and Outsiders: Paradise and Reality in Mallorca*, Oxford: Berghahn.
Wallace, H. (2000) 'Europeanisation and Globalisation: Complementary or Contradictory Trends?', *New Political Economy*, 5, 369–82.
Walzer, M. (1983) *Spheres of Justice. A Defense of Pluralism and Equality*, New York: Basic Books.
Walzer, M. (1990) 'The Communitarian Critique of Liberalism', *Political Theory*, 18, 6–23.
Weber, M. (1946) From Max Weber: Essays in Sociology (translated, edited and with an introduction by H. H. Gerth and C. Wright Mills), London: Routledge.
Weiler, J. H. H. (1996) *The Selling of Europe*, working paper # 96, Jean Monnet Center, New York: NYU School of Law.
Weiss, A. (2005) 'The Transnationalization of Social Inequality: Conceptualizing Social Positions on a World Scale', *Current Sociology*, 53, 707–28.
Weiss, F. and Wooldridge, F. (2002) *Free Movement of Persons within the European Community*, The Hague: Kluwer.
Wellman, B. (2001) 'Physical Place and Cyberplace: The Rise of Personalized Networking', *International Journal of Urban and Regional Research*, 25, 227–52.

Wickham, J., Moriarty, E., Bobek, A. and Salamońska, J. (2009) 'Working in the Gold Rush: Polish Migrants' Careers and the Irish Hospitality Sector', in S. C. Bolton and M. Houlihan (eds), *Work Matters: Critical Reflections on Contemporary Work*, Basingstoke: Palgrave Macmillan.

Wiener, A. (1998) *European Citizenship Practices: Building Institutions of a Non-State*, Boulder (CO): Westview Press.

Wihtol de Wenden, C. (2014) *Faut-il ouvrir les frontières?* Paris: Presses de Sciences Po.

Williams, A. M. and Baláž, V. (2009) 'Low Cost Carriers, Economies of Flows and Regional Externalities', *Regional Studies*, 5, 677–91.

Wilson, I. (2011) 'What Should We Expect of "Erasmus Generations"?', *Journal of Common Market Studies*, 49, 1113–40.

Woolfson, C. (2007) 'Labour Standards and Migration in the New Europe: Post-Communist Legacies and Perspectives', *European Journal of Industrial Relations*, 13, 199–218.

Wright, E. O. (1985) *Classes*, London: Verso.

Wuthnow, R. (2002) *Loose Connections*, Cambridge (MA): Harvard University Press.

Zimmer, O. (2003) *A Contested Nation: History, Memory and Nationalism in Switzerland, 1761–1891*, Cambridge: Cambridge University Press.

Zimmermann, A. and Favell, A. (2011) 'Governmentality, Political Field or Public Sphere? Theoretical Alternatives in the Political Sociology of the EU', *European Journal of Social Theory*, 14, 489–515.

Zitt, M., Ramanana-Rahary, S., Bassecoulard, E. and Laville, F. (2003) 'Potential Science-Technology Spillovers in Regions: An Insight on Geographical Co-location of Knowledge Activities in the EU', *Scientometrics*, 57, 295–320.

Zweig, S. (2014) *Appels aux Européens*, Paris: Bartillat.

Index

Ackers, D. 39
Ackers, L. 82
Action Plan for Mobility, European Commission 44
Adey, P. 150
Alaminos, A. 85
Albert, M. C. 155, 156, 174
Aledo Tur, A. 82
Alfieri, A. 19
Allport, G. W. 171
Ambrosini, M. 147
Amsterdam Treaty 27
Anderson, B. 72
Andreotti, A. 142
Anghel, R. G. 72, 95
Animal rights 159
Arab Maghreb Union (AMU) 11
Arango, J. 96
Archibugi, D. 19
Aron, R. 25
Arsene, C. 84
Association of South-East Asian Nations (ASEAN) 11
Asymmetric shock 43
Attachment to Europe 130–7
Auer, P. 46
Authoritarianism 153
Azmanova, A. 153

Bachan, R. 73
Baczynska, G. 75
Bade, K. xi, 45, 149
Bader, V. M. 160
Baglioni, L. G. 139, 62
Bailly, F. 55
Baláž, V. 97
Baldoni, E. 24, 161
Baldwin-Edwards, M. 96
Balibar, E. xii
Barberis, E. 73
Barnard, C. 2, 29, 161, 163
Barou, J. 82
Barrett, A. 72

Barry, B. 60
Bauböck, R. 2, 6, 7, 160
Bauman, Z. 151, 165, 174
Beck, U. xii, 151, 165
Beckfield, J. 161, 173
Bellamy, R. 123
Bellucci, P. 171
Bendix, R. 5
Benson, M. 82
Berezin, M. 3, 171
Berger, P. A. 153, 168
Bernardi, F. 167
Bettin Lattes, G. 82, 125
Beyers, J. 128
Billig, M. 124
Blanchflower, D. G. 75
Blasius, J. 86
Blatter, J. 7
Block, L. 135
Blome, K. 161
Blondel, J. 161
Bobbio, N. 4, 5
Bonifazi, C. 167
Borjas, G. J. 146, 159
Bourdieu, P. 170
Bousiou, P. 82
'Bowling alone' thesis 122
Boy, D. 114
Brague, R. 128, 171
Braun, M. 84, 155, 156, 168, 174
Braunerhjelm, P. 43
Broeders, D. 164
Brubaker, R. 3, 19
Bruter, M. 127, 131
Buller, H. 82
Burrell, K. 73
Büscher, M. 151

Caiani, M. 169
Campbell, D. 75
Canovi, A. 49
Capitalism 151
Carens, J. H. 160

201

Caribbean Community 11
Caritas-Migrantes 74
Carlier, J.-Y. 36, 161
Carlino, G. 166
Carmel, E. 17, 32
Carrera, S. 32
Casado Díaz, M. 82
Casey, J. P. 11
Castells, M. xii, 151, 161, 174
Castles, S. 54, 98, 147, 148
Catanzaro, R. 73, 94
Chase-Dunn, C. 9
Checkel, J. 171
Churchill, W. 19–20
Cicchelli, V. 82
Cingolani, P. 75, 94
Citizenship 3, 5, 19
  Dual 7
  European 24–7
  Light 7, 107, 121–2
  Knowledge of 121
  Material vs formal 162
  Multiple 7
  Post-national 3, 5–6
Clark, K. 72
Class consciousness 126
Claval, P. 150
Cold War 94
Collard, S. 82
Collective identity 123
  Formation 125–7, 171
Colombo, A. 73, 94
Common Travel Area 162
Commuting 83
Cook, J. 73
Cram, L. 127
Cremers, J. 162
Cresswell, T. 148, 150, 174
Critchley, J. 20
Csedő, K. 72
Cultural policies 128
Culturalism 125
Cyrus, N. 73, 95

D'Amato, G. 85
Dalton, R. J. 141
Dawson, R. E. 125
De Bruycker, P. 29
De Federico de la Rúa, A. 173

De Gasperi, A. 20, 162
De Guchteneire, P. xii, 11, 160
De Vries, C. E. 128
Delanty, G. xii, 161, 171
Deleuze, G. 12, 174
Delhey, J. 129
Della Porta, D. 169
Delors, J. 25
Déloye, Y. 105
Der Spiegel 76
Deutsch, K. W. 128, 129, 137, 142, 171
Diasporas 58–9, 68–70
Díez Medrano, J. 131, 171
Domestic work 73
Doyle, O. 118
Drake, H. 82
Dreher, A. 8
Drinkwater, S. 72
Duchêne, F. 20
Duchesne, S. 131, 170
Duffy, D. 72
Dustmann, C. 167
Düvell, F. 73, 95, 96

Eade, J. 73, 96
Easton, D. 125
Economic Community of West Africa (CEAO) 11
Economic convergence, EU 146–7, 166
Eder, K. xii, 83, 87, 128, 169, 171
Edwards, E. E. 128
Eichenberg, R. C. 141
Elliott, A. 150
Ellis, A. 170
Elster, J. 126
Emirbayer, M. 127
Engbersen, G. 52
Engelen, E. 160
Enlargements of the EU 30–1, 52–8, 97
Erasmus programme 41–3, 142, 165
Erbe, J. 107
Eriksen, E. O. 107
Erikson, R. 113, 119, 168
Ethnic business 73–4
Eucross project 159, 172

EURES 37–9, 164
Euro 127
Eurobarometer 1, 106, 108, 121, 129, 130, 133, 134, 136, 138–40, 155, 157, 159, 166, 171, 172
Euro-crisis 74–7
Euronews 32
European Citizens Charter 27
European Coal and Steel Community (ECSC) 20–2
European Commission xiii, 13, 30, 32, 37, 38, 42–4, 55, 56, 58, 70–4, 84, 116, 124, 155, 156, 159, 163, 164, 166, 169
European Constitution 28, 162
European Court of Justice (ECJ) 7, 24, 31, 165
European Economic Community (EEC) 22
European elections 106
European identity 130–7, 170
European Internal Movers' Survey (EIMSS) 84, 155–6, 170
European Parliament elections 114–20
European passport 25, 127
European Regional Development Fund (ERDF) 37
European solidarity 29, 123
European Travel Commission 11
Europeanization 161
Euroscepticism 32, 105
Eurostars 83
Eurostat 11, 13, 53–5, 57, 61, 63, 65, 67, 74, 76, 147, 173

Faas, D. 128
Faini, R. 176
Faist, T. 7, 104
Falchi, G. 51, 166
Favell, A. 12, 54, 81, 83, 84, 94, 98, 145, 150, 155, 161, 172
Federalism 19–20
Fernández, O. 173
Ferrera, M. 3, 22, 29, 39
Fertig, M. 166
Feudal obligations 159, 174
Fibbi, R. 85
Fidrmuc, J. 118

Fischer, C. 122
Fligstein, N. 129, 161
Flipo, A. 75, 97
Florida, R. 46, 47
Føllesdal, A. 105
Foster, N. 3, 32, 42, 98, 108, 109, 124, 141, 159, 165, 169
Foucault, M. 12
Four freedoms 2
Fox, J. 7
Franklin, M. 2, 107
Frognier, A. P. 131
Fromm, E. 153
Front National 33
Fullin, G. 167

Gabel, M. 141
Galassi, F. 82
Garapich, M. 73
Gaspar, S. 135
Gastarbeiter 50–1, 76
Gaston, N. 181
Geddes, A. 4, 161
Gellner, E. 44
Gerhards, J. 172, 173
GESIS 174
Giddens, A. 126, 151
Giubboni, S. 28, 29, 161–3
Giugni, M. 118
Glaeser, E. L. 166
Glick Schiller, N. 85
Globalization 8–11, 147–8, 151, 160, 161
Glöckner-Rist, A. 168
Goel, M. L. 108
Goldthorpe, J. H. 113, 119, 168
Goodin, R. E. 160
Goodwin, J. 127
Gouldner, A. W. 153
Grabowska, I. 96
Grande, E. xii, 165
Greenacre, M. J. 86
Greenstein, F. 125
Grundy, S. 128
Guattari, F. 12, 174
Guild, E. 36, 52, 161
Guiraudon, V. xiv, 4, 41, 81
Guth, J. 134
Gutiérrez, P. 131

Index

Haas, E. B. 171
Habermas, J. 19, 165
Habitus 170–1
Hadler, M. 84
Hajer, M. 12
Hakhverdian, A. 105
Haller, M. 105, 141, 143
Hampton, K. 174
Hansen, P. 6
Harris, J. R. 146
Harvey, D. 12, 150
Havel, V. 165
Havinga, I, 19
Herm, A. 55
Hess, R. D. 125
Hinderliter Ortloff, D. 128
Hirschl, R. 160
Hix, S. 17, 105, 173
Hoggart, K. 82
Holman, D. 75
Hooghe, L. 12, 105, 128, 131
Høyland, B. 17
Huber, A. 82
Hukou system 11–12
Hüller, T. 128
Human capital density 47, 167
Human geography 150

ILO 167
Immerfall, S. 124
Income inequality, EU 147, 173
Individualization 4–8, 159
Intercultural competence 89, 91–2, 101
Ireland, P. 118
ISCO codes 167

Jamieson, L. 128
Janelle, D. G. 150, 151
Janiak, A. 145, 166
Jensen, O. B. 12
Jones, B. S. 172
Jones, T. 73
Joppke, C. xii, 6, 7, 31, 107, 122, 160, 161
Jordan, B. 95
Judt, T. 93
Jung, J. K. 141

Kaczmarczyk, P. 58
Kaina, V. 142, 143
Kant, I. 19
Kaplan, G. 173
Karolewski, I. P. 142
Kaufmann, V. 153
Kellerman, A. 153
Kennedy, P. 82, 174
Kępińska, E. 97
Kesselring, S. 82
Kim, S. 135
King, R. 81, 82, 147
Kleingeld, P. 19
Klingemann, H. D. 114
KOF Index 8–9, 160
Kohli, M. 170
Koikkalainen, S. 84
Koopmans, R. 107
Koryś, I. 94, 95
Kosic, A. 95
Koslowski, R. 149, 173
Kostoris Padoa Schioppa, F. 46
Kriesi, H. 153
Krings, T. 75, 97
Kuhn, T. 83, 142, 172, 174

Labour flexibility 72–3, 96–8
Labour markets 70–2, 83
Landuyt, A. 20
Languages 173
Lash, S. 151
Latour, B. 151
Lawton, H. 75
Le Galès, P. 142
Le Roux, B. 168
Lebon, A. 51, 166
Legitimacy of the EU 105–7
Lewis, J. 128
Leyshon, A. 150
Lieberson, S. 68, 69
Limmer, R. 85
Lindberg, L. 105
Lisbon strategy 44
Livi Bacci, M. xi, 50
Local identities 131–3
Locals and cosmopolitans 153
Lowi, T. J. 35
Lucassen, J. 149

Lucassen, L. 149
Lűtzeler, P. M. 171

Maas, W. 21, 24, 27
Maastricht Treaty 26
Marcinelle 49
Marks, G. 12, 105, 131
Marradi, A. 172
Marsh, D. 126
Marsh, M. 107
Marshall, T. H. 5
Martin, D. 161
Martinelli, A. 173
Marxism 12, 126
Maslauskaite, K. 166
Massey, D. 152, 174
Matei, S. 120
Mau, S. 3, 11, 138, 164, 172
Mayer, N. 114
Mayne, R. 20
Meaning of Europe 159
Meardi, G. 73, 94
Meil, G. 85
Mérand, F. 161
Merriman, P. 150
Merton, R. 152, 153, 174
Metz-Göckel, S. 73, 94
Mewes, J. 138
Meyer, J. 6
Meyers, E. 11
Miera, F. 73
Migration
 and legitimacy 47
 and unemployment 45–6, 167
 Definition 1, 19, 148–9
 East-West 54–8, 93–8
 Industry 73
 Internal 145–6, 159
 Interstate (US) 145–6, 173
 Irregular 95–6
 Lifestyle 82, 91
 Retirement 82
 Shuttle 97–8
Mikkeli, H. 171
Milbrath, L. W. 108
Miller, M. J. 54, 147, 148
Miller, N. 163
Mitchell, K. 82, 83

Mobility
 and productivity 46
 and welfare 29, 161, 163
 Children's 82
 Definition 1–2
 Forms of 2, 81, 148–51
 Scientists' 82
 Virtual 172, 174
 Women's 82
Moch, L. P. 50, 149
Molle, W. 51
Monetary union 43
Monnet, J. 20, 22
Mood, C. 172
Morales, L. 118
Moravcsik, A. 105
Morawska, E. 72, 96
Morelli, A. 22
Morin, E. 128, 171
Morokvasic, M. 82
Moskal, M. 98
Motility 153
Mouhoud, E. M. 45
Moveact project 156–7
Mubi Brighenti, A. 159
Mulé, R. 82
Multi-level modelling 139–40
Multiple correspondence analysis
 (MCA) 86, 168
Mundell, R. A. 43
Muxel, A. 112, 155, 174

National identity 131–3
Nationalism 44, 107
Nation-building 123–4
Nebe, T. 47, 54, 94, 129, 155, 171
Nelson, B. 134
Network society 151
Neundorf, A. 120
Nice Treaty 28
Nissen, S. 141
Nordic Council 11
North-American Free Trade
 Agreement (NAFTA) 11, 145

O'Keeffe, D. 24, 161
O'Leary, S. 161

206 *Index*

O'Reilly, K.   82
Ohmae, K.   xii
Ohnmacht, T.   153
Oil crisis, 1973–74   51
Okolski, M.   52, 58, 94
Olsen, E. D. H.   25, 41
Onomastic sampling   155
Orlandini, G.   28, 161–3
Oudinet, J.   45

Padilla, A. M.   89
Padoa Schioppa, F.   46
Pajares, M.   73
Palmer, H.   141
Pascouau, Y.   32
Paul, R.   32, 104
Paxton, P.   122
Pécoud, A.   xii, 11, 160
Permissive consensus   105
Perrineau, P.   107, 114
Pettigrew, T.   170
Pinder, J.   19
Pioneur project   84, 155–6
Pocar, V.   159
Poiares Maduro, M.   31
Policies, typology   35
Political participation   108–12
Political party membership   110–11
Political socialization   120–1, 125, 171
Politicization   112–13
Portes, A.   85
Posted workers   162, 166
Potot, S.   95
Poulain, M.   52
Prado, P.   82
Prejudice   171
Prewitt, K.   125
Public sphere   107
Pugliese, E.   50
Puhani, P. A.   45
Putnam, R. D.   122
PVV, party   33

Rabikowska, M.   73
Raffini, L.   169
Ralph, D.   83
Ram, M.   73
Rea, A.   73

Recchi, E.   45, 51, 54, 84, 85, 89, 99, 112, 139, 142, 155, 156, 161, 166–72, 174
Reding, V.   43
Referenda, May 2005   28, 105
Regularization of immigrants   95, 97, 167
Reichel, D.   7
Reif, K.   107, 150
Response-set   172
Reyneri, E.   96, 167
Ribas-Mateos, N.   96
Richardson, T.   12
Risse, T.   127, 131, 134, 171
Robertson, R.   148, 160
Ródenas Calatayud, C.   50
Roeder, A.   135, 164
Rogers, N.   161
Rogers, R.   51
Role-set   151
Roma citizens   x, 32
Romero, F.   50, 162
Roos, C.   2
Rossini, D.   49
Rother, N.   47, 85, 129
Rouanet, H.   168
Roudometof, V.   141
Ruiz-Gelices, E.   82
Rumford, C.   xii, 161

Salamońska, J.   45, 167
Sandu, D.   97
Santacreu, O.   84, 85, 155, 156, 174
Sapir, A.   43
Sarkozy, N.   32
Sassatelli, M.   124, 128, 170
Sassen, S.   xii, 151
Scannell, R.   161
Schachter, J.   173
Scharpf, F. W.   105
Scheingold, S.   105
Schengen agreement and information system   39–41, 164–5
Schissler, H.   128
Schmidt, C. M.   166
Schmidt, V.   105, 107
Schmitt, H.   107
Schmitter, P. C.   105
Schneider, C.   75

Schneider, M. 125
Schneider, N. F. 85
Schulhofer-Wohl, S. 173
Schuman, R. 20
Scott, D. S. 83
Searing, D. 126
Segatti, P. 141
Self-employment 73
Sennett, R. 12
Shachar, A. 160
Shamir, R. 174
Shaw, J. 163
Shaw, S.-L. 150
Sheehan, M. 73
Sheller, M. 151
Shore, C. 44
Siedentop, L. 105
Sigalas, E. 83, 142
Simmel, G. 126, 127, 170, 171
Single European Act (SEA) 26
Sjaastad, L. A. 146
Skeldon, R. 81
Smith, D. P. 147
Smith, T. 135
Social assistance 29, 161, 163
Social classes 168
Social integration 86–93, 99–102, 129
Social mobility 72, 85
Soysal, Y. 5–7, 128
Spaak, P.-H. 20
Space-set 151–3
Spatiality 127
Spill-over 171
Spinelli, A. 20
Stalford, H. 82
Stanisić, N. 146
Statistische Bundesamt 76
Status-set 151
Steinmetz, R. 141
Stoeckel, F. 128
Stråth, B. 171
Structuralism 125
Strudel, S. 116, 117, 156
Student mobility 41–3, 82–3
Support for the EU 105–7
SVR [Sachsverständigenrat deutscher Stiftungen für Migration und integration] 135
Switzerland 161, 163

Taglioli, A. 173
Tajfel, H. 171
Tambini, D. 85, 155, 174
Tarrius, A. 81
Taviani, P. E. 21
Teichler, U. 82
Theiler, T. 44
Theodos, B. 173
Thorogood, D. 55, 181
Tilly, C. 149
Timmerman, C. 82
Todaro, M. P. 146
Torpey, J. 3, 19
Tourism 148–9, 173
Trade union membership 110–11
Transactionalism 128
Transitional measures
 see also enlargements
 of the EU 30–1
Transnationalism 85, 137–41, 172
Trans-Tasman Travel Arrangement 11
Trenz, H.-J. 129, 169
Triandafyllidou, A. 94, 95, 156
Trust in EU institutions 106, 169

UKIP, party 33
United Nations 2, 6, 19, 148
Universal Declaration of Human Rights 160
Urry, J. xii, 150, 151

van der Eijk, C. 107
van der Mei, A. P. 23, 161
van Mol, C. 82, 83
van Mourik, A. 51
Van Steenbergen, M. 173
Vertovec, S. 85
Verwiebe, R. 83, 87, 135
Vigneswaran, D. 12
Viruela Martinez, R. 73
Vogel, D. 95
Voting 114–20, 169–70

Waldren, J. 82
Wallace, H. 161
Walzer, M. 2
Wasmer, E. 145, 166
Weber, M. 126
Weiler, J. H. H. 7

Weiss, A.   153, 168
Weiss, F.   161
Wellman, B.   174
White Paper on European
    Governance   169
Wickham, J.   174
Wiener, A.   161
Wihtol de Wenden, C.   160
Williams, A. M.   97
Williams, D.   97
Wilson, I.   83, 142

Winqvist, K.   55
Wivel, A.   141
Wooldridge, F.   161
Woolfson, C.   94
Wright, E. O.   126
Wuthnow, R.   122

Zimmer, O.   161
Zimmermann, A.   12
Zitt, M.   166
Zweig, S.   166

The manufacturer's authorised representative in the EU is Springer Nature Customer Service Centre GmbH, Europaplatz 3, 69115 Heidelberg, Germany. If you have any concerns regarding our products, please contact ProductSafety@springernature.com

Printed and bound by CPI Group (UK) Ltd, Croydon, CR0 4YY

23/03/2026

02076458-0012